The Human Rights Paradox

Critical Human Rights

Series Editors
Steve J. Stern ❦ Scott Straus

Books in the series Critical Human Rights emphasize research that opens new ways to think about and understand human rights. The series values in particular empirically grounded and intellectually open research that eschews simplified accounts of human rights events and processes.

Human rights are both always and never universal. Advocates assert that fundamental rights belong to everyone, no matter who they are and regardless of context or extenuating circumstance. Yet people can only realize their rights by asserting them in particular places and attending to specific contexts of struggle, alliance, and conflict. *The Human Rights Paradox* is the first book to embrace fully this contradiction—and to draw out the consequences for human rights as historical experience and origins story, as contemporary social advocacy and mobilization, and as future horizon of emerging environmental and intergenerational rights. Through theory as well as case studies from Africa, Latin America, South and Southeast Asia, and the United States, the authors demonstrate that the imperative of human rights is a product of relationships by social actors who entangle the global and the local so profoundly that one domain cannot exist apart from the other.

The Human
Rights Paradox

Universality and Its Discontents

**Edited by Steve J. Stern
and Scott Straus**

The University of Wisconsin Press

The University of Wisconsin Press
1930 Monroe Street, 3rd Floor
Madison, Wisconsin 53711-2059
uwpress.wisc.edu

3 Henrietta Street
London WC2E 8LU, England
eurospanbookstore.com

Copyright © 2014
The Board of Regents of the University of Wisconsin System
All rights reserved. No part of this publication may be reproduced, stored in a retrieval system,
or transmitted, in any format or by any means, digital, electronic, mechanical, photocopying,
recording, or otherwise, or conveyed via the Internet or a website without written permission
of the University of Wisconsin Press, except in the case of brief quotations embedded in critical
articles and reviews.

Printed in the United States of America

Library of Congress Cataloging-in-Publication Data

The human rights paradox : universality and its discontents / edited by Steve J.
Stern and Scott Straus.
    pages   cm — (Critical human rights)
  Includes bibliographical references and index.
  ISBN 978-0-299-29974-3 (pbk. : alk. paper) — ISBN 978-0-299-29973-6 (e-book)
  1. Human rights. 2. Human rights—History. 3. Human rights advocacy.
  I. Stern, Steve J., 1951–, editor of compilation. II. Straus, Scott, 1970–, editor of compilation.
  III. Series: Critical human rights.
  JC571.H769684   2014
  323—dc23
                                                              2013027992

Contents

The Human Rights Paradox

Introduction

Embracing Paradox

Human Rights in the Global Age

STEVE J. STERN AND SCOTT STRAUS

Human rights are paradoxical. On the one hand, human rights are transcendent. Human rights gain power and purchase because they are said to belong to all people no matter who they are or where they are. On the other hand, the idea of human rights conferred on us all by virtue of being human is a convenient fiction. Humans realize their rights only in particular places with particular instruments and with particular protections.

Many scholars recognize elements of this paradox. One of the most consistent themes in the literature on human rights is the absence of international enforcement mechanisms. The human rights of people all over the world may be declared or even promised in law. But the mechanisms by which to enforce those declarations and promises are woefully weak. In the end, universal human rights are achieved in specific states with institutions that enjoy mechanisms to protect rights or through specific transnational networks of civil society actors who pressure governments to change (Hafner-Burton and Tsusui 2005; Hathaway 2002; Ignatieff 2001; Keck and Sikkink 1998; Simmons 2009).

In this book, we seek to deepen the human rights paradox beyond the problem of enforcement. Rather than creating an analytical framework where there are discrete spheres of the global, the national, and the local in which human rights operate, we argue that human rights are constituted ineluctably by a paradoxical intersection between the universal and the specific. When human rights exist, they are always simultaneously global and local. In other words, human rights are both always and never universal and global. Ditto for the local: human rights are only imaginable with appeal to the global and the universal, but they are only concrete when they are local. This paradox, we claim, structures human rights. In every human rights situation and in every human rights activist, there will necessarily be mutually constitutive global and local dimensions, and those dimensions will often be in tension.

The power of globalization offers an imperfect but instructive parallel. Some argue that globalization "flattens" the world (Friedman 2005). Thomas Friedman employs the metaphor to describe how global communication, transportation, and technology create opportunities for new players to participate and profit in a global marketplace. But the metaphor is evocative for conceptualizing how globalization across many spheres—from international organizations whose transnational oversight of matters ranging from fiscal policy to criminal justice to internal rebellion—squeeze spheres of sovereign action and immunity by states. The metaphor continues—from corporations and investors able to operate in real-time and just-in-time rather than lag-time contexts across global markets to transnational advocacy groups and nongovernmental organizations for whom electronic posting and instant communication enhance reach and shift "on the ground" realities—all of which steamrolls the local. Globalized values, connectivity, networking, and integration across national state borders and continents have acquired such velocity, ubiquity, and visibility that it can appear as if the local is being eviscerated. Indeed, the apparent power of globalization is such that it can even eviscerate the distinction between the "universal," understood as an imperative or value that transcends historical context and in a sense human agency, and the "global," understood as transnational relationships so strong and dynamic that they flow across conventional borders of nation, locale, or culture.

Yet appearances can also deceive and beg for critical analysis. World culture includes strong multidirectional influences and a robust heterogeneity of ideas and relationships. The world is not becoming a "world society" with a single system and culture (Lechner and Boli 2004, 1). Nor are world politics simply converging around a single coherent set of ideas around how to structure the state (Kupchan 2012). Rather, when observed empirically, places around the world exhibit striking and resilient variety and "mélange," or dynamic mixing

Steve J. Stern and Scott Straus

between global and local cultural forces (Pieterse 2003). Politics are becoming divergent, even if political ideas in one place constantly influence and shape ideas in another place. In short, the universal and the global unfold in deep tension and indeed interdependence with the local. One is unimaginable without the other.

Human rights are the same. For human rights, whose power and strength derive in part from international assertions of transcendent values that must be respected absolutely, rather than violated by state rulers who use contextual descriptions of crisis to justify a set-aside of fundamental rights, the paradox is both peculiar and challenging. The idea of universalism in human rights establishes a bulwark against claims to cause harm in the name of specific situations—whether they be wars, coups, protests, or deep deprivation. To borrow from Ruti Teitel's (2011) apt phrase, human rights are a form of "humanity law"—laws beyond states and state sovereignty. Yet human rights as animated by people who claim rights—either as advocates or as individuals who seek protection—always inhabit very specific situations. To borrow the mixing metaphor, human rights are always a "mélange" of the global and the local. Human rights simultaneously belong both to "humanity" and to very specific locales and people. To understand what this means, we need to value not only general theory but also specific stories grounded in particular times and places.

※

Consider the art of Sarhua, a Quechua-speaking village of the high Andes renowned for its tradition of *tablas* (painted boards) depicting the idyllic life of the community. The village was also engulfed by the violence of the war, initiated in 1980, that pitted Peruvian state forces against the Maoist insurgents known as Shining Path. The war subjected rural Andean peoples and other civilians to massive human rights violations including cruel vengeance raids, bodily mutilation and sexual assault, and murder and disappearance. Unlike elsewhere in Latin America, where one-sided responsibility fell on state agents and paramilitary forces aligned with the state, in Peru the insurgents were responsible for somewhat more than half the dead. Shining Path lost the war, which wound down by the mid-1990s, but the violence took the lives of some 69,000 persons and displaced hundreds of thousands. One legacy of the war, evident before it wound down, was the creation of a national human rights movement by brave activists whose social capital and human networks varied but ranged from the global to the local. A second legacy emerged after the fall in 2000 of the regime of Alberto Fujimori—the president who at first received credit for vanquishing Shining Path, then succumbed to scandal and disgrace for corruption and power seeking. Peru embarked on a formal national truth commission process, and this opened up additional space for the making of human rights sensibilities and activism including artistic forms of truth telling.[1]

Sarhua's *tablas* traditionally featured multiple art panels arranged as a vertical storytelling strip. They originated as ritual house gifts by co-godparents to the family with whom they shared obligations including labor reciprocity. In the 1970s, Sarhua's artists began adapting *tabla* art and aesthetics to the emerging market for folk art, in part by shrinking the giant boards to manageable size and sometimes to only one scene. Sarhua's art of Andean authenticity, instantly recognizable and unique, began to show up in museum exhibits, private collections of foreigners, and respectable Peruvian middle-class homes, as well as the homes of Sarhuino villagers and urban migrants. To this day, Sarhua's art exerts an aesthetic charm featured as a point of pride in websites promoting Andean/Peruvian tourism.

But what about the war experience? The war between Maoist insurgents and military forces reached genocidal proportions in the Ayacucho region, whose rural indigenous peoples adapted in varied ways—from organizing community self-defense patrols to fleeing to cities or safer rural areas. Sarhua's district sat amid some of the hardest-hit provinces within Ayacucho. By the early 1990s, some Sarhuino artists began to adapt *tablas* to a new purpose—that of telling the war experience of their community. One striking painting, *Community Council*, poignantly sums up that experience. It depicts in its center a community assembly of villagers, surrounded by mountains and invoking the protection of the local Apusuyo (mountain spirit). Driven to desperation by assaults from both sides, they agree they will serve community unity and one another, above all else, with humility. They will not align themselves with sides in the war—neither Shining Path nor the military—but they will offer hospitality (food) to anyone who visits. Outside the protective mountains are the two armed threats: insurgent guerrillas dressed in rural Andean clothes on the left, soldiers in uniform on the right.[2]

Stripped from local context notwithstanding its depiction of local experience, the artistic representation fits well with globally influential languages of human rights. It depicts a clear boundary between perpetrator and victim, and resonates with the idea of the innocent victim whose innate right to bodily integrity—life itself—is under threat of cruel violation. The representation also resonates with the sometimes influential idea of the victim "caught between two sides"—between a state, which tramples the human rights of vulnerable citizens it is obligated to protect but has converted into the demonized enemy,

Steve J. Stern and Scott Straus

and an insurgent force, which ignores humanitarian laws of war and brutalizes socially humble people as it wages its campaign of supposed liberation.

Yet if one digs deeper into the context of community life and artistic production, one discovers that art, like other forms of truth telling and memory making after atrocity, may include silences that complicate generic human rights categories. The civil war in Ayacucho generated fratricidal dynamics within rural villages. People differed and evolved in their adaptations. Some persons including children were forcibly recruited and socialized into one or another side. The local politics of intra- and intercommunity abuse and privilege *before* the 1980s war—from cattle rustling and land grabs to sexual assault and domestic violence—inclined some to seize hold of the war crisis for vengeful or opportunistic ends or for moral justice. Many villagers believed in education as social progress and valued kinship relationships; such stances encouraged some *comuneros* to accept as valid (or possibly valid) the ideas of revolution then influential among youth in provincial universities and also among school teachers. The war crisis and its attendant dynamics of coerced complicity could also produce inner doubts, and sometimes political and spiritual rebirth through Protestant conversion.

Taken together, such dynamics meant that *comuneros* in Ayacucho participated in the war: as social actors assessing politics and society in local and national contexts, deciding how best to survive or even to assert rights in dangerous times, and learning through trial and error. Community members engaged in acts that turned them into perpetrators as well as victims of violence. Such situations generated touchy secrets about internal fissures and violence that afflicted communities in the early years of the war; some were later put aside as communities reconstructed a sense of unity and sought social repair from the state and nongovernmental organizations.[3]

In the case of Sarhua, as the anthropologist Olga M. González (2011) has brilliantly shown, the *tablas* that depict the war experience also evince some discretion about difficult community secrets. They sidestep the mystery disappearance and probable murder of the *comunero* Narciso Huicho, a local tyrant and land grabber who opportunistically denounced alleged insurgents; the subsequent assassination of the *comunero* "Justiniano," who opposed Huicho but escalated the war by supporting Shining Path; and the initial base of support for both Justiniano and Shining Path. It is worth recalling that in the early 1990s when the war *tablas* were created to tell the story, alleged sympathy with Shining Path continued to expose people to great risk. The discretion is understandable.

Yet it goes too far to say that "Community Council" tells an untruth in the simple sense. Art happens at the intersection of experience and imagination.

Metaphor and license may serve to capture the deep truths lived in crisis situations. Literalism may miss the point: the community assembly happened in the central plaza, not huddled in an enclosure surrounded by mountains. What *comuneros* wanted, though, was that sense of protection and rebalancing within an Andean landscape of belonging and relationships with spirit-ancestors. Most important, the depiction of the assembly decision captures a deep social and psychological truth—but one that *eventually* became real and dominant. The representation of community unity and political distancing in the face of violent threat was a point of *arrival*—the outcome of a painful and contradictory community process of learning, anchored in local relationships yet including an awareness of the value of human rights affirmation in other contexts (González 2011).

The problem is that such art, if freed from its back-story context and taken as a point of departure rather than arrival, ratifies rather than problematizes preconceived universal categories of human rights thought. Such an approach does not tell us how and why, and with what limitations, apparently broad notions of right, violation, and innocence may come to resonate. Even a work of art undeniably authentic and instantly recognizable as such, even a work of art whose point is indeed the grounded telling of local experience of a human rights crisis, is vulnerable to an unthinking fitting into the common sense categories of the global age.

❦

This book argues that tensions of the universal and the local in human rights constitute a paradox, and that embracing this paradox can move human rights scholarship in fruitful new directions. The entanglements of the universal and the local amount to a necessary irresolvable contradiction—a relationship between logics of thought and action that create strain and can push actors in divergent directions, yet without whose combined and mutually constitutive effect human rights lose force as value, practice, and scholarship.

Human rights acquire power precisely from internationally supported assertions of a transcendent claim—transhistorical, transnational, and universal. Certain fundamental rights are innately endowed upon people, by virtue of their humanity, regardless of particular circumstances. The crises of state rule and the dynamics of war do not constitute a context that justifies setting them aside. The human rights architecture in the world seeks to provide a set of instruments—including law and legal precedents, treaties and declarations of principle, specialized international organizations, and tribunals and organized action networks, not only by states but also non-state organizations—

Steve J. Stern and Scott Straus

all of which embody the universality of human rights. Those instruments can and do provide tools to mobilize, document, "name and shame," and prosecute oppression around the world.[4]

Yet the chapters in this volume also reveal how fundamental the local and the specific—in a word, grounded contextual analysis—turn out to be for any human rights story. Human rights abuses occur in particular times and places. Likewise, the responses to those abuses and the capacity to live in their aftermath take place in particular times and places. Locality shapes meaning—what constitutes an abuse, how one understands that it transgresses what is morally permissible. Locality shapes divergence—the probabilities, and the sometimes unexpected twist, that drive human rights paths and outcomes in some directions rather than others, and that also define the articulations with supralocal actors and universal values that can gain traction. In other words, locality shapes human response. Actors assert, mold, pull at, and change human rights destinies within their specific contexts of lived experience and struggle, always inflecting human rights stories with their interpretation and their strategies. Human rights abuse is thus always local, always political, and always historical, and the fight for human rights is also always local, political, and historical. In this sense, there is no transcendent universal in the empirics of human rights.

The claim of the book is that this contradiction always structures human rights. There can be no human rights without a claim to the universal, to the transnational, and to transcendent principle. But there can also be no human rights without locality, politics, history, and actors. The issue is not simply a problem of "vernacularizing" human rights—that is, translating universal principles into local context (Merry 2006). The issue is a more profound tension, one that persistently pulls human rights practice and understanding in twinned yet often countervailing directions simultaneously. Precisely because it is not self-evident that the logics of these doubled directions are smoothly harmonious, human rights analysis falls into a trap if it focuses uniquely on one or the other. The necessity to see, to mediate, and to coordinate the mutually constitutive tensions of the universal and the local: this constitutes a fundamental paradox of human rights, as scholarship and as practice.[5]

Human rights, therefore, is a story of "universality and its discontents." Here we acknowledge but do not reduce discontents to a shorthand word for discrimination—the idea that some people in some parts of the world are not in reality included in the circle of those deemed fit or ready for human rights. Such exclusions matter and do indeed figure into the ways people deploy, resist, neglect, or interpret universalist assertions of right. For purposes of this book, however, we also understand discontents as locally grounded experience, that is, the lived achievements, frustrations, and emerging contentious issues among actors who struggle for human rights and for whom part of the struggle lies in the gaps between the local and the global. Such actors find themselves impelled to build and mediate and improvise on a foundation of material created simultaneously from "global" and "local" forces. It is the only foundation possible, perhaps, but it is vulnerable to cracking.

But are we dealing with one paradox, or several? We seek in this book not only to embrace paradox but also to unpack it. In reality, this book's chapters address several closely related issues. We may think of this bundle as distinct dimensions of the larger tension we have elucidated. Each issue is critical in its own right for understanding human rights, yet each also draws analytical force from the tension between universal affirmation and local struggle.

Taken together, these chapters address three implications of the human rights paradox that we underline. They do so mainly through case study analysis informed by theory or academic discipline. Here we express each in methodological terms, as a "necessity" useful to advance scholarship:

(a) *The necessity for deeply contextualized multilevel analysis, simultaneously attentive to local as well as global terrains of struggle over human rights, and to grounded study of efforts at mediation across distinct levels of human action.* By implication, a recognition of the always multilevel ways in which human rights operate immediately speaks to a need for multidisciplinary insights on human rights. In this volume, each contributor is grounded in his or her discipline. Multidisciplinarity does not mean the abandonment of disciplinary rigor, approaches, methods, and theory. To the contrary, careful empirical, disciplinary-rooted research from multiple perspectives is an asset in the face of a necessarily multilevel phenomenon. To engage a plurality of knowledge sites and vehicles is not only to recognize the idea that human rights issues arise in different parts of the world and in societies with distinct trajectories of human action and culture. It is also to recognize the need for cross-disciplinary conversation—grounded not in the dissolution of academic disciplines but in awareness that each can lend unique powerful insight.

(b) *The necessity to focus on human agency and relationships in the making and unmaking of human rights, such that victims are not reducible to victims only, and such that understandings of rights are not merely diffused or imported from a "global" field of politics or culture.* The analyses in this book, each of which is sensitive to the particular and the specific, make this clear. The making of human rights abuse and the surviving of such abuse often entail complex relationships. Human rights discourse provides a language to name and respond to that abuse; that language can be both powerful and essential for recognizing injustice and for providing a framework for justice. But when such language in turn displaces the local context in which the abuse and response take place, it can create new myopias. Indeed, in some cases such as postgenocide Rwanda—where an authoritarian regime has successfully downplayed its abuses by invoking a global human rights narrative about genocide—substituting local understanding with universal human rights categories can lead to dangerous appraisals of the situation (Straus and Waldorf 2011). The same is true in places like the Democratic Republic of Congo, where overplaying the universal in place of the local has quite serious negative repercussions on the ground (Autesserre 2012).

(c) *The necessity to conceptualize new horizons of human rights precisely because relational dynamics of action, thought, and communication in global and local settings give rise to a shifting history and future of urgent fundamental rights attached to the human, rather than eternal transcendent rights that emerge after a formative point of historical origin.* Recognizing the importance of the historically grounded sets us up to think about the ways in which the present will change—and how, as change occurs, so too will human rights. The foundational human rights discourse laid down in key documents such as the Universal Declaration of Human Rights and the pantheon of core international human rights treaties have proven remarkably flexible. But there is always a risk that once named, such frameworks limit what a human rights agenda— whether scholarly or practical—can envision. Yet careful attention to locality, as well as to changes in the global arena, can yield appreciation of new human rights challenges or old ones that have not yet been named. Recognizing the relational underpinning of the paradox of the global and the local helps to make any human rights analysis more flexible, more accommodating of facts and insights that lie outside the dominant paradigm, and more open to emerging and urgent rights.

Each dimension just discussed raises analytical challenges in its own right. Each also relates to the larger paradox we have highlighted here: fundamental human rights that are at once profoundly transcendent and profoundly rooted, as assertion and experience and struggle, and for which an inescapable tension between the universal and the local pulls in distinct directions.

We are certainly not the first to recognize the importance of the local. Careful empirical studies of globalization in the cultural realm show how influence is multidirectional (Pieterse 2003). Within the human rights field, a number of important studies already recognize clear tensions between the local and the global (Clarke and Goodale 2010; Englund 2006; Goodale 2006; Goodale 2009; Goodale and Merry 2007; Merry 2006; Shaw, Waldorf, and Hazan 2010). Our claims build upon and are consistent with these and other works. Like Marc Goodale and Sally Merry (2007) and like Rosalind Shaw and Lars Waldorf (2010), we do not see the local as simply an appendage to the global. Introducing the local is also not only a question of translation and legitimation—that is, of vernacularizing the practice of human rights (Goodale and Merry 2007; Merry 2006). Similarly, we do not aim to reverse the primacy of the global with a primacy of the local, creating a new romanticization of all things local (Goodale 2009). Nor are we claiming that all human rights are "hybridized," whereby the global is inflected with the local. Rather our claim is that there is a necessary tension between the global and the local that *structures* human rights. The global and the local are always present in human rights—*always in tension yet mutually constitutive*. That is the central theoretical claim of our book, and we argue that these dimensions should be a central point of departure for scholarship and practice on human rights.

What do we mean by the local? In general, we mean the particular and the contextual, in the sense of rooted in specific places and relationships so pervasive that they give rise to a sense of the "locale" as a sited experience of community and contention about rights, values, and obligations. The scale of the locale may vary, from the small-scale community of limited national visibility to larger communities of regional or other subnational identity to communities of peoples who self-identify with the nation-state and its public sphere. Indeed, as Sidney Tarrow has aptly put it, transnational activists themselves "are a subgroup of rooted cosmopolitans," that is, "actors rooted in specific national contexts, but who engage in contentious political activities that involve them in transnational networks of contacts and conflicts" (Tarrow 2005, 29).

What is important as we unpack the "local" is to recognize that it unfolds on distinct scales of human action and consciousness. Sometimes, the "local" refers to a field of actors influential at the national level and who see themselves as such. Some national-level elite actors may even be oblivious to the distinction between the capital city as a subnational community—one locale among others, with its own distinctive history of struggles, relationships, norms, and expectations—and the capital city as the outsized political symbol

Steve J. Stern and Scott Straus

of the nation—that is, the place able to take on the conceit of acting as if its inhabitants and their urban community are the nation. Sometimes, the scale of the local is more "provincial," in the sense of referring to regional or subregional communities whose actors and lived experiences are less consciously aligned with national imaginaries and influence. The local actors may lament or denounce their peripheral leverage or visibility within the nation. In such cases, the "global" or the "universal" may often be refracted through relationships between logics of the nation and its periphery. At the extreme (see Meghan Foster Lynch's chapter 3), the "global" aspect of a human rights moment may drop out altogether. In other words, the tension may be present even when it appears to be invisible.

Transnational refugee camps and cross-border regions that witness human displacement and migration offer another variation. In many locations, "local" relationships of kinship, livelihood, and language may remain quite strong even across borders and even in the context of "global" spaces, such as refugee camps organized and run by international actors. Refugees often are aware and play off a doubled awareness of local and international relationships and environments. In addition, even when displaced from their locale and placed in a transnational space of a camp, refugees often reproduce a version of their local communities, ties, and preferences—sometimes with detrimental effects (Lischer 2005; Todd 2010). Here again in these cross-border spaces the "local" demonstrates remarkable staying power, even when situated in a "transcendent" space of a refugee camp, and actors find themselves constantly negotiating the tensions between the local and the universal.

When we refer, therefore, to contextualized multilevel analysis attentive to local as well as global terrains of struggle and mediation over human rights, we understand that from a theoretical standpoint we are advocating for triple-level cognizance of place-based contexts (subregional or regional, national, and sometimes self-consciously international), in tension with a transcendent, universal imperative. Even in regions or subregions distant from national capitals, some actors may arrive at an awareness of multileveled fields of action, and they may literally migrate back and forth across fields of social network and experience.

Consider Sarhua once more. Some Sarhuinos experienced life in Lima as well as Sarhua. Some transnational and national actors rooted in metropolitan Lima built relationships in Ayacucho and Sarhua. In Peru as elsewhere, the locale, the nation, and the transnational all engendered communities of experience, ideas, and struggle on issues related to human rights. Such communities overlapped but did not erase their distinctive normative and social logics.[6]

The chapters in this book reflect in diverse ways the multilevel contexts of action and experience that emerge when we unpack the local. In some chapters, the "local" and the "national" are very closely associated. For others, the locale as a field of experience is sharply distinct from the national, and the global may be refracted through the national. In still others, the global—whether understood as universalizing theory that has become influential, or as vehicles of transnational communication and relationship building—is itself contextualized and in that sense provincialized.

※

A brief guide to the chapters and how they relate to the book's argument will be useful. Although most of the chapters address most of the themes highlighted above, they do so with different emphases. We have organized chapters in three clusters that serve distinctly to underscore and elaborate the implications of multilevel contextual analysis, human agency, and emerging new horizons.

A first cluster of three chapters draws out the implications of contextualized analysis sensitive to multiple scales of human action and influence. By focusing seriously on local as well as international social forces, and on the ways human agency creates a history of contingency—shifting possibilities and probabilities, within specific contexts—these studies turn familiar global narratives inside out. Assumptions of diffusion and a related chronology of linear displacement—one big idea gives way to the next big idea—lose ground. Analytical priority on the moment of global origin or global tipping loses much of its point. Once we are drawn into the vortex of tension between the local and the universal, the making of human rights history and the challenge of making a human rights future look sharply different.

In chapter 1, Geoffrey Robinson, a historian, demonstrates how East Timor's conjoining of independence and human rights struggles pushes us to rethink the history of human rights "from the ground up." The chapter not only elucidates the ups and downs of the human rights struggle in East Timor as an important case study in its own right when analyzed in local and international contexts simultaneously; it also shows that precisely because human rights struggle merged with the politics of anticolonial struggle, common narratives of global displacement and turning points mislead us: they push human actors and their projects to the margin in our field of vision. Although Robinson emphasizes as foil the influential interpretation by Samuel Moyn (2010) of human rights as a mid-1970s transition premised on the failure of political projects and self-determination struggles, Robinson's deeper point

Steve J. Stern and Scott Straus

lies elsewhere. The very terms of debate—the quest for the decisive moment of origin or turning point, on a global scale—are misplaced. By studying human action and politics at the intersection of the local and the global, Robinson echoes Marc Bloch's (1953) cautionary note about the "idol of origins" in historical scholarship.[7]

Bridget Conley-Zilkic's chapter on the U.S. Holocaust Memorial Museum and the global upsurge in memorial museum projects considers the tension between the universal and the local from a different perspective. Here the focus is on social actors who make museum work happen and—as in the case of the author herself, who is a former research director at the Committee on Conscience at the Museum—are acutely conscious of both peril and promise. On the one hand, human rights museum work often unfolds within a field of constraint defined by the nation-state. Museums risk ratifying state power and an empty transnational discourse—the universalizing gesture toward other cases reduced to a story of suffering by victims, and stripped of the specific contexts that shape the urgent moral and political issues that have arisen, and the likely consequences of a given action. On the other hand, precisely because museums have shifted toward an ethos of engaged visitor-centered experience and are institutions of unusual credibility about history, museums of conscience can create a space of "interruption" grounded in specific historical experience. The museum can invite the visitor to enter a space of disorienting experience that unsettles cultural and political commonplaces. Working within the gap between the universal and the historical while embracing the inescapable dialogue between them: museums of conscience have a perhaps unique capacity to draw people into this work.

A third chapter within this cluster offers a distinct twist by placing improbable historical contingency—the unexpected—in the center of the analysis. Meghan Foster Lynch's study of Hutus and Tutsis in Burundi, in the wake of the 1993 assassination of the first elected Hutu president, Melchior Ndadaye, turns upside down the usual focus. Instead of analyzing why atrocities against Tutsi citizens happened in much of Burundi, she asks why they did *not* happen in Rumonge, where violence could have been expected. The result is a remarkable analysis of how and why people "waged peace" rather than war. Lynch, a political scientist, shows that part of the explanation derives from considering how local actors and leaders engaged in their own political learning process, based on their own readings of historical experience. Significantly, however, Lynch does not idealize human agency even as she focuses on it. She enables us to see limits: what the waging of peace was up against, when and why it broke down, how the probabilities and contexts in play were at once local and national. Her story is also one of a human rights moment—of human protection and the avoidance of violence—but one seemingly taken without reference to universal principles. As such, the remarkable Burundi case also stands as a caution not to assume we may "read" the global and universal into the making of every human rights moment. At the same time, and as Lynch observes, this unusual limit-case may offer an instructive practical lesson for transnational human rights activists who work at the intersection of local and global claims.

Taken together, the studies by Robinson, Conley-Zilkic, and Lynch demonstrate that analysis attentive to context and human actors opens up fresh approaches to human rights as global historical narrative. The story does not reduce to diffusion from global to local terrain, nor to translation of the global into the particular, nor to a history of the decisive global moment. Human rights stories often unfold more dialectically and creatively and synergistically, at the paradoxical space of intersection between local and supralocal contexts populated by social actors seeking to interpret, shape, and mediate. The space is one of historical contingency—a field of probabilities with multiple paths taken and not taken, not a highway of inexorability. The actors who populate such fields of probability are specific and varied—from political activists pressing for national self-determination and an end to atrocity, to institutional memory makers seeking to educate through interruption, to community leaders determined to wage peace over war. Such actors are aware of the contexts that root them and frame their choices and opportunities, even as they seek to create new possibilities. Such stories can generate a history of globally significant events and transitions in world culture of human rights, but one whose methodology of research and explanation does not derive singularly from the global level of analysis itself, nor do they elide ongoing heterogeneity of action and contexts that give rise to divergent histories of human rights.[8]

A second cluster of chapters builds on the first but shifts the focus. Once we take as a theoretical given the necessity of contextualized analysis cognizant of multiple scales of struggle and agency in the making and unmaking of human rights, what happens to fundamental categories of transcendent human rights thought? Here our authors offer a fresh look at three major categories: victim, truth, and justice.

In chapter 4 of this book, health demographers Patrick Vinck and Phuong N. Pham use comparative research, notably in northern Uganda, eastern Congo, and Cambodia, to ask difficult questions. What do survivors want? Who considers themselves victims of atrocity? How do victim-centered ideas compare to those of the professional human rights community? Does our model of victim rely implicitly on the idea of an innocent minority, whose violation of fundamental rights leads them to want to return to "normalcy" after a period

Steve J. Stern and Scott Straus

of repair? What happens if some victims have also been perpetrators of horrific atrocity? Vinck and Pham unpack a fundamental category of human rights law and action. Experiences in specific contexts shape the meanings of "victim" in sometimes unexpected ways.

Similarly, in chapters 5 and 6, respectively, the anthropologist Noa Vaisman and the political scientist Jo-Marie Burt prod us to consider how meanings of "truth" and "justice" evolve and relate to social actors. The generic meaning of "truth" in South American human rights communities after military dictatorships of the 1970s was violent atrocity perpetrated but denied by the state. As Vaisman shows, however, the Argentine context also attached particular generational meanings to truth. The central mechanism of state terror was to disappear people—not only permanent abduction followed by torture and death but also denial of knowledge and records of the kidnapped prisoner. The disappeared included thousands of young women, some of them pregnant, and the perpetrators adopted or trafficked in those women's babies. The children turned into a key issue, politically and culturally and, eventually, legally. In this context, "truth" meant the genetic ancestry of persons who grew up as children of their parents' kidnappers—and the contested ethics of identification, affective ties, and individual choice. As Vaisman also shows, and as children of the disappeared asserted their own generational voice and praxis in a group called H.I.J.O.S., another sensitive issue emerged over time. Many persons disappeared in the 1970s were politicized and thought of themselves as advocates of social justice or revolution. Did focus on their political values play into the hands of state terror—since everyone has human rights, and since the discourse that some do not deserve rights had to be resisted—or was it important to honor the victims by embracing their projects? Likewise, did assertion of political values as such, with reference to both past and present, create new lines of division that weakened human rights? How did strains in the human rights community on this issue intersect with generational dynamics? Truth was elusive, fundamentally because of state terror and denial—but it was also elusive because people reconsidered and argued about what was important to document and remember, and why.

Jo-Marie Burt's contribution, in chapter 6, is to interrogate the meaning of justice if one sees through local and global lenses, simultaneously. Her case study is the trial of Alberto Fujimori, the disgraced former president of Peru who was convicted in his own country in 2009 on human rights charges and sentenced to twenty-five years in prison. When seen from the perspective of global justice and international human rights law, the Fujimori affair constitutes a major advance. It set an important legal precedent on a knotty issue—immunity for heads of state and former heads of state. Chile's extradition of

Fujimori to Peru in 2007 was also notable because it was an affair of South-to-South transitional justice, rather than pressure from the global North on the weaker South. When seen from within the Peruvian context, however, Burt shows that the Fujimori affair ended up becoming a high-profile exception that seemed, in the medium run, to prove the rule of impunity. The conviction in some ways galvanized rather than stopped the impunity bloc and a backing away from justice. At this level of analysis, the political inflections bounded the case as a one-off rather than a precedent. The consequences of justice were contingent and they unfolded in distinct contexts simultaneously.

To understand the confounding implications, it may be helpful to take a cue from sensibilities about time that have historically inflected Latin American literature.[9] Time is more than linear motion forward, in a sequence where event A is displaced by or makes possible the arrival of event B, which is subsequently displaced by event C, and so on. Time may also be an illusion or a puzzle—simultaneous forward and backward motion on different tracks, apparent forward movement only to find that one has traveled in a circle back to the start, a travel escapade into a regional time-space of alternate reality that does not end offering refuge, however, from the familiar. Precisely because distinct actors rooted in distinct contexts pushed to draw meaning from a singular trial of consequence, Burt's interrogation of justice underscores Robinson's cautionary tale about historical chronology.

Taken together, our second cluster of chapters demonstrates that categories closely associated with human rights as transcendent value—the victim of violation by a perpetrator, the truth that undermines the denial and cover-up, the justice that restores balance—are themselves historically constructed. Social experience, political action, and moral appeal shape and shift what such terms can mean, and unfold in distinct yet related contexts simultaneously. This heterogeneity occurs even when the ostensible substantive focus is the same: a regional genocide, or a national scandal of kidnapping accompanied by child theft, or a precedent-setting trial of a former president.

One may take the implications another step: the meaning of "human rights" shifts as a result of human action in multiple contexts. As Winifred Tate (2007) has shown in a superb study of human rights activism in Colombia, as the language of human rights became perceived as internationally influential or hegemonic, varied social actors with distinct political agendas—and including those historically hostile to human rights—will find reasons to engage it. They will seek to build a human rights doctrine of their own, to embrace and redefine the category of victim, to create strategies such as the endless bureaucratic loop of apparent concern. In Colombia, where the line between "local" and "international" actors promoting human rights blurred in the 1990s and

Steve J. Stern and Scott Straus

early 2000s, military officers eventually found themselves impelled to engage. What human rights can mean does indeed shift over time as a result of human relationships of necessity and opportunity. These relationships shape, build, and deflect the climate of legal right and moral appeal.

The contested historicity of human rights brings us to the third cluster of chapters in this book. If fundamental human rights—not only the substantive meaning or content of the rights but also the vehicles of their assertion—are profoundly relational and historical, what new horizons of human rights are unfolding in the present and the future?

In chapter 7, Fuyuki Kurasawa provides a powerful analysis of the promise and perils of social media technology for a "global civil society" of human rights activism. The explosion of web-based modes of sharing information—from Twitter to crowdsourcing to new platforms being developed seemingly weekly—creates exceptional possibilities for human rights activism in the global age. Yet critics worry that such new technologies also significantly limit human rights engagement; today human rights might mean sitting behind one's computer in perfect comfort, a form of "slacktivism." Kurasawa, a sociologist, perceptively reviews but ultimately sets aside as too limited these terms of debate between techno-idealists and techno-skeptics. The irony of new social media is that even as they fortify global voice and connection through a digital politics of representational activism, they also create a set of new contradictions and problems, including possibilities for new forms of state surveillance and problems of reducing complex situations to short tweets. Kurasawa shows that analysis at the level of disembodied global technologies can provide little insight on local situations—and may overlook unintended consequences including impact, saturation, credibility, and invisibility. The point is not that the new technologies of activism are valuable or useless, but rather that their value is contingent rather than intrinsic. We need empirical and situational analysis to draw out both the promise and peril of representational activism. In making these points, Kurasawa smartly demonstrates how even for new information communications technology—which seemingly provides all kinds of new global possibilities for human rights—the local and the specific are fundamental.

In an age of global climate change, the question of access to water is one of the new frontiers of human rights. Should there be an explicitly articulated, universal right to water? In chapter 8 Philippe Cullet, a legal scholar, provides insight into the issue by examining India. The country is a particularly valuable case in which to explore the issue because Indian governments face an enormous challenge in providing access to clean water to its billion people, many of whom are poor, and because the state's constitution establishes some legal room for conceptualizing water as a human right. Cullet's chapter is an expert, detailed analysis of how the Indian Supreme Court's decisions have created a legal framework on the right to water and how that framework has and has not shaped government policy on water. His analysis makes many compelling points. But one of the most powerful is the way in which any universal mandate for a right to water cannot be understood without recourse to local conditions. The local enters at the judicial level—it is the specificity of the Indian Supreme Court's interpretations that are especially important. But more generally, states are the principal institutions to realize any social-economic right, including the right to water. As such, any right to water will always be embedded in a national government's, a regional government's, and a local government's capacity to put an abstract human right into practice. In India's case, policies on access to water translate into highly specific counts of distances to water sources and of liters per day for villagers. At the same time, they are also part of an evolution, within and beyond India, toward neoliberal approaches to policy making, which turn the state toward a role as facilitator of access to the water market rather than provisioner of water as a right. Cullet's attention to these and other details shows just how locally embedded any discussion of a human right to water must become, both as legal doctrine and political reality.

The last chapter in the volume completes the book's circle by reconsidering grand theory, but in a highly innovative way. In chapter 9, the political theorist Richard P. Hiskes forces us to reread Thomas Hobbes, who is not generally considered a towering figure in the pantheon of human rights theorists. Hiskes builds a strong case to show how human relationships and the ability to establish promises and contracts are fundamental to Hobbes's theory of the state and of rights. From this, in a highly original move, Hiskes derives a new theory of human rights in which relationships form the core of human rights. A human right is at base something that guarantees the ability to have human relationships; without them, in a Hobbesian framework, the lives of humans are much diminished, even "subhuman."

Hiskes's emphasis on rights derived from human relationships rather than on rights derived from individual and natural rights opens a new way to conceptualize contemporary human rights problems. Hiskes rereads the language of the Universal Declaration of Human Rights to argue that its human rights are also conceptualized in social and relational terms. Hiskes furthermore makes a compelling case for seeing relational and situational rights as fundamental for other human rights philosophers. He argues that all rights are situationally embedded. Hiskes continues by showing how a relational view of human rights is in fact fundamental to many contemporary human rights challenges, in particular environmental ones and especially the right to water.[10]

Steve J. Stern and Scott Straus

Environmental harms and regimes to protect against environmental harms are fundamentally about relations between human beings, especially relations between humans across generations. Here we have another perspective that highlights time and place.

From this innovative theoretical perspective, Hiskes brings together many of our themes: the necessity for contexts, both local and transnational/universal; the making of rights through relationships and experience (i.e., via human agency rather than providentially given); the emerging horizon of new issues that may challenge some of the very premises (i.e., the autonomous right-endowed individual of liberal society, rather than communities of future generation). Hiskes also underscores the value of cross-disciplinary talk—here, in a volume most of whose contributors put theory on the back burner in order to talk more effectively to others, we have someone who brings us back to consider how an explicit study of theory can illuminate our concerns.

Taken together, we have three quite different but very complementary chapters in this final section on new horizons in human rights. Each one focuses on a contemporary problem—from innovations in information and communications technology to the right to water in India to environmental rights—but ends up reiterating the fundamental tension between the universal and the local that we argue structures the field of human rights. Kurasawa shows us how even in a global age of space-time compression, much turns on how, where, and by whom the technology is used. Twitter can become a vehicle for human rights documenting and organizing, but similar technologies also can provide a platform for state surveillance. Cullet shows us how any resort to the notion of a universal right to water is immediately embedded in very detailed and political questions over location, volume, and need—all highly local issues. And Hiskes shows us, in a theoretical vein, how the universal call for human rights is always enmeshed in webs of human relations; it is in a way always local.

❧

We argue in this volume that the tensions of the universal and the local constitute a paradox of human rights in the global age that ensued in the wake of the Cold War, and that embracing such paradox can move human rights as a field of study in fruitful directions. In conceptualizing human rights as stories of "universality and its discontents"—manifest in highly contextualized and multiscaled analysis, attendant to human agency and relationships and mediation, open to new horizons of fundamental right that emerge relationally and historically, and receptive to intellectually cosmopolitan conversation across disciplines and regions—we do not intend to throw out the baby with the bath water. Precisely because we live in an age of globalization, we have emphasized grounding and context. Put differently, the dynamics of globalization itself are also grounded. They are not a transcendent über-force but rather a product of human agency and invention in a specific world-historical context.

Yet even as we argue for the importance of grounded local analysis that calls into question chronologies, social categories, and conceptualizations of transcendent right at the global level, we do not advocate a setting aside of global analysis. On the contrary, we have observed that mutual constitution by the universal and the global on the one hand, and national and local on the other, can create dramatic strain—a double-pull in distinct directions, rather than harmony of purpose. The successful push to establish Fujimori's accountability by building on a convergence of local and global action against impunity gave way to the sense that such convergences are at best fleeting. To advance justice, activists would have to navigate both the intractable gaps and the synergistic potentials of local and global logics of human rights action. The inauguration of the U.S. Holocaust Memorial Museum galvanized another kind of tense drama of the double-pull. As Bridget Conley-Zilkic explains, the ceremony created a complication of conscience. Bill Clinton's call to draw the universal lesson seemed too provincial and empty, too oblivious to the global imperative to stop mass atrocity in its southeastern European context, to proceed without a call to conscience. The point, then, is not to dismiss the global or to replace one primacy with another but rather to embrace the mutually constitutive tension between the universal and the local. The tension creates a paradox good to think with—and a condition of human rights struggle good to advocate with. For as Conley-Zilkic puts it so eloquently in her study of the Holocaust Memorial Museum and the controversy about Bosnia-Herzegovina that hovered over its 1993 inaugural, "history and headlines do speak to each other." Struggles for human rights within specific local contexts gain power from universalistic historical lessons and assertions drawn from other contexts. This reality yields some analytical peril, but it also yields something crucial— hope in times of peril.

Afterword: An Image of Encounter and Mis-Encounter

The cover image of this book is a photograph of a screening in Northern Uganda of the video *Kony 2012*, the centerpiece of a human rights

Steve J. Stern and Scott Straus

campaign by the nonprofit group Invisible Children. The image captures an intersection among the necessarily multiple levels at which human rights operate, and thereby offers one fascinating, if extreme, example of the core argument of this book. The image draws out the range of emotion, including bewilderment, which may emerge from encounter and mis-encounter among global and local actors involved in the making of a human rights moment, but rooted in different contexts.

Kony 2012 went viral on social media including YouTube, but was controversial in part because it decontextualized and misrepresented the very human rights problem that was the subject of the film. While they did not defend Joseph Kony and the Lord's Resistance Army against charges of abducting children into a rebel army that committed brutal human rights crimes, critics of Invisible Children noted that the video ignored the reality of a long-standing civil war including state violence, the absence of Joseph Kony from Uganda for years, and the decline of the Lord's Resistance Army as a local presence in Ugandan social conflicts.

In this image, we see an effort to reinsert the film back into the local context of Gulu, the place of victimization emphasized in the film. For further discussion of social media as they relate to human rights, please consult the excellent chapter in the volume by Fuyuki Kurasawa.

Notes

1. For narrative, analysis, and statistics of the war, the fundamental starting point is the national truth commission report: Comisión de la Verdad y Reconciliación Perú 2003 (hereafter CVR 2003), esp. vols. 1, 4, 9, also published online at www.cverdad .org.pe, and ably summarized in one volume as *Hatun Willakuy: Versión abreviada del Informe Final de la Comisión de la Verdad y Reconciliación, Peru* (2004). The CVR's careful revision of the estimated toll from perhaps 30,000 lives to 69,000 lives was a major shock. On Peru's human rights movement, see Youngers 2003; for spaces opened up for artistic truth telling, see Milton 2007 and Milton 2014.

2. On Sarhua's *tablas* tradition and its transformations, we have relied on the beautifully researched and illuminating historical ethnography by Olga M. González (2011). See also Nolte Maldonado 1991; for promotion in tourism and fair trade websites, see, e.g., www.visitperu.com/artesanias_ing/sarhua.html and www.lucuma.com/content/artists/LSSSHA01_Sarhua Tradition.pdf (last accessed August 19, 2012).

3. For more on Peru and the conflict there, see Degregori 2012; Del Pino Huamán 2003; Gamarra 2010; O. González 2011; Heilman 2010; La Serna 2012; Stern 1998; and Theidon 2004.

4. There are many works that view human rights as a set of transcendent claims embodied in international law, covenants, and declaration of principle—and the history of obstacles and pathways to effective assertion of such claims. For example, see Carey,

Gibney, and Poe 2010; Falk 2009; Ishay 2004, Lauren 2003; and Robertson 2002. By and large, these texts give short shrift to the tension between the global and the local that we argue structures human rights. For a complementary perspective, focused on the making of transnational activist networks of "naming and shaming," and setting the history of human rights NGOs within a broader context that includes more local agency, see Keck and Sikkink 1998 as well as Risse, Ropp, and Sikkink 1999. For a poignant and courageous reflection by a human rights activist about the ways particular context—in this case, war and mass atrocity by insurgents in Peru—pulled against the imperatives of classic transcendent doctrine, see Basombrío 1998. For the irony that the increasing influence of international human rights norms drives all kinds of social actors, including some historically hostile to human rights, to embrace them discursively while building strategies to blunt their force or to instrumentalize them, see the superb study by Tate 2007. For debate on historical chronologies and origins of human rights, see the discussion below in relation to the essays in Part I of this book. Our understanding of deep tension between the imperative of the universal and that of the local has been influenced by our own work on cases that proved iconic in world culture of human rights at distinct historical moments: the brutal Chilean dictatorship of Augusto Pinochet that began with the 1973 bombing of the presidential palace, while democratically elected Salvador Allende remained inside to defend the constitutional government; and the 1994 genocide in Rwanda whereby the state orchestrated the massacre of at least half a million civilians while most international actors withdrew their forces. Each case provides a sobering example of both the limits and the power of human rights as an assertion of innate rights that transcend the particular contexts used by violent regimes to justify or explain away atrocity. One might say that the Chilean case served as a galvanizing example in the making of transnational human rights networks and norms since the early 1970s, notwithstanding the local dynamics that undergirded the dictatorship and its afterlife. The Rwanda case showed that even after transnational activists had built much normative acceptance of human rights in international culture, transnational engagement proved unreliable in the mid-1990s while the impact of local dynamics—both during the genocide and in the instrumentalization of its memory by the post-atrocity state—remained powerful. For the case studies, see Stern 2006; Stern 2010; Straus 2006; and Straus and Waldorf 2011.

5. To be sure, this is not the *only* human rights paradox. An important stream of research in recent years is that while human rights are articulated as universally applicable international treaties and norms, and are designed most often to override state sovereignty in order to protect civilians, it is domestic, usually democratic, institutions that breathe concrete power into human rights. In other words, while human rights are international in concept, they are often made concrete through domestic institutions. On these points, see Hathaway 2002; Ignatieff 2001; and Simmons 2009. Another paradox recognized in the literature stems from the ways in which some states sign treaties with little, if any, commitment to them and without any formal enforcement mechanisms to force states to comply with their commitments. But the spread of such laws and norms empower global NGOs to pressure states to comply (Hafner-Burton and Tsutsui 2005).

Steve J. Stern and Scott Straus

6. For more on these points, see González 2011 and Milton 2014.

7. For more on the history of human rights, and in contrast to Moyn on the specifics of periodization and origins, see Hunt 2007. Robinson's essay in this volume cites other recent influential work by historians. An area in need of special mention, however, is the historiography of antislavery as a central feature in the remaking of rights norms in the Atlantic world. For more, see Blackburn 2011 and the seminal work of Davis 1975, cf. Davis 2006.

8. Kathryn Sikkink's (2011) superb study of the emergence of an international norms cascade of accountability for human rights crimes is a sophisticated example of the promise of such an approach. For a different but complementary global analysis of transitional justice, see Olsen, Payne, and Reiter 2010. These books succeed in coordinating multiscaled and highly contextualized analysis in a convincing manner. Yet even in these works, the analytical emphasis on the emergence and diffusion of global norms creates some risk that divergent histories are acknowledged mainly as variations or as influential founding examples that fit into the larger scheme. In short, the centrality and the intractable paradox of the tension between the universal and the local may be minimized. For case studies attentive to international dimensions and advances but that also serve as cautionary tales on justice despite the norm cascade, see Collins 2010; Cruvellier 2010; Huneeus 2010; and Shaw, Waldorf, and Hazan 2010 as well as chapter 6 by Jo-Marie Burt in this volume.

9. A more developed interpretation of temporal sensibilities and literary culture of "boom" writers in relation to Latin American historical experience is given in Stern 1999. For trenchant analysis of the colonial foundations of contemporary literature, and on literary dynamics of myth and history in Latin America, respectively, see Adorno 2007 and González Echevarría 1990, cf. González Echevarría 1985.

10. A profound implication of the relational theory of human rights developed by Hiskes is precisely that new forms of mobilization and meanings of justice developed by communities of poor people may come to critique the narrowness of widely accepted international norms that focused especially on executions, disappearances, and torture as core rights for the integrity of life. In the post–Cold War world, people may come to press the case in new ways and with increasing force that environmental and socioeconomic matters are themselves constitutive of life and violence. For a probing exploration of environmental justice issues, see Nixon 2011. For a critique in South Africa of the limits of postapartheid democracy and its human rights regime when viewed from the perspective of life's necessities, see Zuern 2011.

References

Adorno, Rolena. 2007. *The Polemics of Possession in Spanish American Narrative.* New Haven, CT: Yale University Press.

Autesserre, Séverine. 2012. "Dangerous Tales: Dominant Narratives on the Congo and their Unintended Consequences." *African Affairs* 111, no. 443: 202–22.

Basombrío, Carlos Iglesias. 1998. "Sendero Luminoso and Human Rights: A Perverse Logic that Captured the Country." In *Shining and Other Paths: War and Society in*

Peru, 1980–1995, edited by Steve J. Stern, 425–46. Durham, NC: Duke University Press.

Blackburn, Robin. 2011. *The American Crucible: Slavery, Emancipation and Human Rights*. London: Verso.

Bloch, Marc. 1953. *The Historian's Craft*. Translated by Peter Putnam. New York: Vintage.

Carey, Sabine, Mark Gibney, and Steven Poe. 2010. *The Politics of Human Rights: The Quest for Dignity*. Cambridge: Cambridge University Press.

Clarke, Kamari Maxine, and Mark Goodale, eds. 2010. *Mirrors of Justice: Law and Power in the Post–Cold War Era*. New York: Cambridge University Press.

Collins, Cath. 2010. *Post-Transitional Justice: Human Rights Trials in Chile and El Salvador*. University Park: Pennsylvania State University Press.

Comisión de la Verdad y Reconciliación Perú. 2003. *Informe final*. 9 vols. Lima: CVR.

———. 2004. *Hatun Willakuy: Versión abreviada del Informe Final de la Comisión de la Verdad y Reconciliación, Peru*. Lima: Comisión de Entrega de la CVR.

Cruvellier, Thierry. 2010. *Court of Remorse: Inside the International Criminal Tribunal for Rwanda*. Translated by Chari Voss. Madison: University of Wisconsin Press.

Davis, David Brion. 1975. *The Problem of Slavery in the Age of Revolution, 1770–1823*. Ithaca, NY: Cornell University Press.

———. 2006. *Inhuman Bondage: The Rise and Fall of Slavery in the New World*. New York: Oxford University Press.

Degregori, Carlos Iván. 2012. *How Difficult It Is to Be God: Shining Path's Politics of War in Peru, 1980–1999*. Edited by Steve J. Stern. Madison: University of Wisconsin Press.

Del Pino Huamán, Ponciano. 2003. "Uchuraccay: Memoria y representación de la violencia política en los Andes." In *Jamás tan cerca arremetió lo lejos: Memoria y violencia política en el Perú*, edited by Carlos Iván Degregori, 49–95. Lima: Instituto de Estudios Peruanos.

Englund, Harri. 2006. *Prisoners of Freedom: Human Rights and the African Poor*. Berkeley: University of California Press.

Falk, Richard. 2009. *Achieving Human Rights*. New York: Routledge.

Friedman, Thomas. 2005. *The World Is Flat: A Brief History of the Twenty-First Century*. New York: Farrar, Straus and Giroux.

Gamarra Carrillo, Jefrey. 2010. *Resiliencia social y cambio en comunidades campesinas afectadas por conflicto armado interno: El caso de las comunidades de Incaraccay y Tanquihua en la provincia de Cangallo, Ayacucho*. Lima: IPEDEHP. Available at www.ipedehp.pe/. Last accessed June 11, 2012.

González, Olga M. 2011. *Unveiling Secrets of War in the Peruvian Andes*. Chicago: University of Chicago Press.

González Echevarría, Roberto. 1985. *The Voice of the Masters: Writing and Authority in Modern Latin American Literature*. Austin: University of Texas Press.

———. 1990. *Myth and Archive: A Theory of Latin American Narrative*. Cambridge: Cambridge University Press.

Goodale, Mark. 2006. "Introduction to Anthropology and Human Rights in a New Key." *American Anthropologist* 108, no. 1: 1–8.

———. 2009. *Surrendering to Utopia: An Anthropology of Human Rights*. Stanford: Stanford University Press.

Goodale, Mark, and Sally Merry. 2007. *The Practice of Human Rights: Tracking Law between the Global and the Local*. New York: Cambridge University Press.

Hafner-Burton, Emilie, and Kiyoteru Tsustui. 2005. "Human Rights in a Globalizing World: The Paradox of Empty Promises." *American Journal of Sociology* 110, no. 5: 1373–1411.

Hathaway, Oona A. 2002. "Do Human Rights Make a Difference?" *Yale Law Journal* 111:1935–2042.

Heilman, Jaymie. 2010. *Before the Shining Path: Politics in Rural Ayacucho, 1895–1980*. Stanford: Stanford University Press.

Huneeus, Alexandra. 2010. "Judging from a Guilty Conscience: The Chilean Judiciary's Human Rights Turn." *Law & Social Inquiry* 35, no. 1: 99–135.

Hunt, Lynn. 2007. *Inventing Human Rights: A History*. New York: W. W. Norton.

Ignatieff, Michael. 2001. *Human Rights as Politics and Idolatry*. Princeton, NJ: Princeton University Press.

Ishay, Michelle. 2004. *The History of Human Rights: From Ancient Times to the Globalization Era*. Berkeley: University of California Press.

Keck, Margaret, and Kathryn Sikkink. 1998. *Activists beyond Borders: Advocacy Networks in International Politics*. Ithaca, NY: Cornell University Press.

Kupchan, Charles. 2012. *No One's World: The West, the Rising Rest, and the Coming Global Turn*. New York: Oxford University Press.

La Serna, Miguel. 2012. *The Corner of the Living: Ayacucho on the Eve of the Shining Path Insurgency*. Chapel Hill: University of North Carolina Press.

Lauren, Paul Gordon. 2003. *The Evolution of International Human Rights: Visions Seen*. Rev. ed. Philadelphia: University of Pennsylvania Press.

Lechner, Frank, and John Boli. 2004. *The Globalization Reader*. London: Blackwell.

Lischer, Sarah Kenyon. 2005. *Dangerous Sanctuaries: Refugee Camps, Civil War, and the Dilemmas of Humanitarian Aid*. Ithaca, NY: Cornell University Press.

Merry, Sally Engle. 2006. *Human Rights and Gender Violence: Translating International Law into Local Justice*. Chicago: Chicago University Press.

Milton, Cynthia E. 2007. "At the Edge of the Peruvian Truth Commission: Alternative Paths to Recounting the Past." *Radical History Review* 98:3–33.

———, ed. 2014. *Art from a Fractured Past: Memory and Truth-Telling in Post–Shining Path Peru*. Durham, NC: Duke University Press.

Moyn, Samuel. 2010. *The Last Utopia: Human Rights in History*. Cambridge, MA: Belknap Press of Harvard University Press.

Nixon, Rob. 2011. *Slow Violence and the Environmentalism of the Poor*. Cambridge, MA: Harvard University Press.

Nolte Maldonado, Rosa María Josefa. 1991. *Quellcay: Arte y vida de Sarhua, comunidades campesinas andinas*. Lima: Terra Nuova.

Olsen, Tricia, Leigh Payne, and Andrew Reiter. 2010. *Transitional Justice in the Balance: Comparing Processes, Weighing Efficacy*. Washington, DC: United States Institute of Peace.

Pieterse, Jan Nederveen. 2003. *Globalization and Culture: Global Mélange*. Lanham, MD: Rowman and Littlefield.

Risse, Thomas, Stephen Ropp, and Kathryn Sikkink, eds. 1999. *The Power of Human Rights: International Norms and Domestic Change*. New York: Cambridge University Press.

Robertson, Geoffrey. 2002. *Crimes Against Humanity: The Struggle for Global Justice*. New York: New Press.

Shaw, Rosalind, and Lars Waldorf, with Pierre Hazan. 2010. *Localizing Transitional Justice: Interventions and Priorities after Mass Violence*. Stanford: Stanford University Press.

Sikkink, Kathryn. 2011. *The Justice Cascade: How Human Rights Prosecutions Are Changing World Politics*. New York: W. W. Norton.

Simmons, Beth. 2009. *Mobilizing for Human Rights: International Law in Domestic Politics*. New York: Cambridge University Press.

Stern, Steve J., ed. 1998. *Shining and Other Paths: War and Society in Peru, 1980–1995*. Durham, NC: Duke University Press.

———. 1999. "The Tricks of Time: Colonial Legacies and Historical Sensibilities in Latin America." In *Colonial Legacies: The Problem of Persistence in Latin American History*, edited by Jeremy Adelman, 135–50. New York: Routledge

———. 2006. *Battling for Hearts and Minds: Memory Struggles in Pinochet's Chile, 1973–1988*. Durham, NC: Duke University Press.

———. 2010. *Reckoning with Pinochet: The Memory Question in Democratic Chile, 1989–2006*. Durham, NC: Duke University Press.

Straus, Scott. 2006. *The Order of Genocide: Race, Power, and War in Rwanda*. Ithaca, NY: Cornell University Press.

Straus, Scott, and Lars Waldorf, eds. 2011. *Remaking Rwanda: State Building and Human Rights after Mass Violence*. Madison: University of Wisconsin Press.

Tarrow, Sidney. 2005. *The New Transnational Activism*. New York: Cambridge University Press.

Tate, Winifred. 2007. *Counting the Dead: The Culture and Politics of Human Rights Activism in Colombia*. Berkeley: University of California Press.

Teitel, Ruti. 2011. *Humanity's Law*. Oxford: Oxford University Press.

Theidon, Kimberly. 2004. *Entre prójimos: El conflicto armado interno y la política de la reconciliación en el Perú*. Lima: Instituto de Estudios Peruanos.

Todd, Molly. 2010. *Beyond Displacement: Campesinos, Refugees, and Collective Action in the Salvadoran Civil War*. Madison: University of Wisconsin Press.

Youngers, Coletta. 2003. *Violencia política y sociedad civil en Perú*. Lima: Instituto de Estudios Peruanos.

Zuern, Elke. 2011. *The Politics of Necessity: Community Organizing and Democracy in South Africa*. Madison: University of Wisconsin Press.

Who Makes Human Rights?

1

Human Rights History from the Ground Up

The Case of East Timor

GEOFFREY ROBINSON

In the past few years, standard accounts of the history of human rights have been subjected to serious critique and revision. As part of that effort, a handful of historians have advanced provocative and insightful new accounts of the origins and development of human rights, the relationship between individual and collective rights, the role of human rights in struggles for decolonization, and the relationship between international and local movements for the advancement of rights (Burke 2010; Goedde et al. 2012; Hoffmann 2011; Moyn 2010; Weitz 2008). In the hope of contributing in some way to this encouraging trend, I want to share here some observations based on my experience working for, and writing about, human rights in the former Portuguese colony of East Timor—a tiny half-island that experienced invasion, unlawful occupation, genocide, and armed humanitarian intervention, all in the last quarter of the twentieth century. Quite apart from its intrinsic interest I believe a careful, historical analysis of a nontypical case like East Timor's can illustrate how distinctively universal human rights ideals and norms play out in different local contexts. I also hope that a close-grained account of this kind might serve to underscore how important, and intellectually rewarding, it can be to take seriously the experiences of people whose lives are actually affected by human rights violations, and whose actions and ideals are so vital in shaping the movements to end them.

East Timor is promising terrain for such an exploration, not only because its history has been so profoundly shaped by human rights but also because the movement for human rights there was rather different from many others of the same era, especially those that have formed the empirical basis for much of the theorizing, old and new, about human rights history.[1] Perhaps most importantly, East Timor's human rights movement was inextricably linked to the struggle for self-determination—or more precisely, national liberation. In that sense, it was more similar to the anticolonial struggles of the 1940s, 1950s, and 1960s than to the human rights movements of the late twentieth century in Eastern Europe. Like those earlier anticolonial liberation struggles, too, it was an inescapably political movement, in the sense that it explicitly challenged state power from the moment of Indonesia's invasion in December 1975 until the overwhelming vote for independence in August 1999. In marked contrast to those movements, however, East Timor's anticolonial movement continued beyond the end of the Cold War, a matter of timing that arguably enhanced the political significance of human rights in the movement after 1989 and contributed substantially to the achievement of independence some ten years later.

Against this backdrop, I examine more closely a number of claims in the recent literature, which strike me as important but are also open to question on both empirical and analytical grounds. The first of these is related to the difficult subject of origins and turning points in the history of human rights. Much of the new work quite sensibly takes aim at conventional treatments that trace the origins of the contemporary human rights idea and movement to some more or less distant starting point. Hoffmann, Weitz, and others have criticized what they see as the heroic or triumphalist character of standard human rights narratives, insisting instead on the highly contingent and contested quality of that history. Samuel Moyn takes particular issue with the oft-repeated claim that the human rights discourse of the late twentieth century can be traced to the debates and mentalities of the European Enlightenment. Moyn is perhaps even more dismissive of the view that the Universal Declaration of Human Rights of 1948 marks a critical turning point in the modern history of human rights. Describing such standard accounts as teleological, and as little more than "church" history, he insists that the true point of origin is 1977, the year in which he claims human rights finally took hold in the popular imagination.

A number of the new historians have likewise questioned the significance for the modern human rights movement of the United Nations and the body of human rights covenants and institutions it has spawned since 1945. Against the grain of most standard accounts, they characterize the UN and its

Geoffrey Robinson

institutions as the sterile creations of powerful post- or neo-imperial states, whose actual commitment to human rights was doubtful, and whose interests and power ensured that the individualist human rights ideals articulated in UN declarations and covenants would not have any real resonance for most of the world's population.[2] Indeed, in Moyn's view, it was only when human rights discourse was finally removed from the halls of the UN and championed by popular social movements and NGOs like Amnesty International (AI) that it finally took hold in popular consciousness, laying the foundation for its emergence as a hegemonic discourse in the last quarter of the twentieth century.

Moyn's case for declaring 1977 as the pivotal year for human rights rests on an argument about broad ideological and normative shifts in the late 1960s and 1970s, which he takes to have had global ramifications. The principal condition for the emergence of human rights at this time, he argues, was the demise or "death" of the older political utopias, especially socialism and anti-colonialism, which had dominated the political and ideological landscape since the 1940s. As these came to be seen as unviable in the late 1960s and 1970s, Moyn contends, the stage was set for their "displacement" by human rights, a new utopian vision whose appeal lay in its explicit turn away from maximalist political schemes, and its embrace of a minimalist, moral ideal that was above and beyond politics. Yet, he argues, if the popular appeal of human rights lay in its embodiment of a minimalist "antipolitics," it was Jimmy Carter's explicit articulation of that ideal as a foundation of U.S. foreign policy in January 1977 that finally secured its position as hegemonic discourse.

Running through this argument, indeed lying at its very heart, is the claim that human rights only "works" as a new utopia because it is avowedly, and intrinsically, apolitical, or even antipolitical. The evidence for this claim is drawn, for the most part, from the statements of the Eastern European dissidents and their supporters who decided in the late 1960s that politics as usual was no longer an option, and that the only way forward lay in adopting a moral position outside of and above politics. The claim is also underscored by reference to the founding principles and operating mandate of Amnesty International, the leading international human rights organization of the era, which explicitly rejected association with any ideological position, insisting that its exclusive goal was to protect and promote the rights of the individual.

These are important interventions, and they arguably mark a decisive turn in our understanding of the history of human rights. And yet, when they are viewed against the historical evidence from East Timor, some serious problems arise. For the sake of simplicity, these may be summarized as follows.

First, whatever importance it may have had globally, the year 1977 was decidedly not a pivotal one for human rights in East Timor, except in the perverse sense that it signaled the deepening of a genocide that left at least one hundred thousand people dead. Other years—notably 1983, 1989, 1991, 1999, and 2001—were vastly more significant for the human rights movement there. Perhaps more to the point, East Timor's experience suggests that it is analytically unhelpful to think of human rights history in terms of globally significant turning points or junctures. Second, the human rights ideals, covenants, and institutions of the UN were not in any sense irrelevant or uninspiring to East Timorese. On the contrary, like many involved in movements against racism and colonialism in the late 1940s and 1950s, East Timorese embraced those ideals and mechanisms, and used them to extraordinarily powerful political effect in their struggle for human rights and independence. Third, human rights did not "displace" the old utopias of anticolonialism and armed struggle in East Timor—nor did those old utopias "die." Even as it changed over the years, East Timor's struggle deftly combined demands for human rights and national self-determination, and employed both the rhetoric of revolutionary war and the discourse of human rights morality. What occurred, then, was not a matter of "displacement"—or of "death" and "birth"—but a conjoining of different elements into a new whole. Finally, and most emphatically, the adoption of human rights discourse inside East Timor did not represent a turning away from politics but rather the embrace of a powerful new tool for the achievement of explicitly political ends. As in so many places with experience of egregious state violence, notably in Latin America, Africa, and elsewhere in Asia, in East Timor resistance to violence constituted an intentional and ultimately effective challenge to state power. Accordingly, human rights ideals and movements were understood—by state authorities and by civil society alike—to be intrinsically political in their aims and their effects.

This chapter develops these observations through an account of the human rights movement in and for East Timor from 1975 to the present, then goes on to reflect on the possible significance of that history for the wider history of human rights. While I recognize the problems inherent in seeking general conclusions from specific historical experiences, I hope that a closer look at this case might, at a minimum, add a layer of complexity to the wider history of human rights, highlight some problem areas, and perhaps also open some new avenues of inquiry.

Human Rights in East Timor

If what we now call human rights violations—arbitrary killing, torture, rape, political imprisonment, and so on—have a very long history in

East Timor, the same cannot be said of the movement to promote and protect such rights. That movement, and the discourse of human rights that formed an integral part of it, did not appear in any meaningful form until after the Indonesian invasion of December 1975. From that time to the present, the movement has followed an uneven trajectory, which makes any simple account of its development over time problematic. Indeed, following Hoffmann, it is worth emphasizing that far from tracing a steady arc of progress, the history of that movement has been marked by more or less constant contestation and contingency. Some sense of these discontinuities can be gleaned by thinking of the movement in terms of four distinctive periods: 1975–1981, 1981–1991, 1991–1999, and 1999–2012.

Genocide and Humanitarian Crisis: 1975–1981

The years 1975–81 marked a low point in respect for basic human rights in East Timor, but also the start of an international campaign aimed at addressing the widespread and systematic abuse that characterized these years. In some respects, East Timor's experience in this period appears as a clear example of the explosion of human rights activism in the late 1970s that Moyn has posited. In other ways, though, the story of the movement that emerged in and for East Timor at this time suggests something very different and much more complex.

As in many other countries, the human rights movement in East Timor grew out of, and in response to, the experience of systematic state violence. Indonesian forces invaded East Timor in early December 1975, just one week after a left-leaning nationalist party, Fretilin (Frente Revolucionária de Timor Leste Independente, or Revolutionary Front for an Independent East Timor) had declared the territory's independence from Portugal. The invasion and subsequent occupation resulted in the death of at least one hundred thousand, and possibly as many as two hundred thousand, of a pre-invasion population of about six hundred fifty thousand (CAVR 2006, pt. 6, 13). Most died of starvation and disease as the direct result of an Indonesian military campaign in which civilians were forcibly relocated into concentration camps. The campaign—dubbed "encirclement and annihilation"—entailed the deployment of some forty thousand combat troops and the intensive aerial bombardment of one Fretilin base area after another, using low-flying counterinsurgency aircraft such as OV-10 Broncos. All told, the campaign resulted in the forcible displacement of at least three hundred thousand people into concentration camps, where malnutrition and disease were rampant and many died (USAID 1979). In addition, tens of thousands of suspected supporters of independence were deliberately killed or died as a result of torture at the hands of Indonesian military authorities or their local proxies. The scale of the killing in the first four years of the occupation was such that many scholars have described it as genocide (Robinson 2010).

The news of Indonesia's invasion of East Timor and its counterinsurgency operations there were condemned by the UN, and met with angry protests and demonstrations by church groups, trade unions, and peace groups, especially in Australia, Portugal, the Netherlands, the United Kingdom, and the United States. To a remarkable degree, however, Indonesia managed to conceal the nature of its operations and the extent of the humanitarian crisis that was the result. It did so in part by cutting off all means of communication and preventing visits to the territory by any international media or independent observers. Indonesian authorities were ably assisted in these efforts by powerful international actors, most notably the U.S., Australian, and British governments, which saw Indonesia's staunchly anticommunist New Order regime as a vital ally in the Cold War. Without the conscious support of these states, it is safe to say that the invasion and the genocide would never have happened.

The United States played an especially critical role. The December 1975 invasion, for example, was launched less than twenty-four hours after a meeting in Jakarta between President Suharto and President Gerald Ford and Secretary of State Henry Kissinger. The transcript of that meeting captures something of the Cold War logic, and perhaps also the cynicism and fatigue, that prevailed within the Ford administration in the months after the fall of Saigon in April 1975. It reveals, for example, that Kissinger and Ford gave Suharto repeated assurances that the United States understood Indonesia's "problem" and "intentions" in East Timor, and would not object if Indonesia found it necessary to take "drastic action" there (US DOS 1975). The transcript also shows that Kissinger advised Suharto on how "we" might evade provisions of U.S. law that explicitly forbade the use of U.S.-supplied weapons for purposes other than self-defense.[3] Considering that roughly 90 percent of the military equipment used in the invasion was supplied by the United States, Kissinger's concern about legality was not an idle one.

Less often discussed was the role played by the Carter administration, which, like its predecessor, viewed Indonesia as an indispensable anticommunist ally in an increasingly hostile region at a troubling juncture in the Cold War. American military assistance sent an especially clear message of support to the regime despite its very poor record on human rights. In 1978, the year of the deadly "encirclement and annihilation" campaign and the second year of Carter's human rights presidency, U.S. arms sales and transfers to Indonesia spiked to more than $129 million (IPS 1982). Especially important among

Geoffrey Robinson

these transfers were the versatile, low-flying OV-10 Broncos, which were ideal for counterinsurgency operations in East Timor's difficult terrain.[4] By any reasonable measure, the introduction of these weapons at that juncture contributed directly to the massive forced displacements of 1977–79 and therefore also to the genocide. Meanwhile, the Carter administration and its Western allies worked assiduously to block meaningful international action in response to the invasion and to conceal the truth about its human consequences. Their reasons for doing so were straightforward and familiar. Indonesia was considered to be an important Cold War ally; East Timor was not.

Thus, while President Carter's embrace of human rights may have galvanized the growth of a global human rights movement in the late 1970s, as Moyn has claimed, the emergence of a campaign for human rights in East Timor at this time had little if anything to do with the pronouncements of Carter or his Western allies. On the contrary, it emerged in response to egregious acts of violence against civilians, and in direct opposition to what its chief supporters saw as the culpable complicity of the U.S., Australian, and British governments in that violence.

Moreover, far from building upon the credibility of a burgeoning global human rights movement or discourse, the campaign for East Timor was built largely from scratch by a small handful of activists, scholars, trade unionists, and others, with only limited support from major international human rights organizations like Amnesty International. The movement drew upon the expertise of scholars like Benedict Anderson, Elizabeth Traube, and Noam Chomsky, and channeled reliable information to editorial writers at key media outlets like the *New York Times* and *Washington Post*. It was largely due to these efforts that the U.S. Congress briefly demonstrated serious concern on the issue and threatened a reevaluation of U.S. policy.[5] While the election of Ronald Reagan in November 1980 effectively put an end to demands for meaningful change in U.S. policy on East Timor, the work of church and secular solidarity groups at this juncture bore long-term dividends. Crucially, these groups, and the political and media networks they had forged, laid the groundwork for a continued awareness of East Timor during the lean years of the 1980s, and for the groundswell of international criticism that grew in strength in the 1990s (Kohen 2004, 8–9).

The success of that nascent movement rested, in some measure, on the description of the situation inside East Timor as a "humanitarian" rather than "human rights" or "political" crisis. That approach was driven, in part, by the facts on the ground. But, according to one of the principle U.S. architects of the campaign, Arnold Kohen, the choice of terminology was also intended to garner the widest possible political support for East Timor.[6] In the United

States and elsewhere, the framing of the problem in humanitarian terms was still deemed to be less threatening to potential allies on the Right and in the powerful Roman Catholic Church than framing it in terms of either national liberation or human rights. In other words, even after "human rights" discourse had supposedly become hegemonic, those directly involved in the campaign for East Timor saw no strategic advantage—and some clear disadvantages—in framing their appeals in that language.

The focus and language of international campaigners at this stage was also shaped by the views of those inside East Timor who were the source of what little information was then available. The Roman Catholic Church was especially important. Notwithstanding its colonial origins, by the late 1970s the East Timorese Church had become the moral center of resistance to Indonesian rule. In large part, that was because, following the invasion, it had been completely cut off from the Universal Church, and many of its priests had joined the population and Fretilin in the mountains. Against that backdrop, the local church developed a theology and practice rooted in the ideals of social justice, service to the people, and self-reliance. Those ideals were articulated in a remarkable document written by the East Timorese religious in 1981:

> The people are aware that their faith comes from God whose Word takes the form of social justice. This justice derives from the justice of God in His relations with His people. This justice must be built by the people themselves based on faith and co-operation with God and with one's fellow men who are still the sacrifices of oppression. For us, living the faith without serious endeavors for the building of social justice is the same as making faith merely foreign and mystical. Creating justice together with the present Indonesian government is not possible, or not yet, although the people desire justice greatly. (Archer 1995, 122)

The explicit focus on social justice in this document highlighted an important dimension in local church thinking that influenced East Timorese views of the occupation and laid the foundation for future international appeals in the language of humanitarianism and human rights.[7]

Significant as it was, the church view was not the only one available. Through the late 1970s and early 1980s, in fact, the overwhelming preoccupation among East Timorese resistance leaders was with national liberation. Inspired principally by the independence movements in Portuguese colonies in Africa, East Timor's nationalists invoked the language and ideas of revolutionary anticolonialism, and adopted armed struggle as their primary mode of resistance. To that extent, East Timor's domestic experience was consistent

Geoffrey Robinson

with Moyn's suggestion that the goals and language of revolution and national liberation *preceded* the emergence of a discourse of human rights and the formation of a human rights movement.

On the other hand, the continuing appeal of these revolutionary ideals and methods well into the 1980s—when they were conjoined with but did not displace human rights discourse—raises questions about Moyn's claim that human rights emerged only when the old utopias had "died." That may be an apt description of the sequence of events in the Soviet Union and Europe in the mid-1970s, but it does not in any meaningful sense capture the historical dynamic in East Timor, or for that matter in much of Asia, at this time. Indeed, the mid-1970s arguably marked a high point in the appeal of revolutionary ideals in the region.[8] Thus, even after the mass killing, forced relocation, and genocide of the late 1970s, the political discourse inside East Timor was overwhelmingly framed in terms of national liberation, with human rights still only a dim flicker on the horizon.

Human Rights and Diplomacy: 1981–1991

If the late 1970s marked the first signs of a human rights movement against a backdrop of armed struggle in the name of national liberation, the next decade saw a gradual shift toward the language of human rights and a strategy of diplomacy and nonviolent political action. Yet even as the discourse of human rights was more openly adopted in the 1980s, revolutionary language and armed resistance were never completely abandoned, and the bedrock demand for independence remained. Once again, the shift was not a simple case of the "displacement" of old utopias with a new one but of different utopias being conjoined into a new amalgam. To understand how and why that happened, and what the implications were, one needs to look closely at political and sociological developments inside the country, and at the complex relationships that developed between human rights and political activists inside East Timor and abroad.

Inside East Timor, the shift toward the language of human rights began a few years after the near total destruction of the armed resistance in late 1979. In the reorganization and reorientation that followed, one segment of the independence movement, led by Xanana Gusmão, sought consciously to move away from the strategy and rhetoric of armed resistance and revolution, and to focus on the international diplomatic struggle. In that context, they sought to frame the movement's concerns and goals in terms of universal human rights, including the right to self-determination. This move reached a critical turning point in 1983, the year in which Gusmão negotiated a ceasefire with Indonesian military authorities, called for an official Amnesty International delegation to be allowed to visit East Timor, and ordered Fretilin officials to start preparing human rights reports—including lists of civilians killed, disappeared, tortured, and detained—for international dissemination. The new approach was stimulated, among other things, by a growing awareness among some resistance leaders that the strategy of armed resistance and the language of militant anticolonialism had failed to win the sympathy of the wider international community, and may even have undermined it.

Yet while some inside the movement accepted that logic, others were reluctant to abandon revolutionary goals and methods. Out of this debate a new formula gradually emerged in which individual human rights were viewed as an integral element in a wider struggle for self-determination. The key slogans continued to be "Independence or Death!" "Long Live East Timor!" and "The Struggle Continues!" But these demands were now joined with appeals for the protection of basic human rights and for justice. In 1987 Xanana Gusmão declared, for example, that the National Council of the Maubere Resistance (CNRM), formed in that year, "was committed to building a free and democratic nation, based on respect for the freedoms of thought, association and expression, as well as complete respect for Universal Human Rights" (Webster 2003, 14).

The shift to a human rights discourse at this time was also the consequence of significant sociological developments inside East Timor and Indonesia. By the late 1980s a new generation of East Timorese had emerged who had no memory of Portuguese rule, and who had declining patience with the failing guerrilla strategy of their elders (Carey 2003, 47–48; Fernandes 2011). Starting in the mid-1980s, some of these young people took advantage of the opportunity to attend universities in Indonesia. By chance, their arrival in Indonesia coincided with a renaissance of Indonesia's own student movement. In this heady new environment, East Timorese students eagerly absorbed and adapted the human rights language and tactics that their Indonesian peers had started to deploy in their opposition to Suharto's authoritarian New Order. They also sought out international contacts and began to read whatever critical scholarship and reporting was available. Among other things, they became avid consumers of neo-Marxist scholarship as well as the publications of AI and other human rights organizations.[9] Interestingly, it was at about this time that East Timorese began to compare their movement both to the Indonesian nationalist struggle against the Dutch and to the Palestinian intifada (Cox and Carey 1995, 40; Gomes 1995).

The development of a human rights discourse and movement inside East Timor also coincided with the active engagement of major international human rights organizations—notably AI—starting in the mid-1980s. The release of

AI's first major report on human rights in East Timor in 1985 helped shift the terms of the international discourse about East Timor to the protection and promotion of human rights (Amnesty International 1985). That trend in turn lent weight to the use of human rights discourse inside East Timor and Indonesia. It would be a mistake, however, to conclude that the change in direction was initiated solely by AI or other international organizations. In fact, AI's engagement at this time was triggered largely by the efforts of individuals and clandestine groups inside East Timor, including the Catholic Church and Fretilin, which by the early 1980s had begun to gather accurate information about the human rights situation there and arrange for its dissemination abroad long before the Internet made such practices routine.

The shift toward the language of human rights and away from revolutionary politics—but not away from demands for self-determination—was also encouraged by the local Catholic Church. A key figure was Msgr. (later Bishop) Carlos Filipe Ximenes Belo, appointed in 1983 (Kohen 1999). While Bishop Belo and other church leaders did not openly advocate East Timorese independence, they sought consistently to defend the population against human rights abuses by Indonesian security forces, while demanding that they be given an opportunity to decide their own political future. In a letter written on February 11, 1989, to UN Secretary-General Pérez de Cuéllar, Bishop Belo repeated a demand for peaceful self-determination he had made as early as 1984:

> [T]he people of East Timor must be allowed to express their views on their future through a plebiscite. Hitherto the people have not been consulted. Others speak in the name of the people. Indonesia says that the people of East Timor have already chosen integration, but the people of East Timor themselves have never said this. Portugal wants time to solve the problem. And we continue to die as a people and as a nation. (Belo 1989)

Beyond the principled positions taken by its clergy, the unique advantage of the Catholic Church in East Timor lay in the fact that it was administered directly from Rome (via the papal nuncio in Jakarta) and not as part of the Indonesian Roman Catholic church. While that did not prevent Indonesian authorities from trying to interfere in its work, it gave East Timor's Catholic Church a vital measure of autonomy. More generally, the arrangement eventually provided the local church with an extraordinarily wide network of international support that Indonesian authorities were powerless to obstruct (Archer 1995, 126).

East Timor's human rights movement and discourse were also stimulated by the end of the Cold War. After 1989, the preoccupation with fighting communism—which had so profoundly influenced Western foreign policy toward Indonesia and other countries for four decades—grew increasingly difficult to sustain. Without the overriding imperative of anticommunism, there was no plausible reason for Western governments *not* to extend their ostensible concern for the promotion of human rights to all states in the region, regardless of their political complexion. That political shift provided an unexpected opportunity for those genuinely committed to human rights to push their governments to match rhetoric with action. Partly for this reason, and perhaps also as a guise for other economic and strategic objectives, the promotion of human rights became an explicit foreign policy objective of an increasing number of Western states after 1989, establishing something like a new international norm (Robinson 1996, 74). These broader international trends also seem to have been a factor in the Suharto regime's decision to "open up" East Timor following a state visit there in late 1988, and to embrace a policy of political "openness" (*keterbukaan*) for Indonesia as a whole in 1989.

Against this backdrop, and armed with exciting new ideas about human rights and politics, East Timor's youth burst loudly onto the political scene in October 1989. The occasion was an eagerly awaited visit to East Timor by Pope John Paul II. As the pope concluded his celebration of a huge outdoor mass, before the largest contingent of foreign media since the invasion, several young people began to shout and unfurl hand-painted banners bearing pro-independence slogans, most of them in English. The reaction of Indonesian security forces was swift and harsh. The demonstrators were detained by the military and badly beaten in custody. But the visit and the demonstration had sent a clear signal to outside observers—and especially to Catholics around the world—that it was right to support the cause of human rights in East Timor (Kohen 1999, 145).

The incident marked the start of a new approach by the resistance. Impressed by the courage and creativity of the new generation, Gusmão endorsed their plans for direct, nonviolent action aimed at an international audience. The timing of that decision was no accident. Closely attuned to developments on the international stage, Gusmão had quickly seen the strategic potential offered by the Western rhetorical embrace of human rights after the collapse of the Berlin Wall and by the Suharto regime's version of "perestroika" the same year. He also saw clearly the political opening that Western states provided the following year when, following Iraq's invasion of Kuwait, they justified their attack on Iraq on the grounds that large nations cannot be permitted to invade their smaller neighbors (Robinson 1996).[10]

A Transnational Movement: 1991–1999

The new strategy of direct nonviolent protest reached its tragic, but historically pivotal, apex on November 12, 1991, when Indonesian security

Geoffrey Robinson

forces opened fire on a peaceful demonstration of young people at the Santa Cruz cemetery in the capital, Dili, leaving an estimated 270 dead (Amnesty International 1991a; Cox and Carey 1995). Captured on film by a visiting British journalist, and then broadcast on television around the world, the massacre galvanized opinion inside East Timor and internationally.[11] The result was an unprecedented international condemnation of Indonesia's human rights record in East Timor and the initiation of some of the first concrete measures designed to compel the Indonesian government to clean up its act (Cox and Carey 1995, 52–53; Robinson 1996). After Santa Cruz, in fact, Indonesia remained permanently on the defensive with respect to East Timor, leading its foreign minister, Ali Alatas, to describe the territory famously as "a pebble in our shoe."[12]

The Santa Cruz massacre of 1991 led to the formation of dozens of new international solidarity groups and gave a new visibility and cachet to the work of older organizations, like AI, Tapol, ACFOA, and A Paz é Possível em Timor Leste. Among the most important of the new solidarity groups was the U.S.-based East Timor Action network (ETAN), but it was only part of a vast transnational network that emerged at this time.[13] Together, these organizations worked aggressively after 1991 to raise public awareness about the situation in East Timor and to demand that key decision makers in their own countries adopt policies consistent with their rhetorical support for human rights.

Santa Cruz also stimulated adjustments in the strategy of the resistance inside East Timor. Without ever renouncing the armed struggle or the goal of independence, the resistance itself began to focus even more systematically on diplomatic and political efforts, and to invoke the language of human rights with greater frequency. That strategy drew upon and at the same time helped transform the worldwide network that linked the resistance to international human rights organizations, the UN, solidarity groups, and the Roman Catholic Church. Paradoxically, even as the movement inside East Timor began to balance its demands for independence with the language of universal human rights, after 1991 the international movement gradually came to embrace and emphasize the demand for self-determination and decolonization.

For those who had decided that East Timor's best hope lay in gaining the sympathy and support of the international community, it made sense to reach out ever more energetically to human rights organizations like AI and Human Rights Watch. As the lines of communication developed through the 1990s, East Timorese quickly learned how to present information in language that would be most readily understood by an international audience. Indeed, the skillful use of the language of universal human rights by East Timorese—

including the judicious use of terms like "extrajudicial execution," "disappearance," "prisoner of conscience," and so on—rendered the movement immediately more "legible" and credible in the eyes of those large organizations, and thereby enhanced both their stature and their visibility internationally. Even members of the armed resistance began to adopt it. In 1994, for example, a former Falintil commander, Paulino Gama, wrote:

> We members of the East Timorese resistance are not murderers as some people have tried to depict us, but simply nationalist soldiers dedicated to the defence of our country in the face of Indonesian invasion, occupation, and genocide. We are dedicated to upholding the fundamental principles of the Universal Declaration of Human Rights (1948), such as the avoidance of arbitrary violence and arrest, respect for human life, and the protection of the lives and dignity of all prisoners of war. (Gama 1995, 99)

Though routinely mocked by skeptics on the Right and the Left—and regarded as an institution of little real importance by some revisionist historians of human rights—the UN also played a vital role in East Timor, and its procedures and institutions were used to powerful strategic effect for two decades. In the UN and in the body of human rights law that developed under its auspices after 1945, many East Timorese found a basis for hope that their dream of national independence was legitimate and could be achieved. More concretely, the UN set in motion various institutional mechanisms that helped ensure that the East Timor question was not forgotten, and provided both the legal and political framework through which independence was ultimately achieved (Gunn 1997).

The annual meetings of the UN Special Committee on Decolonization, for example, became a vital forum for reporting on Indonesian human rights violations in East Timor, and for demanding immediate independence. Likewise, especially after 1991, the much-maligned UN Human Rights Commission initiated credible investigations into Indonesian human rights practice in the territory.[14] These investigations, and the reports that resulted from them, often placed Indonesia under a most unwelcome spotlight and constituted a significant form of political pressure. The Department of Political Affairs in the UN Secretariat also played a role by keeping the East Timor issue on the UN agenda even as powerful governments sought to have it removed. And while East Timor was removed from the agenda of the General Assembly before the 1983 session, it was done on the condition that the UN Secretary-General would continue to seek an internationally acceptable solution to the problem. It was under that arrangement that in May 1999 Portugal, Indonesia, and the UN reached agreement on plans for the referendum that finally led to East Timor's independence. Thus, however ambiguous or politically compromised the language and covenants of universal human rights may appear to international legal scholars and historians, those ideals and covenants served as a genuine inspiration to a generation of East Timorese activists and brought tangible political results.

Paradoxically, the links between East Timor's resistance and various international bodies were further strengthened after the capture and trial of Xanana Gusmão in late 1992. In the years of his imprisonment in Jakarta, Gusmão's stature grew, particularly in international circles. He began to emerge, Mandela-like, as an internationally respected statesperson and indeed received a visit from Mandela in July 1997. Gusmão took advantage of his time in prison to develop his ties with a range of international human rights and solidarity organizations and individuals whom he knew to be sympathetic to the cause of independence. Through these interactions, he deepened his understanding of international affairs and human rights and, on that basis, adjusted his approach to the resistance.

The growing importance of these international linkages, and of human rights, in Gusmão's thinking was revealed soon after his incarceration. In June 1993 he authorized several young East Timorese to enter the embassies of Finland and Sweden in Jakarta to seek political asylum. The action was carefully planned to have the maximum possible international impact, and to that end explicitly invoked universal human rights ideals and norms. The timing, for example, coincided exactly with the UN World Conference on Human Rights in Vienna, while the letter that the group presented to the embassy officials made careful use of the language of international human rights (Amnesty International 1993a, appendix 1). Moreover, with the help of Gusmão's future wife, the Australian Kirsty Sword, essential information about the asylum seekers was communicated in advance to select individuals and organizations outside of Indonesia (Sword-Gusmão 2003, 56–66). As a consequence, when the young people entered the embassies on June 23, an international network was poised to act. Amnesty International's first report on the action was released within twenty-four hours, prompting Foreign Minister Alatas to accuse the organization of orchestrating the action to embarrass the Indonesian government (Amnesty International 1993b).

A further international development that served to undermine Indonesia's position came in 1996 when José Ramos-Horta and Bishop Belo were jointly awarded the Nobel Peace Prize.[15] The Prize dramatically increased international awareness of the East Timor issue, and gave a new visibility and legitimacy to the international solidarity network that had worked for so many years in the shadows. Perhaps most importantly, it helped to shift the international discourse in the direction of demands for self-determination and independence, striking precisely the balance between concern for individual human rights and the right to self-determination that East Timor's resistance movement and its local Catholic Church had started to articulate in the 1980s. In a clear expression of the new approach, in September 1997 a group of Nobel Prize laureates and other prominent human rights figures wrote an open letter to President Suharto calling on him to work with Nelson Mandela and UN Secretary-General Kofi Annan to find a lasting solution to the East Timor problem (Open Letter 1997).

Framed as a matter of human rights through peaceful self-determination, by the late 1990s East Timor's struggle had gained a new credibility abroad and had won the support of a far wider constituency than had supported the idea of a revolutionary war of liberation. Among its more powerful advocates were political conservatives and Roman Catholic Church leaders, for whom human rights were seen as a relatively benign alternative to more radical demands. The embrace of a universal human rights discourse also enhanced East Timor's stature and credibility in the eyes of the UN and major human rights organizations like AI and Human Rights Watch. Meanwhile, fueled by evidence of systematic human rights violations inside East Timor and by significant changes in international attitudes toward human rights after the Cold War, the transnational movement on behalf of East Timor had grown dramatically in size and influence. While that did not bring an immediate end to human rights violations, or to Indonesian rule, it laid the foundation for the dramatic political achievements of the next two years.

Intervention and Independence: 1999–2012

The year 1999 marked the apex of the human rights movement around the issue of East Timor both inside East Timor and internationally. In that year, the movement contributed powerfully to the political resolution of the East Timor question through a UN-supervised referendum on independence. It was also instrumental in bringing about a swift and unusual UN-backed armed intervention to stop spiraling post-ballot violence that had threatened to escalate into genocide in mid-September 1999 (Robinson 2010). These achievements were not in any sense inevitable. Nor could they be said to mark the "triumph" of East Timor's human rights movement. On the contrary, they were highly contingent, the product of unexpected acts of conscience and courage by ordinary people, and of momentary adjustments in calculations of national interest. As such, they were vulnerable to relapse. And indeed, within a year or two, the influence of the movement both outside and inside East Timor had virtually evaporated.

Geoffrey Robinson

In May 1998 Indonesian President Suharto resigned in the face of a severe economic crisis and widespread pro-democracy and human rights demonstrations. Anxious to prove his human rights credentials and under increasing pressure from local and international human rights organizations, in early 1999 the new president, B. J. Habibie, proposed that East Timorese should be given an opportunity to vote on their future political status. Indonesia's military commanders felt compelled to accept Habibie's initiative, but it soon became clear that they planned to do everything possible to thwart it. Their strategy involved the mobilization of East Timorese militia groups to disrupt the referendum with threats and acts of violence. Nevertheless, by May 1999 a set of agreements had been brokered by UN Secretary-General Kofi Annan under which the UN would carry out a referendum in August.

Those agreements were reached despite serious reservations and resistance by key states, most notably the United States and Australia, which were anxious to avoid upsetting good relations with Indonesia's military. In fact, as late as February 1999, U.S. government officials were actively considering alternatives to a referendum—including a colonial-style settlement based on consultation with a few hand-picked representatives of the different parties.[16] The pro-Indonesian position of these states continued without significant interruption in the months leading up to the August vote, despite mounting evidence of official Indonesian involvement in systematic violence against suspected supporters of independence. Calls from human rights organizations and from within the UN itself for action to stop the violence were answered with bland assurances that the Indonesian authorities could be relied upon to maintain order.

The problem came to a head in the days immediately after the referendum in which, despite credible threats of massive violence and retaliation, 78.5 percent of voters opted for independence. When the result of the vote was announced on September 4, 1999, Indonesian forces and their local militia proxies launched a widespread campaign of violence that left at least fifteen hundred people dead, destroyed some 70 percent of the infrastructure in the country, and forcibly displaced an estimated four hundred thousand people from their homes. For ten days, key states maintained their position that the violence could be controlled by the very Indonesian forces that were organizing it. Then, in a dramatic about-face, the United States and other governments lent their support to the idea of an armed international intervention to stop the violence. A few days later, in another highly unusual move, the UN Security Council authorized the deployment of a multinational force to East Timor. That force landed less than a week later and by the end of the month the worst of the violence had ended.

The decision to intervene in mid-September 1999 was the consequence of an unusual confluence of events and trends that distinguished that moment decisively from the late 1970s when, in the face of similar violence, key states chose to stand by and do nothing. Among the more important factors were: (1) the availability of shocking images and reporting made possible by the substantial media presence on the ground as the violence descended; (2) the courage displayed by East Timorese, and some UN staff, in the face of the violence; (3) the decision by Xanana Gusmão not to respond to the violence in kind; (4) the personal commitment of UN Secretary-General Kofi Annan to preventing the escalation of the violence to genocide; and (5) the unusual, if temporary, openness among world leaders to the idea of "humanitarian intervention" that prevailed at the end of the millennium.

Crucially, the intervention was also due to the prior existence of a sophisticated and credible worldwide network of solidarity and human rights organizations with expert knowledge of East Timor. Over the years, that movement had established channels of access and influence not only to the media but also to government and legislative decision makers and to various UN bodies. That essential groundwork—for years considered a rather hopeless task carried out by naive idealists—meant that when the crisis came, the lobbying effort did not have to begin at square one. The network was also instrumental in creating a broad consensus that the problem in East Timor was fundamentally about human rights and self-determination, and in quickly organizing massive demonstrations and media campaigns in major capitals. By all accounts, the results of these efforts were concrete and impressive.

If 1999 marked the dramatic high point of the human rights movement for East Timor, the following decade saw its drastic demise. At the height of the crisis of 1999, and in the months immediately after, there were repeated calls by world leaders for those most responsible for the violence—specifically Indonesian military authorities—to be brought to justice, if necessary before an international criminal tribunal. More than a decade later, not a single Indonesian official had been successfully tried for crimes related to the events of 1999, and the idea of an international criminal tribunal had effectively been shelved. In retrospect it is depressingly easy to see that the strength and influence of the international human rights movement for East Timor all but evaporated within a year or two of its greatest achievement. The decline was partly due to the desire on the part of major states, notably the United States and Australia, to restore cordial relations with the Indonesian military. It was hastened by a decisive shift in international norms with respect to human rights following the attacks of September 11, 2001.

Geoffrey Robinson

Perhaps even more depressing for human rights activists, though not altogether surprising, these years also saw the decline of the legitimacy of human rights discourse and norms *inside* East Timor. After the achievement of independence in 2002, political leaders like Xanana Gusmão and José Ramos-Horta—who had once appealed forcefully to the ideals of universal human rights and made skillful use of available human rights language, institutions, and mechanisms to achieve their goals—now heaved them overboard in the name of "political stability" and the pursuit of good relations with Indonesia. That shift was expressed most clearly in their persistent opposition to bringing those responsible for past crimes against humanity to justice, in particular through an international criminal tribunal.[17] It was also evident in their strong support for a joint Indonesia-East Timor Commission on Truth and Friendship (CTF), which was clearly designed to undercut demands for justice and to restore good relations with Indonesia (Robinson 2011, 1007–21).

In some ways, the about-face of East Timor's leaders is easy to understand. A tiny, fledgling state, impoverished and decimated by long years of occupation and war, and still sharing a vulnerable border with Indonesia, East Timor could not reasonably be expected to take the lead in the costly and complex process of bringing to justice some of Indonesia's most powerful officials. Moreover, even if the government had wished to take on this task, it would have been seriously hampered by the lack of resources, capacity, and expertise in the country's new judiciary. At the same time, these concerns might easily have been addressed by simply remaining neutral or lukewarm on the matter of justice for the perpetrators. Yet both Gusmão and Ramos-Horta campaigned actively against an international criminal tribunal, against what they termed punitive justice, and in favor of a vaguely defined reconciliation in the form of the CTF. Whatever their reasons for doing so, in adopting those positions East Timor's leaders undermined profoundly the arguments for an international tribunal and placed an almost insurmountable obstacle in the path to securing justice for the crimes of 1999 and the quarter century of Indonesian rule.

And yet this is not the whole story. For one thing, since 1999 East Timorese have made significant advances in seeking the truth about the history of human rights in the country and in establishing mechanisms for reconciliation and justice. In 2000, for example, East Timor's fledgling judiciary, with substantial UN assistance, began to conduct something close to a serious investigative and judicial process, in accordance with accepted international standards. The process was set in motion by an UNTAET statute establishing Special Panels for Serious Crimes within the Dili District Court to try serious crimes, including crimes against humanity.[18] Under the same statute, the norms of international law were adopted as the basis on which such crimes would be prosecuted and tried. UNTAET also established a Serious Crimes Unit (SCU) with a mandate to investigate serious crimes that had occurred between January 1 and October 25, 1999, and to prosecute those responsible for such crimes.[19]

After a series of false starts and delays, in 2002 these mechanisms began to achieve some notable successes. By late 2004, indictments had been filed against a total of 391 individuals, most of whom were charged with crimes against humanity.[20] Those indictments accounted for roughly half of all the killings reported to have been committed in 1999. Notably, those indicted included the former TNI Commander, General Wiranto, six other high-ranking TNI officers, and the former governor of East Timor. Of the 391 individuals indicted, some fifty had been convicted and sentenced to jail terms by late 2004, and two had been acquitted.

Of course, the picture was not all rosy. For one thing, as the SCU mandate expired in 2005, the vast majority of those indicted remained at large in Indonesia, effectively beyond the court's jurisdiction.[21] And there was virtually no chance that any of the senior officials and officers who had been indicted— that is to say, the managers and planners of the violence—would ever be tried through East Timor's judicial process. The main reason was that the government of Indonesia categorically refused to extradite any suspects to East Timor or even to recognize the competence of East Timor's courts to try them. As a consequence, the only cases that had actually been tried by late 2004 were those of low-ranking local militiamen. This situation led to growing frustration among East Timorese, who noted with dismay that it was only East Timorese of lowly means who were being caught up in the judicial net, while the big fish went free. Still, given the fact that East Timor had no functioning judiciary in 2000 and few qualified lawyers, prosecutors, or judges, the serious crimes process was a remarkable achievement—an example of effective and meaningful international cooperation and assistance.

By far the most comprehensive human rights effort to date was conducted by East Timor's Commission on Reception, Truth and Reconciliation (Comissão de Acolhimento, Verdade e Reconciliação, CAVR). Although formally established by UNTAET regulation in 2001, the CAVR was in fact an initiative of a coalition of East Timorese political figures, human rights activists, and international experts. An autonomous body that operated independently of the government, it was given a broad mandate to establish the truth about the pattern of human rights and violence that had occurred during the period from 1974 to 1999, to write a comprehensive report of its findings, to assist victims of the violence, to promote human rights, and to foster reconciliation among East Timorese.[22]

Geoffrey Robinson

In carrying out this mandate, between 2002 and 2005 the CAVR held fifty-two public hearings in East Timor's districts and eight national public hearings in Dili, gathered and analyzed 7,200 victim statements, conducted several workshops for the worst-affected victims of violence, and processed 1,404 depositions from individuals requesting adjudication through a Community Reconciliation Process (CRP) established and implemented by the CAVR. In the course of that work, it amassed what is arguably the most comprehensive body of material on East Timor's modern history, comprising tens of thousands of pages of testimony, thousands of pages of documents, and many hundreds of hours of audio- and videotape. Based on a careful analysis of that material, the CAVR produced a detailed final report, *Chega!* (Enough!). The report concluded that both Indonesia and other states bore responsibility for the crimes committed in East Timor, and it spelled out detailed recommendations for different parties, including the Indonesian government, the United Nations, and various member states.

The UN and key states praised the CAVR's work, and expressed fulsome support for its findings. The same was true of East Timor's political leaders, most of whom said they welcomed the report; they promised to review its findings carefully and to implement its recommendations. A special session of East Timor's Parliament was convened to mark the submission of the report, on the symbolically important date of November 28, 2005, the thirtieth anniversary of the country's declaration of independence. And in January 2006 President Gusmão formally presented the report to the UN Secretary-General and addressed the Security Council on the question of justice and reconciliation.[23] This was all very good. The problem was that none of those who praised the report in principal were prepared to back it in practice by actually implementing its recommendations. Key international players declined to act or to insist on UN action, most probably because they did not wish to create difficulties for Indonesia or for East Timor's leaders. As a result, more than seven years after the report was formally presented to East Timor's Parliament, that body had not even debated it. Nor had any government agency made any move to implement even its most benign recommendations—such as compensation to the victims of past violence or the creation of memorial sites. This inaction on the part of the government and the international community provided further evidence, if any were needed, that the early consensus on the urgent need to bring the perpetrators of violence to justice had dissipated.

Despite these setbacks and obstacles, it needs to be stressed that there are many East Timorese, particularly outside of government, who have not abandoned the human rights ideals that were so central to their struggle for independence. The result is that many East Timorese are now deeply critical of their own leaders for their apparent about-face. The drastic decline in the strength of the international movement notwithstanding, they continue to demand justice for past crimes, and the principled promotion and protection of human rights inside East Timor.

Reflections

Though admittedly cursory, this account of the human rights movement in and for East Timor since 1975 provides some food for thought about the revisionist claims described at the outset and about the history of human rights more generally.

To begin with the question of origins and turning points, the evidence from East Timor highlights a serious problem in Moyn's claim that 1977 marks a universally important historical juncture. For while the timing of the rise of the East Timor human rights movement in the late 1970s fits reasonably well with that claim, both the character of the movement and the logic of its emergence are completely at odds with the general argument. Indeed, despite its timing, the human rights movement that emerged in East Timor in the late 1970s had virtually nothing in common with the larger transformation and movement that Moyn describes. Rather than being inspired or encouraged by President Carter's embrace of human rights in 1977, for instance, it emerged in defiant opposition to his administration's complicity in the genocide in East Timor. Far from being buoyed or stimulated by a "hegemonic" international human rights movement, it was built from scratch by a small handful of activists and academics who were all but ignored by major human rights organizations for at least a decade. Likewise, the movement inside East Timor was begun by a handful of local Catholic priests operating in near total isolation from the Universal Church, which provided no meaningful support until the late 1980s. In these early years, moreover, the movement did not even use the language of human rights, preferring the less controversial language of humanitarianism. In short, far from being part of a global phenomenon or contagion, the movement that emerged in these years was entirely a grassroots affair that grew, quite literally, from the bottom up and survived against extraordinary odds.

A related problem is that the shift to the discourse of universal human rights in East Timor that eventually took place in the 1980s did not, in fact, signal the "death" of earlier utopias, like national liberation, as Moyn suggests it ought to have done. On the contrary, the two goals and discourses were seen as intrinsically connected—gross violations of human rights were understood to stem directly from the denial of sovereignty and accordingly could only be secured through complete independence. In other words, like many anticolonial movements of the postwar period, the human rights movement in East Timor did not emerge from the ashes of the discredited ideal of self-determination; it was instead essential (both in theory and in practice) to the achievement of that ideal. This was not a case of "death" and "birth," or of "displacement" but of the two ideals and two discourses finding resolution in a single whole.

The history of human rights in East Timor also serves as a useful reminder that, as Mark Mazower has written of the United Nations, "origins are not destiny" (Mazower 2009). However compromised or inadequate the Universal Declaration of Human Rights (UDHR) and other human rights instruments may have appeared at the time of their promulgation, and however cynically they may have been used by political leaders in the years after, for many East Timorese they were a source of genuine inspiration and offered an important moral and legal foundation for their struggle. The same was true of the UN itself, whose institutions provided the essential political and legal framework within which independence was achieved and systematic human rights violations were ended. In that sense, East Timor was reminiscent of the anticolonial and antiracialist movements of the 1940s, 1950s, and 1960s that, as Burke, Anderson, and others remind us, found in the UN and its human rights covenants and bodies powerful rhetorical and legal support for their political objectives.

The engagement with human rights ideals and UN mechanisms, then, was not, as Moyn suggests, a naïve diversion from the "real" work of politics that brought no tangible change. On the contrary, for those inside East Timor, this work was intrinsically political, in the sense that it entailed direct and intentional challenges to the Indonesian state. The same was true outside of East Timor where human rights campaigning, though much less dangerous, directly contested the legitimacy of powerful states. It is worth stressing that this work contributed to fundamentally important political outcomes in the real world, notably a referendum that led to East Timor's independence and an international intervention that stopped a possible genocide. East Timor was hardly unique in this respect. Indeed, in many societies plagued by systematic state violence, human rights quite naturally become an important site of political struggle and, as Sikkink and others have argued, that work can result in meaningful political change (Sikkink 2011).

Turning to the wider history of human rights, East Timor's experience suggests that broad shifts in international norms, ideological formations, and legal regimes can influence the dynamic of local human rights movements. The dramatic expansion of the movement for East Timor around 1989, for example, is consistent with a broader global pattern of intensified human rights activism after the fall of the Berlin Wall. Likewise, the UN-backed intervention in East Timor of September 1999 occurred, in part, because of the widespread support for the idea of "humanitarian intervention" that briefly prevailed at the end of the millennium. Finally, the demise of the East Timor human rights movement after independence parallels almost exactly the global decline in human rights idealism after September 11, 2001.

At the same time, the evidence from East Timor raises questions about a tendency in some of the literature to think of the history of human rights in terms of globally significant origins or turning points, whether 1789, 1948, 1977, or some other date. Even a cursory glance at the movement in East Timor shows that the history of human rights is far more complicated than such approaches might suggest. While the debate about origins and turning points may be important, it would seem that more attention should be paid to the processes through which human rights ideas and movements change, including the reasons why they succeed and fail, and why they take the different forms they do. The answers to such questions are unlikely to be found in global ideological trends alone, but require attention to the specific political and sociological conditions prevailing in different locales. Those dimensions are especially important if there is to be any hope of accounting for variations in the trajectory of human rights movements over time and place.

If East Timor is any guide, historians of human rights will also need to resist the temptation to place Europe and the United States (and occasionally Latin America) at the center of the narrative. More specifically, we will need to stop portraying human rights movements elsewhere—especially in Africa and Asia—as essentially derivative, or as second-rate efforts by westernized elites guided by human rights leaders in Geneva, London, or Washington, DC. The case of East Timor suggests that the reality has been far more complex, and that whatever one may say of their ultimate "origins," the spread of human rights ideals, strategies, and movements has not been unidirectional. If there has been a global surge in the human rights ideal in the past half century, some part of the explanation must lie in the initiative of local populations responding to specific conditions—notably the experience of extreme state violence, racism, and colonialism—rather than in the benevolent efforts of outsiders or in broad ideological realignments.

Pursuing this line of thought a little further, historians may need to look more carefully at the ways in which international and local human rights movements have interacted with and influenced one another. As the story of East Timor shows, local NGOs and political movements do not operate in a vacuum. They choose and adapt discourses, strategies, and tactics that make sense locally and seem likely to resonate and to have credibility internationally.

Geoffrey Robinson

In doing so, they sometimes change their own character and their goals. At the same time, they influence the character of the international movements and discourses with which they become involved. This complex pattern of inter-action is well captured by the idea of networks of exchange, in which ideas, information, innovations, strategies, and tactics move in all directions, not just from the center to the periphery (Keck and Sikkink 1988).

East Timor's example also reminds us of the importance of contingency, or mere happenstance, in the history of human rights. The dramatic expan-sion of the human rights movement after 1991, for example, was partly attrib-utable to the fact that the Santa Cruz massacre of November that year just happened to be caught on video tape and then broadcast around the world. Likewise, the singular success of the human rights movement for East Timor in 1999 depended on such unpredictable contingencies as the availability of shocking images of militia violence; the individual acts of courage by many East Timorese and foreigners in 1999; and the personal intervention by key figures like Kofi Annan and Xanana Gusmão. Even more important, perhaps, that success depended on the unique confluence of such contingencies at the precise moment when the international credibility of human rights arguments and the idea of humanitarian intervention were at their height. Any general history of human rights needs somehow to take account of such conjunctures.

To do all of these things, historians will need to think harder about sources and methods. For a start, we must look beyond the published statements of well-known political, cultural, and intellectual figures, and examine the words and actions of less-visible people and movements, as well as the local sociology and politics in which they are embedded. In other words, we will need to engage in, or at least take account of, close-grained microhistories of particular movements, and then locate those movements squarely in a wider political and normative context. The point of such studies should not be to romanticize local human rights heroes—and certainly not to replace general, panoramic histories of human rights—but to explore more fully the ways in which less immediately visible movements and actors have helped to shape and transform national and international human rights ideas, actions, and strategies. In a word, the challenge will be to tell the history of human rights from the ground up.

Notes

1. Indeed, it is striking that East Timor is virtually absent from most of the gen-eral histories of human rights, including more recent works, which have continued to focus by and large on the dynamics of human rights movements in the Soviet Union, Eastern Europe, and Latin America. A handful of recent studies explore

the history of human rights in various African and Asian settings (Burke 2010; Eckert 2011; Hoffmann 2011; Klose 2011; Moses 2011).

2. There are two notable exceptions to this trend (C. Anderson 2003; Burke 2010). Both works highlight the critical importance of the UN and its human rights mechanisms in struggles against colonialism and racism in the late 1940s and 1950s.

3. The use of U.S.-supplied weapons for offensive purposes was explicitly forbidden under the Foreign Assistance Act of 1961 and the U.S.-Indonesia Mutual Defense Agreement of 1958.

4. Anderson notes that the Carter administration supplied these systems secretly, while telling Congress that no such transfers were taking place (B. Anderson 1998, 133).

5. In 1979–80, for example, Congress held three separate hearings on East Timor—in December 1979, February 1980, and June 1980—highlighting the duplicitous role of successive U.S. administrations in the invasion and genocide, and providing the essential, albeit short-lived, political pressure that permitted the International Committee of the Red Cross (ICRC) and other agencies to conduct their humanitarian work.

6. Arnold Kohen, interview with author, November 1, 2010.

7. A key figure in that transformation was Msgr. Martinho da Costa Lopes, vicar general and then apostolic administrator of the diocese of Dili in the crucial first decade of the occupation. A fearless and outspoken critic of Indonesian rule, he was removed from his position by the Vatican in 1983, after which he lived in Lisbon until his death (Lennox 2000; Kohen 2004, 10).

8. It was in 1975, after all, that armed revolutionary movements seized power in Vietnam, Cambodia, and Laos and continued to pose a serious threat to military regimes in the Philippines and Thailand—not to mention East Timor.

9. Nug Kacasungkana, interview with author, Dili, September 25, 2008.

10. Gusmão mentioned the significance of Kuwait in a September 1990 interview with the Australian lawyer Robert Domm (Cox and Carey 1995, 37).

11. Carey, among others, has compared Santa Cruz to South Africa's Sharpeville massacre in its historic importance (Cox and Carey 1995, 55).

12. Many years later, Ali Alatas used the same phrase in the title of his book about Indonesia's struggles to retain East Timor—*The Pebble in the Shoe: The Diplomatic Struggle for East Timor* (Alatas 2006).

13. Brad Simpson recounts a careful history of ETAN (Simpson 2004). David Webster describes the wider transnational solidarity movement (Webster 2003).

14. The UN Special Rapporteur on Torture visited the territory in 1991 and issued a report in time for the 1992 meeting of the Human Rights Commission. The Commission passed a consensus statement on human rights in East Timor that year and a stronger one in 1993. In December 1994 the UN Special Rapporteur on Extrajudicial, Summary, or Arbitrary Executions visited East Timor and issued a highly critical report later that same year.

15. The committee stated that it had awarded the prize to the two men "for their work towards a just and peaceful solution to the conflict in East Timor . . . [and] to honour their sustained and self-sacrificing contributions to a small but oppressed people" (Norwegian Nobel Institute 1996).

16. I learned about those efforts during a working dinner with Secretary of State Madeleine Albright in February 1999; I was asked at that time by State Department officials to propose alternatives to an open, democratic vote.

17. President Gusmão was especially cautious in this regard. Prime Minister Mari Alkatiri called for the establishment of an international tribunal in a neutral third country (see "East Timor PM Wants International Tribunal to Try Indonesian Officers," *Associated Press*, May 30, 2003).

18. The statute was UNTAET Regulation No. 2000/15, "On the Establishment of Panels with Exclusive Jurisdiction over Serious Criminal Offences," June 6, 2000. The serious crimes over which these panels had jurisdiction were genocide, war crimes, crimes against humanity, murder, sexual offenses, and torture.

19. After East Timor's independence on May 20, 2002, the SCU began to operate under the legal authority of the General Prosecutor of the Democratic Republic of Timor-Leste (Democratic Republic of Timor-Leste, Deputy General Prosecutor for Serious Crimes, Serious Crimes Unit, "Serious Crimes Update V/03," Dili, May 28, 2003).

20. Democratic Republic of Timor-Leste, Deputy General Prosecutor for Serious Crimes, Serious Crimes Unit, "Serious Crimes Update V/03," Dili, May 28, 2003; United Nations, Security Council, "Summary of the Report to the Secretary-General of the Commission of Experts to Review the Prosecution of Serious Violations of Human Rights in Timor-Leste (then East Timor) in 1999," May 26, 2005, 3, Annex I of UN Security Council document S/2005/458, July 15, 2005.

21. In May 2003, 169 of 247 indictees were in Indonesia (see Democratic Republic of Timor-Leste, Deputy General Prosecutor for Serious Crimes, Serious Crimes Unit). In May 2005, the figure was 339 of 391 indictees (see United Nations, Security Council, "Summary of the Report to the Secretary-General of the Commission of Experts," 4). In August 2006, the UN Security Council renewed the mandate of the Serious Crimes Unit to investigate but not to prosecute such crimes (United Nations, Security Council, Resolution 1704 [August 25, 2006]).

22. The CAVR was established under UNTAET regulation 10/2001 (July 13, 2001). Its final report, *Chega!* was published in early 2006 and is available at http://www.cavr-timorleste.org/en/chegaReport.htm.

23. Security Council Report, "Update Report No. 7: Timor-Leste," January 2006.

References

Alatas, Ali. 2006. *The Pebble in the Shoe: The Diplomatic Struggle for East Timor.* Jakarta: Aksara Karunia.

Amnesty International. 1985. *East Timor: Violations of Human Rights; Extrajudicial Executions, "Disappearances," Torture, and Political Imprisonment, 1975–1984*. London: Amnesty International.

———. 1991a. "East Timor: The Santa Cruz Massacre." November 14.

———. 1991b. "East Timor: After the Massacre." November 21.

———. 1993a. "Indonesia and East Timor: Seven East Timorese Seek Asylum." June 23.

———. 1993b. "Indonesia and East Timor: Seven East Timorese Still in Danger." July 5.

Anderson, Benedict. 1998. "Gravel in Jakarta's Shoes." In Benedict Anderson, *The Spectre of Comparisons: Nationalism, Southeast Asia, and the World*, 131–38. London: Verso Press, 1998.

Anderson, Carol. 2003. *Eyes Off the Prize: The United Nations and the African American Struggle for Human Rights, 1944–1955*. New York: Cambridge University Press.

Archer, Robert. 1995. "The Catholic Church in East Timor." In Carey and Bentley 1995, 120–33.

Belo, Carlos Filipe Ximenes (bishop). 1989. Letter from Bishop Belo to UN Secretary-General Xavier Pérez de Cuéllar. February 11.

Burke, Roland. 2010. *Decolonization and the Evolution of International Human Rights*. Philadelphia: University of Philadelphia Press.

Carey, Peter. 2003. "Third World Colonialism, the *Geração Foun*, and the Birth of a New Nation: Indonesia Through East Timorese Eyes, 1975–99." *Indonesia* 76:23–68.

Carey, Peter, and G. Carter Bentley, eds. 1995. *East Timor at the Crossroads: The Forging of a Nation*. Honolulu: University of Hawaii Press.

Comissão de Acolhimento, Verdade e Reconciliação de Timor Leste (CAVR, Commission for Reception, Truth and Reconciliation in East Timor). 2006. *Chega!* Dili. http://www.cavr-timorleste.org/en/chegaReport.htm.

Cox, Steve, and Peter Carey. 1995. *Generations of Resistance: East Timor*. London: Cassell.

Eckert, Andreas. 2011. "African Nationalists and Human Rights, 1940s–1970s." In Hoffmann 2011, 283–300.

Fernandes, Clinton. 2011. *The Independence of East Timor: Multidimensional Perspectives—Occupation, Resistance, and International Political Activism*. Toronto: Sussex Academy Press.

Gama, Paulino. 1995. "The War in the Hills, 1975–85: A Fretilin Commmander Remembers." In Carey and Bentley 1995, 97–105.

Goedde, Petra, William Hitchcock, and Akira Iriye, eds. 2012. *Human Rights in the Twentieth Century: An International History*. London: Oxford University Press.

Gomes, Donaciano. 1995. "The East Timor Intifada: Testimony of a Timorese Student Activist." In Carey and Bentley 1995, 106–8.

Gunn, Geoffrey. 1997. *East Timor and the United Nations: The Case for Intervention*. Lawrenceville, NJ: Red Sea Press.

Hoffmann, Stefan-Ludwig, ed. 2011. *Human Rights in the Twentieth Century*. New York: Cambridge University Press.

Hunt, Lynn. 2007. *Inventing Human Rights: A History*. New York: W. W. Norton.

Institute for Policy Studies (IPS). 1982. "Background Information on Indonesia, the Invasion of East Timor, and U.S. Military Assistance." Washington, DC: Institute for Policy Studies.

Keck, Margaret, and Kathryn Sikkink. 1998. *Activists beyond Borders: Advocacy Networks in International Politics*. Ithaca, NY: Cornell University Press.

Klose, Fabian. 2011. "'Source of Embarrassment': Human Rights, State of Emergency, and the Wars of Decolonization." In Hoffmann 2011, 237–57.

Kohen, Arnold. 1999. *From the Place of the Dead: The Epic Struggles of Bishop Belo of East Timor*. New York: St. Martin's Press.

———. 2004. Testimony before the CAVR. Dili. March 15.

Lennox, Rowena. 2000. *Fighting Spirit of East Timor: The Life of Martinho da Costa Lopes*. London: Zed Books.

Mazower, Mark. 2009. *No Enchanted Palace: The End of Empire and the Ideological Origins of the United Nations*. Princeton, NJ: Princeton University Press.

Moses, Dirk. 2011. "The United Nations, Humanitarianism, and Human Rights: War Crimes/Genocide Trials for Pakistani Soldiers in Bangladesh, 1971–1974." In Hoffmann 2011, 258–82.

Moyn, Samuel. 2010. *The Last Utopia: Human Rights in History*. Cambridge, MA: Harvard University Press.

Norwegian Nobel Institute. 1996. "The Nobel Peace Prize for 1996." October 11.

Open Letter to President Suharto. 1997. Kabar dari Pijar, September 11.

Quataert, Jean H. 2009. *Advocating Dignity: Human Rights Mobilizations in Global Politics*. Philadelphia: University of Pennsylvania Press.

Ramos-Horta, Jose. 1997. *Funu: The Unfinished Saga of East Timor*. Trenton, NJ: Red Sea Press.

Robinson, Geoffrey. 1996. "Human Rights in Southeast Asia: Rhetoric and Reality." In *Southeast Asia in the New World Order*, edited by David Wurfel and Bruce Burton, 74–99. New York: Macmillan.

———. 2010. *"If You Leave Us Here, We Will Die": How Genocide Was Stopped in East Timor*. Princeton, NJ: Princeton University Press.

———. 2011. "East Timor Ten Years On: Legacies of Violence." *Journal of Asian Studies* 70:1007–21.

Sikkink, Kathryn. 2011. *The Justice Cascade: How Human Rights Prosecutions Are Changing World Politics*. New York: W. W. Norton.

Simpson, Brad. 2004. "Solidarity in an Age of Globalization: The Transnational Movement for East Timor and U.S. Foreign Policy." *Peace & Change* 29:453–82.

Sword-Gusmão, Kirsty. 2003. *A Woman of Independence: A Story of Love and the Birth of a New Nation*. Sydney: Macmillan.

Tanter, Richard, Mark Selden, and Stephen R. Shalom, eds. 2001. *Bitter Flowers, Sweet Flowers: East Timor, Indonesia, and the World Community.* New York: Rowman and Littlefield.

United States, Agency for International Development (USAID). 1979. "Situation Report No. 1. East Timor, Indonesia-Displaced Persons." October 19.

United States, Department of State (US DOS). 1975. Telegram 1579 from U.S. Embassy Jakarta to Secretary of State. "Ford-Suharto Meeting," Document 4, "East Timor Revisited." National Security Archive, December 6. http://www.gwu.edu/~nsarchiv/NSAEBB/NSAEBB62/.

Webster, David. 2003. "Non-State Diplomacy: East Timor 1975–99." *Portuguese Studies Review* 11:1–28.

Weitz, Eric. 2008. "From the Vienna to the Paris System: International Politics and the Entangled Histories of Human Rights, Forced Deportations, and Civilizing Missions." *American Historical Review* 113:1313–43.

Geoffrey Robinson

2

 Rights on Display

Museums and Human Rights Claims

BRIDGET CONLEY-ZILKIC

Introduction

On April 22, 1993, President Bill Clinton stood at the podium erected in front of the U.S. Holocaust Memorial Museum (USHMM). Addressing a crowd of dignitaries assembled for the museum's opening, he stated: "[E]ven as our fragmentary awareness of these crimes grew into indisputable facts, we did far too little. . . . The evil represented in this museum is incontestable. It is absolute. As we are its witnesses, so must we remain its adversary" (Clinton 1993).

Across an ocean in southern Europe, the brutal war in Bosnia-Herzegovina, one of the newly independent states carved out of the former Yugoslavia, was entering its second year of what became known as "ethnic cleansing" in full force. And on that same April day, in Tuzla, a Bosnian government-held town, the American journalist Peter Maas watched the museum's opening ceremonies on TV. It was the moment, he writes, that he began to feel "spiritually sick" (1996, 242).

Maas spent three hours that day interviewing Dr. Nedret Mujkanovic, who had fled along with some of the injured from the besieged town of Srebrenica. Mujkanovic's work in Srebrenica included tending to some sixty thousand people eking out a survival in a town under near-complete blockade and frequent bombing by Bosnian Serb forces. Their health system consisted of two general practitioners and no medical supplies (no aspirin or bandages, let alone heavy-duty pain killers). Under these conditions over nine months, he performed fourteen hundred surgeries, among them countless amputations. Although he didn't know it at the time, in July 1995 the town would finally fall to the Bosnian Serbs forces, who killed some eight thousand Bosnian Muslims, mostly men and boys. The International Criminal Tribunal for the Former Yugoslavia would later decide these murders were genocide.

Clinton's words left Maas filled with disgust and a new sense of his own complicity in the betrayal: "President Clinton was making hypocrites of us all, and there was very little that could be done about it" (Maas 1996, 246). Another journalist who covered the war in Bosnia, David Rieff, also watched the opening of the USHMM in 1993 with disbelief, writing:

> To utter words like "Never again," as Clinton did at the opening of the Holocaust Museum, was to take vacuity over the border into obscenity as long as the genocide in Bosnia was going on and Clinton was doing nothing to stop it. His words were literally meaningless. For if there was to be no intervention to stop a genocide that was taking place, then the phrase "Never again" meant nothing more than: "never again would Germans kill Jews in Europe in the 1940s." (Rieff 1996, 27)

President Clinton was not the only speaker that rainy morning in Washington. Elie Wiesel, an Auschwitz survivor and Nobel laureate, also rose to the podium. He spoke of his experiences during the Holocaust. His family was among the Hungarian Jews, some of the last European Jews to be deported to death camps, well after world leaders knew what was happening and yet chose not—at a minimum—even to warn them of their fate. Raindrops blurred the ink on Wiesel's papers; he turned away from his prepared remarks to address President Clinton directly. Now he spoke of what he had witnessed only months beforehand when he visited a Bosnian Serb–run concentration camp. Wiesel stated: "Mr. President, I cannot not tell you something. I have been in the former Yugoslavia last fall. . . . As a Jew, I am saying that we must do something to stop the bloodshed in that country" (Wiesel 1993).

And thus, the U.S. Holocaust Memorial Museum was opened to the public.

It is no accident that a museum would provide the context for an unexpected and powerful human rights intervention. And, although Wiesel's provocation cannot be understood absent the particular circumstances of Holocaust memorialization and contemporary genocide, the inherent potential of museums to spark new forms of human rights activism is not limited to this framework. In the years since 1993, museums are increasingly testing the waters of engagement on human rights issues.

Returning to the opening scene at the USHMM as our grounding example, I question what museums, given their particular strengths and weaknesses, can uniquely contribute to human rights discourse. This example is unique in important ways, both in terms of the particular place of the Holocaust as a historical event, as well as the landmark position the USHMM occupies on the landscape of Holocaust memorialization and museum practices. It is also an example that I know well, having worked at the museum in its Committee on Conscience (COC), dedicated to issues of contemporary genocide, for ten years.[1] By placing this one example in the context of evolving debates about museums and rights as a model of political contestation, one can begin to see how the issues it raises are relevant to broader debates about the future of museums and their potential to offer a unique contribution to human rights practices.

Museums on the Political Landscape

The term "museums" covers an enormous array of institutional models and practices. This chapter draws heavily on the example of the USHMM because it is most relevant to national history museums, and, more specifically, to memorial museums. Such museums, like all institutions, do not exist in a vacuum and then suddenly become political by choosing to engage with human rights issues. They are embedded in practices, logics, and hierarchies that are unavoidably politicized.

A comprehensive assessment of the cultural-political position of the museum is a more complex project than can be undertaken in this chapter. Here, I simply sketch out three of the most important questions that might guide such an undertaking, each of which has a corresponding body of literature and debates. First, scanning the politico-social horizon, I ask what role museums play in the larger context of the state and power relations. Second, looking inside the museum, I chart the changing context for curatorial decisions about what should be displayed. Finally, I introduce contemporary debates about how a museum addresses and engages its visitors. We begin by returning to the scene of the opening of the USHMM.

When President Clinton rose to the podium that rainy April day, he could look up and see the cherry tree–lined tidal basin, a shallow curve of water in front of the Jefferson Memorial; the Washington Monument soaring into the sky just beyond the museum buildings; and farther on, the White House and the U.S. Capitol. The audience before him included American and international leaders, in addition to Holocaust survivors, supporters of the museum, and those who had worked to create it.

There were undoubtedly political-historical reasons that made it possible for the museum to exist at this location and moment in time (Linenthal 1995). The museum leadership justified it by placing the Holocaust and the museum firmly within U.S. national discourse: "This museum belongs at the center of American life because as a democratic civilization America is the enemy of racism, and its ultimate expression, genocide. An event of universal significance, the Holocaust has special importance for Americans: in act and in word the Nazis denied the deepest tenets of the American people" (Young 1994, 337). Wiesel repeated this sentiment at the opening: "It is because of the passion that we have for Israel, we are Jews, and decent people in America, that we have faith in humanity and in America" (Wiesel 1993).[2] And the approach is reflected in elements of the architecture: displays, quotations from U.S. presidents on the walls, an introductory film narrated from the perspective of an American GI, the opening image in the permanent exhibition of U.S. forces liberating camps, and presentations concerning American responses to the Holocaust, among other details.

This approach marks a sharp departure from Holocaust scholarship that argues vociferously against the search for redemption in the history of the Nazi regime's attempt to murder the European Jews—including, certainly, putting the history at the service, however darkly, of celebrations of national idealism. Articulated most succinctly with Theodor Adorno's statement that "to write poetry after Auschwitz is barbaric," there is a significant body of work asserting the impossibility of representing or redeeming the history of the Holocaust (Spargo and Ehrenreich 2011). Lawrence Langer (1998) describes such efforts as "preempting the Holocaust," by which he means "using—and perhaps abusing—its grim details to fortify a prior commitment to an ideal of moral reality, community responsibility, or religious belief that leaves us with space to retain faith in their pristine value in a post-Holocaust world" (1).[3]

One side note here, which will become more important in relation to the next section, is that too often the philosophical or existential concern with the limitations of representing the Holocaust are translated directly into an argument for its historical, ethical, or political uniqueness. There are important differences. The former focuses on experiences that exist across a threshold of brutality that exceeds communication: it is the destruction of meaning. The latter imposes a hierarchy of meaning derived from analysis of the factual components of the events.

Overall, the richness of these debates about representing the Holocaust impacts the USHMM's exhibitionary and educational practices. However, in terms of framing the rationale for its presence on the National Mall, the museum's leadership clearly opted for a national logic that finds its place within time-worn justifications for national museums. These kinds of museums, many of which emerged out of the collections of princely or private collections and often expanded through colonial plunder and elite patronage, have become a sign of nationhood itself, "part of the checklist for being a nation" (Kratz and Karp 2006, 3). The relationship between the national museum and national imagination is not a simple presentation of histories or objects related to national history; it is instead best described as part of becoming a modern nation through institutions that help the citizen (and outside world) experience the nation as a logical, coherent, and ideal political unit to which they belong.

As powerfully presented in Tony Bennett's (1995) landmark history of museums, *The Birth of the Museum: History, Theory, Politics*, the emergence of the national museum contributed to the production of the modern citizen by providing a public space in which "civilized" behaviors and attitudes might be learned.[4] Positioning the museum within a Foucauldian history of modernity, Bennett argues that it exhibited structured knowledge that helped the citizen perceive progress and receive education in a space that circulated around spectacle—of seeing and being seen in light of the behavioral and pedagogical expectations of the modernizing state—what he terms the "exhibitionary complex" (Bennett 1995, 24, 61).

The status of the museum as both a representation and (re)producer of the ideal socio-political community continues to define its role today. What Bennett frames in critical language is also celebrated by museum advocates as the museums' distinguishing traits on a crowded horizon of pedagogical consumer experiences. For instance, museums enjoy remarkably high levels of social trust (Griffiths and King 2008).[5] A museum visit can be a powerful, almost ritualistic experience. Visiting is intentional, exceptional although potentially repeatable, educational, yet open-ended and self-propelled.[6] For most people the encounter with a museum is measured in terms of a time-constrained, single visit. However, there is strength within this limitation. At the USHMM, for example, nearly 2 million people a year, many of them first-time visitors, enter the doors. While this implies that the institution has only one chance with each visitor, it also means that the total visiting population is annually expanded and represents a broad cross-section of the general public.

Museums can also occupy a place on the social horizon that exceeds any particular visit in terms of their physical presence, capacity to leverage media attention, and role intersecting formal educative practices. And the open invitation to "visit" helps define the national public apart from the conveyance of any particular information associated with the exhibitions' content. Whether one is critical or celebratory of the ways that museums rely on their ability to create and nurture cultural-political community, it must be acknowledged that despite being public in terms of their availability to the general public, they do not constitute a public sphere in the sense of being a neutral forum open for all forms of discussion (Bennett 2006, 49). On this matter, the USHMM is no different from other museums.

While certain elements of the museums' cultural-political status have remained fairly persistent over time, their exhibitions have not. Museums participate in the production of the national subject not merely by mirroring values but by defracting those values through specific contexts and experiences created in their exhibitions. The disjunction between the ideal and the details, which echoes what Stern and Straus have described as a human rights paradox, when presented in exhibitions offer a foothold for politicization and contestation. Over time, in relation to criticism as well as in relation to—and in cases embrace of—broader social-political movements, national museums have changed in important ways. Looking to the same landscape as the USHMM, which itself provides an example of a minority history entering the national imagination, there is also the National Museum of the American Indian, National Museum of African American History and Culture (opening 2015), or particular exhibitions, like those on the civil rights era in the National Museum of American History.

There are several ways to understand these changes. Some may argue that the inclusion of these minority histories signifies the ways that they have already been absorbed into the national consciousness—essentially the taming of their challenge to accepted political relations. Regardless of one's interpretation, at a minimum it can be said that museums—and there are many such examples beyond the U.S. context—are increasingly defining nations in relation to the diversity of their population, even if the limits of plurality remain hotly contested.[7] Other factors have influenced changing exhibitionary practices as well, not least of which are decreases in public funding (Koster 2006).

Museums grappling with these trends have found themselves forced to articulate their social meaning and address their audiences in new ways. Some museums have responded by asserting the relevancy of their established collections to contemporary events. Others have embraced or tested ways of shifting away from the dominance of the expert-curator voice toward visitor-centered experiences (Sandell 2007; Simon 2010; Witcomb 2003). At one end of this spectrum are fantastically creative experiences, and at the other end is the threat of increasingly consumerist approaches to museum pedagogy.

What does this mean as rights go on display?

Bridget Conley-Zilkic

There is no single answer. At a minimum, museums already play a role in human rights discourse inasmuch as they have always related to the production of and reflection on national subjectivity. What concerns the citizen, as the national political subject, concerns rights. While we see contestation and evolution, we can also perceive how museums participate in processes of validation and reproduction of existing norms, rather than offering a challenge to those norms. This conservative potential is even more pronounced when an institution internalizes its relationship to the state instead of foregrounding it as a political fact. It must be acknowledged and accounted for rather than be allowed to merge unexamined within the content of a museum's presentation.

Unexamined, the museum participates in the processes by which human rights do not provide a bulwark against power in the name of a minimal threshold of human sanctity but, as Michel Foucault suggested, rather legitimatizes and reproduces relations of power within a national (or even nationalist) narrative. Rights help define what is normal, common, and thereby beyond all argument. This normative truth, embedded in a discourse of rights, delimits and fixes individuals in their relationship with the state. In the context of a Holocaust museum, there is very little grappling with the history of the Holocaust or with the potential to challenge our practices today if the dark history serves only as a contrast to the shining example of established American nationalism. This is how President Clinton's statements at the opening of the USHMM might have been perceived.

In choosing to include new stories that complicate nationalist narratives, *how* museums tell these stories is just as important as the fact of their telling. In the case of rights discourse, the temptations of hasty summaries of distant crises and a consumerist approach to engaging the public can feed self-satisfaction.

Nonetheless, it is possible to imagine a way of telling histories that challenge the present, and it is also possible to do this in a way that carves out a unique human rights role for museums. But to explore this further, we must also examine the political landscape of human rights practices. For this, we focus on the scene in 1993.

Human Rights on the Political Landscape

In April 1993 international responses to the ongoing war and atrocities in Bosnia-Herzegovina included a UN peacekeeping mission, a spate of negotiation processes, and a massive humanitarian aid effort. International media and human rights organizations covered its brutal images and details.

That very month Helsinki Watch (now Human Rights Watch) issued volume 2 of its report on war crimes in Bosnia-Herzegovina, which it termed "genocide," and called for measures to (1) prevent and suppress genocide, (2) create a war crimes tribunal, (3) effect an armed force to protect the delivery of humanitarian supplies, and (4) deploy UN human rights monitors (Helsinki Watch 1993, 4).

Into this mix of voices, Wiesel issued his plea to President Clinton at the opening of the USHMM. Arguing that one lesson of the Holocaust is that "when people suffer we cannot remain indifferent," he referenced the war in the former Yugoslavia and stated, "People fight each other and children die. Why? Something, anything must be done."

Thus Wiesel tied the legacy of the Holocaust to an ethical stance against human suffering that posits indifference as the harm and action ("something, anything") as the cure. This is consistent with Wiesel's long-asserted position that the Holocaust was both Jewish *and* universal in its nature. Within debates about Holocaust memorialization, this marks a departure from the premise of absolute uniqueness of the Holocaust—the idea that the Holocaust is phenomenologically and ethically unique and therefore beyond compare with any other event. Wiesel's argument marks a subtle shift in this logic, whereby the Holocaust remains a historically, politically, and ethically unique event, which nonetheless operates as a universal ethical principle in relation to what he termed "human suffering." As stated in the 1979 Report of the President's Commission on the Holocaust, largely authored by Wiesel, that recommended the creation of the USHMM: "The universality of the Holocaust lies in its uniqueness: the Event is essentially Jewish, yet its interpretation is universal" (President's Commission 1979).

In maneuvering this shift, Wiesel sets an example that would later echo throughout the broader human rights field and particularly in the antigenocide movement that arose in the mid-2000s. The Holocaust increasingly provides the standard-image book and vocabulary for human rights issues (Levy and Sznaider 2006, 161), which is possible as the Holocaust becomes a reference point and morality tale, rather than a historical event. As Levy and Sznaider argue, "The Holocaust sets the parameters for de-territorialized memory-scapes[,] . . . provides a model for national self-critique, serves to promote human rights as a legitimating principle in the global community, and plainly offers a negative example of dealing with alterity" (201). Embraced by some, this manner of abstracting the Holocaust has been criticized by others for how it reduces the historical complexity and Jewish character of the Holocaust.

One question approaches this shift from a different angle: How does invoking the Holocaust as an ethical absolute to define ongoing events frame

Bridget Conley-Zilkic

our responses to those events? Or, to frame the question in a more general form that might apply to other museums' human rights endeavors: What are the consequences of drawing on historical narratives or fixed collections as ethical imperatives to define the present?

The effect in the case of Wiesel's intervention on Bosnia-Herzegovina was to depoliticize the present by converting the political-military issues and conundrums into ethical-humanitarian absolutes.[8] This was not an incidental effect—it was the intended goal. In Bosnia, this conversion supported the humanitarianization of the conflict and contributed to the range of responses that consistently failed to define the political stakes of the situation, and by focusing primarily on protecting the delivery of humanitarian supplies, it ended up increasing civilian vulnerability to violence (Feher 2000; Rieff 1996). For example, throughout much of the conflict, a more robust engagement with the primary aggressors, the Bosnian Serbs, was rejected for fear that it would disrupt the delivery of humanitarian supplies to civilians. This approach fed, clothed, and provided some minimal medical relief to civilians who, like those in the most extreme case of Srebrenica, remained vulnerable to Bosnian Serb attacks, even genocide. This approach, coupled with an arms embargo, which froze into place a significant arms imbalance that favored the Bosnian Serbs, masqueraded as apolitical, humanitarian intervention.

Wiesel's plea in the name of Holocaust and human suffering to do "anything" did not challenge this core approach. While he faced criticism for "politicizing" the Holocaust with this intervention, what actually occurred was the universalization of the Holocaust as an ethical absolute to depoliticize the present. To the extent that museums try to build a program out of cries to "do something, anything," they walk the border between instigating ethical action and escalating ethical rhetoric absent informed engagement of the history, context, and politics at play in a situation. In this agenda, they do not carve out a new role for themselves, but tread the same challenging ground as professional human rights organizations without offering a comparable suite of investigation and policy tools.

Today's human rights organizations operate by advancing, monitoring, and expanding human rights norms, generally as articulated in major legal or aspirational documents like the UN Genocide Convention, the UN Universal Declaration of Human Rights, or the range of key international conventions and legal standards. The executive director of Human Rights Watch, Ken Roth, succinctly summarizes the methodology and strengths of human rights organizations as naming and shaming: "We must be able to show persuasively that a particular state of affairs amounts to a violation of human rights standards, that a particular violator is principally or significantly responsible, and that a widely accepted remedy for the violation exists." Shaming works, as Sikkink, Ropp, and Risse (1996) argue, because human rights norms today define the international community—which is (my definition) an abstraction of existing power relations articulated through the ideals of liberal rights discourse—and provide the "rules for appropriate behavior" of individual states (11).

These practices are not without their critics. Arguing that "speaking law to politics is not the same thing as speaking truth to power," David Kennedy offers one of the most insightful and concise critiques of human rights practices today (Kennedy 2002, 121). He argues that human rights discourse is hegemonic and absolutist in its articulation of how its rules should govern practices, while nonetheless valuing participation in existing political systems. This argument is often oblivious of its own assumptions and historical development. Human rights discourse offers a narrow view of the problems it seeks to define by foregrounding form (legal mechanisms) over analysis of larger social, political, and economic factors that might enable abuses. It tends to categorize situations with broad strokes of victim versus perpetrator; it reduces incidents of violence to illustrations of general principles; it offers answers, not questions; it treats symptoms; and finally, it excuses and justifies too much.

Human rights as a discourse and professional practice promises more than it can deliver, not only regarding what it can understand but also its potential to exist outside of politics as a neutral tool for achieving justice. While today's human rights paradigm has undeniably reduced suffering in many contexts, it often does so at the cost of avoiding or refusing to acknowledge its own political context. Wendy Brown (2004) argues:

> There is no such thing as mere reduction of suffering or protection from abuse—the nature of the reduction or protection is itself productive of political subjects and political possibilities. Just as abuse itself is never generic but always has particular social and subjective content, so the matter of how it is relieved is consequential. . . . The pragmatist, moral, and antipolitical mantle of human rights discourse tends to eschew, even repel, rather than invite or address these questions. (460)

The law-based, juridical model of human rights is, as all models are, a limited vision of what human rights might be and how they might be enacted. Its contributions and limitations rest in its strategy: envisioning change as an adjustment of government policies to align with universal ethical principles. Politics, therefore, is perceived as responsible primarily to abstract principles—not necessarily to people—even if in practice the goal is for principles to improve the plight of people. But this logic underwriting practice has, as mentioned earlier, consequences. When museums adopt the same logic by converting

Bridget Conley-Zilkic

historical memory into universal ethical imperative, they provide a companion to the abstraction of political, historical, and social context that grounds the juridical model of human rights advocacy. The two approaches to injustice—juridical and historical—do not complicate but reify each other. Failing to recognize the limitations of the dominant juridical model of rights and the struggle to define their own unique contribution, museums can easily fall into discourse that merely amplifies the ethical absolutes already claimed by human rights professionals in leading nongovernmental organizations.

If their role is thus defined, museums are put in the situation of providing sentimentalized amplification of the "real work," work done elsewhere by professional human rights organizations whose unique history, practice, skills, and access were designed for this purpose. In so doing, museums miss an opportunity to define their unique role on the human rights horizon—a role that they play best and that makes significant contributions to the way we understand and enact rights claims.

Memorialization and Interruption: A New Direction for Rights?

The concluding sentence of Elie Wiesel's speech in April 1993 offers a glimpse of the truly unprecedented contribution museums might make to human rights practice. Earlier in his speech, Wiesel spoke of a young Jewish woman in Hungary who, upon reading of the Warsaw ghetto uprising, asked: "'Why are our Jewish brothers doing that? Why are they fighting? Couldn't they wait quietly'—the word was quietly—'until the end of the war?' Treblinka, Ponar, Belzec, Chelmno, Birkenau. She had never heard of these places. One year later, together with her entire family, she was already in a cattle car traveling to the black hole in time, the black hole in history, named Auschwitz." Wiesel's final words returned to this woman. He said: "The woman in the Carpathian Mountain of whom I spoke to you, that woman disappeared. She was my mother" (Wiesel 1993).

This was a human rights intervention that could not be subsumed by a celebration of American exceptionalism; it did not call upon international judicial mechanisms, conventions, or norms. It could not be abstracted into anything else. No other Holocaust story can substitute for this story—against the backdrop of overwhelming history, Wiesel's call to reimagine today ended with the unbearable loss of one person.

Out of this, on a day that resonated with history, memory, and the simultaneous existence of violence that betrayed the promise of new rights-based stabilization, one catches a glimmer of how memorial museums might rewrite rights. In both their approach to history as event and their memorialization practices, these institutions offer a unique contribution to the discourse and practice of human rights.

When historiography is framed by a memorial context, as it is in memorial museums, the presentation is tethered to the documentation of a time-constrained series of events rather than to a narrative of national or international historical progress. No museum or any other form of telling history escapes large historiography altogether, but it is not the ultimate purpose of a memorial museum to explain everything—it is to detail a circumscribed time period. In this, the limitations of presenting the history of traumatic historical events can be understood as a strength: retaining fidelity to the complexity of the events they relate, rather than trying to explain those events in connection to a longer continuum, an endless process of questioning is opened. As long as memorial museums are not frightened of the complications their examples inevitably surface, the historical details will remain a source of unraveling assumptions.[9]

Memorialization—honoring the losses of individual lives (or the impossibility of mourning individual lives due to the large-scale nature of the violence)—rewrites the rules for telling public history and engaging the world today. Memorialization as a rights intervention reverses the relationship between our frameworks for understanding events and the events themselves. It shifts the burden of proof away from the details of events, whose intricacies are itemized. Instead, laid bare and open for question are the national, political, historical, and ethical frameworks that frequently serve as shortcuts for determining appropriate responses. Memorialization suggests that before one can discuss a theory or practice of rights, one must accept humility before the losses exposed. The assertion of rights is not a cure for history, politics, or suffering; it is an attempt to build something different moving forward. Memorialization reminds us that in moving forward, we have not changed history but find new ways to live with it.

To be effective in making linkages from the past to the present, three key strategies emerge: (1) emphasis on clarity about what can be understood from the past and refusal to build programs or issue demands that exceed such insights; (2) a redirection toward the unique context of the events at hand; and (3) an understanding that responses to abuses will always be of a different nature than the abuses themselves—the ethical demands issued by human rights abuses do not convey the types of responses that can be offered, certainly not those responses crafted from afar.

Memorial museums are particularly well placed to make powerful and creative human rights interventions by deploying these strategies.[10] Paul Williams

Bridget Conley-Zilkic

(2007) writes that memorial museums are a form whose popularity has grown since 1990, when only a handful of examples existed, to the present where such museums can be found on every continent, dedicated to diverse historical events: slavery, apartheid, genocide, terrorism (state sponsored or not), totalitarianism, and more.[11] The institutions that fall into this category share in common a sense that the suffering they explore has social and historical meaning often embedded within an imperative to end the violence—and thereby have an inherent political meaning—while also emphasizing the need to honor the individual victims. The tension between these two insights is what creates a unique human rights perspective.

A sign that the form had come of age, the International Council of Museums (ICOM), an international museum professionals' organization created in 1946 that has a consultative status with UNESCO, created an International Committee of Memorial Museums in Remembrance of the Victims of Public Crimes (ICMEMO) in July 2001. They define the purpose of memorial museums as commemorating "victims of State, socially determined and ideologically motivated crimes"; these "crimes" imply a political context and need to examine how states justify and enact violence. They further note the connection between historical sites and the engagement of survivor or victim communities in the museums, thereby emphasizing the ways the historical events they depict are tied to discrete places and people. Finally, the definition also notes that memorial museums present "information about historical events in a way which retains a historical perspective while also making strong links to the present" (ICMEMO 2001). Memorial museums have claimed as part of their institutional template a role in exploring how certain ongoing policies and ideologies participate in abuses and how the history of past violence helps to define our engagement today.

It is a powerful departure from previous practices for museums to include juridical human rights language in their self-conception. But the mere assertion of their human rights role does not solve but only begins the challenge of making meaningful and distinct contributions, rather than a weakened mimicry of the roles played by human rights advocacy organizations today.

It is arguably the role that audiences expect and desire from them. For example, a 2011 report from the Fundamental Rights Agency of the European Union (FRA 2011) looked at Holocaust education in formal settings and at memorial sites in order to build a case for how it might intersect with human rights education. The term "HRE" is defined within juridical terms as education that increases knowledge about human rights and mechanisms that protect them but also imparts the skills needed to promote, defend, and apply human rights in daily life (10). One telling section of the report details a series of focus-group discussions with teachers and students in various European countries.

Discussions of HRE with students, if one can rely on the results of this study, appear to have produced blank stares: "[I]t became clear that the students had barely any concept of HRE" (FRA 2011, 101). The facilitators, intent on their purpose, offered some examples but the students still balked. Human rights, taught as an introduction to international norms, was considered too unfocused, unrelated to school subjects, and boring (97). Researchers found that the disconnect between Holocaust history and HRE was most strongly pronounced when it came to visiting memorial sites and museums (91). What teachers and students sought in site visits was an experience that combined historical knowledge and context with "authenticity," understood as exposure to testimonies, places, and objects in addition to fostering discussions that were based on "real" feelings: "[P]eople should interact in a way not determined by the institution, school, or its hierarchical structures" (104). What is interesting about these expectations is that they were perceived as being antithetical to human rights discourse: "Both teacher and student groups showed a similar level of hesitation concerning Holocaust education and HRE. Although teachers certainly think about lines of connection, which they often explicitly reject, it is obviously very difficult for students to recognize connections of any kind" (105).

One could argue that an appropriate response is to teach Holocaust as a stand-alone historical case without any attempts at making connections to contemporary human rights issues. One could also argue that the solution is to provide students with more information about the norm-building process that informs HRE. To the first response, I argue that our juxtaposition of Bosnia and the opening of the USHMM tells us that whether we like it or not, history and headlines do speak to each other. To the second response, I agree that more could be done, but we should also heed the nature of the students' comments and take up the challenge to human rights discourse reflected therein.

Somewhere between wanting greater context for understanding the Holocaust and how it came to pass, seeking more "authentic" and nonhierarchical encounters with history, and searching for the contemporary relevance of this history, students and teachers' comments reflect not only a desire to understand history but to better understand what makes history possible and how it impacts the world today. This desire cannot be answered by the insertion of norms and a juridical framework, nor does it require a political shortcut through the path of ethical imperatives. Instead, it ought to be understood as a challenge to rethink the hegemonic status of such articulations of rights.

Bridget Conley-Zilkic

To understand the potential for memorial museums to contribute to rights discourse we must learn to think about rights differently. A distinct model for human rights based in the historiographical strength of the memorial museum would function not through abstraction, be it juridical or ethical, but through interruption. In other words, one must let go of the hope that rights stabilize justice in a political system and imagine their disruptive capacity as their real contribution. It is precisely the capacity of memorial museums and sites of conscience to disrupt relations that the students referred to; they wanted conversations that linked to the present but wanted them to be structured as an interruption of accepted practice, not a new set of rules.

To the extent that one can theorize such a vision of memorialization and rights, we need a way to think of rights as a force that destabilizes rather than secures social relations. This is what Jacques Rancière (2004) calls "dissensus" (304)—the moment when the tenets of social order are revealed as incapable of totalizing. Uncertainty, interruption, and destabilization—not national redemption, ethical imperative, or norm building—provide the grounds for dissensual politics. The process of claiming rights cannot be reduced to the application of standards, be they conventions or ethical absolutes. Rights are claimed and expanded through contestation, when, as Rancière states, those who have no rights claim the rights they do not have. This can be undertaken only in a moment of interruption when the example destabilizes the given principles.

This was a strategy that my team and I deployed in the USHMM's 2009 exhibit *From Memory to Action: Meeting the Challenge of Genocide Today*. The exhibit comprised a framework of "genocide" (the legal term) to introduce three cases, eyewitness testimonies, and a challenge to visitors to imagine their own agency in responding to today's threats. We imagined these elements as bound together but in ways that maintained a tension between them.

Unlike other exhibitions at the USHMM, both its permanent exhibition and other temporary ones, the one on genocide does not follow a narrative development. It offers three main entrees to the question of how genocide exists in our lifetime and juxtaposes these approaches without suggesting that they can be subsumed within a single approach. No single case perfectly illustrates "genocide," just as individual stories offer details that can exceed or complicate the larger historical narrative. In addition, the actions of individuals far from the halls of power or the locations of destruction can and often are outside the proximity of change. Nonetheless, when experienced together, these disparate elements gesture to a reality of experienced violence and an interruption of the present day that is a constant political and social challenge.

The success of this effort will ultimately be judged by others. But the experiment in displaying rights as dissensus suggests that museums can forge a unique role on the human rights landscape. This role is not to provide a map for response but to issue a challenge by reexposing the vulnerability of our given frameworks through respect and honor of the unique examples that museums present.

Conclusion

Andreas Huyssen (1995) has argued that "in our century, different political versions of some better future have done fierce battle with each other, but the quintessentially modern notion of the future as progress or utopia was shared by all. It no longer is" (8). At the beginning of the twenty-first century, it is simply too late to believe that our maps for progress, even those grounded in human rights norms and ethical imperatives, do not also leave a trail of monumental suffering in their wake. This is why our exploration of museums' role in human rights engagement is not merely relevant to the work of museums—it is imperative to enrich the discourse and practice of human rights.

There are considerable limitations to the museums' potential role. Combining rights debates with historical examples will not produce obvious insights into how history intersects with the challenges of the day. There will be some who believe that museums should seek to isolate their histories and contexts from social debates. There will also be many people who will want to expand and stabilize the moment of dissensus into a political or ethical program that dissolves what is actually unique in the experience. Nonetheless, it is also possible and a particular strength of memorial museums to transform a public engagement with rights by insisting on a radical commitment to the methodology of memorialization that serves as their foundation.

Notes

1. The creation of such a committee was recommended by the 1979 Report of the President's Commission on the Holocaust, the foundational document for the USHMM. It argued that a "memorial unresponsive to the future would [also] violate the memory of the past." However, the COC was not formed until 1995 and not staffed until 1999. I began working there two years later. See http://www .ushmm.org/genocide/. Please note that all of the opinions expressed in this chapter are mine alone and should not be mistaken as official USHMM positions.

2. I cannot pass over this statement without commenting on the problematic equation of state interest (American and Israeli, and apparently identical), with

the religious community of Judaism, and the unspecified ideas of decency and humanity.

3. There is a great deal of literature on the debates about the instrumentalization of the Holocaust; see, e.g., Cole 1999; Finkelstein 2000; and Novick 1999.

4. There is a significant body of critical work on the museum focused on how these institutions inculcated bourgeois values, particularly vis-à-vis colonial enterprises by displaying empire for a national audience. This approach informs but does not fully grapple with the socio-political dynamics at play as museums take on social justice issues; but see Witcomb 2003.

5. Griffiths et al. found that 77 percent of museum visitors rated them equal or higher in trustworthiness than all other sources of public information. This correlates with the results of a similar study conducted in 2001 by the American Association of Museums.

6. Many museums undertake work well beyond what is visible in their exhibitions, including maintaining archives, a broad range of educational activities, development of resources (including posters, teaching guides, websites, videos, etc.), and research activities. But the nature of the visit to exhibitions is what makes museums a unique type of institution.

7. Debates over representation in South African museums are particularly pointed illustrations of this. The end of apartheid played out with great detail in museum exhibitions; see Coombes 1998 and Witz 2006 for a discussion of ethnography in museum practices. For a brief overview of some controversial exhibitions in recent history, see Bennett 2006, 60–61; Kratz and Karp 2007, 12–14; and Moses 2012.

8. Levy and Sznaider address the treatment of the broader context of Jewish groups like the American Jewish Committee, the American Jewish Congress, and the Anti-Defamation League, which followed suit by similarly deploying Holocaust references in relation to the conflicts of the Balkans (Levy and Sznaider 2006, 159).

9. The practice of returning again and again to the complications of the history to challenge any easy assumptions that an audience might want to make is part of the core pedagogical approach that the USHMM models, particularly in their educational programs. The complexity of their pedagogy is evident in the guidelines they have produced for teachers; see http://www.ushmm.org/education/foreducators/guideline/ (last accessed March 13, 2013).

10. In addition to the International Committee of Memorial Museums in Remembrance of the Victims of Public Crimes (ICMEMO), there are other important official recognitions for including rights in museum practices (The Declaration of Museum Responsibility to Promote Human Rights 2009; Federation of International Human Rights Museums 2010; and the International Coalition of Sites of Conscience [1999]).

11. Studies of museums that address these events have been studied under multiple headings, indicating only some of the strands one would have to explore

in order to fully appreciate their social role: Holocaust museums (there are so many that these deserve special attention as a field in their own right); sites of conscience (located at a historical site); burdensome memory (see Linenthal 1995), museums of human suffering (Duffy 2001), thanatourism (studies analyze the phenomenon of making violent history appeal to tourists), and the newly emerging human rights museums (e.g., Canadian Museum for Human Rights) or coalitions of museums (Federation of International Human Rights Museums [FIHRM], which includes many of the above types of museums as well as others).

References

Bennett, Tony. 1995. *The Birth of the Museum: History, Theory, Politics*. New York: Routledge.

———. 2006. "Exhibition, Difference, and the Logic of Culture." In Karp, Katz, Szwaja, and Ybarra-Frausto 2006, 46–79.

Brown, Wendy. 2004. "'The Most We Can Hope For . . . ': Human Rights and the Politics of Fatalism." *South Atlantic Quarterly* 103, no. 2/3: 452–63.

Clinton, William. 1993. Remarks of President Bill Clinton at the Dedication Ceremonies for the United States Holocaust Memorial Museum. April 22. http://www.ushmm.org/research/library/faq/languages/en/06/01/ceremony/?content=clinton.

Cole, Tim. 1999. *Selling the Holocaust: From Auschwitz to Schindler; How History is Bought, Packaged and Sold*. New York: Routledge.

Coombes, Annie. 1998. "Museums in the Formation of National and Cultural Identities." *Oxford Art Journal* 11, no. 2: 57–68.

Duffy, Terrence. 2001. "Museums of 'Human Suffering' and the Struggle for Human Rights." *Museum International* 53, no. 1: 10–16.

Feher, Michel. 2000. *Powerless By Design: The Age of the International Community*. Durham, NC: Duke University Press.

Finkelstein, Norman. 2000. *The Holocaust Industry: Reflections on the Exploitation of Jewish Suffering*. New York: Verso Books.

Fundamental Rights Agency of the European Union (FRA). 2011. "Discovering the Past for the Future: A Study on the Role of Historical Sites and Museums in Holocaust Education and Human Rights Education in the EU." Luxembourg: Publications Office of the European Union. http://fra.europa.eu/fra Website/research/publications/publications_per_year/2010/pub_holocaust-education_en.htm.

Griffiths, Jose-Marie, and Donald W. King. 2008. *The IMLS National Study on the Use of Libraries, Museums and the Internet*. Washington, DC: Institute for Museum and Library Services. http://interconnectionsreport.org/.

Helsinki Watch. 1993. *War Crimes in Bosnia-Herzegovina*. Vol. 2. New York: Human Rights Watch.

Huyssen, Andreas. 1995. *Twilight Memories: Marking Time in a Culture of Amnesia*. Routledge: New York.

International Committee of Memorial Museums for the Remembrance of Victims of Public Crimes (ICMEMO). 2001. About ICMEMO see http://falstad senteret.no/ic_memo/about.htm.

Karp, Ivan, Corinne Katz, Lynn Szwaja, and Tomas Ybarra-Frausto, eds. 2006. *Museum Frictions: Public Cultures/Global Transformation*. Durham, NC: Duke University Press.

Kennedy, David. 2002. "The International Human Rights Movement: Part of the Problem?" *Harvard Human Rights Journal* 15:101–26.

———. 2004. *The Dark Sides of Virtue: Reassessing International Humanitarianism*. Princeton, NJ: Princeton University Press.

Koster, Emlyn. 2006. "The Relevant Museum: A Reflection on Sustainability." *Museum News* 85, no. 3 (May/June): 67–70, 85–90.

Kratz, Corinne A., and Ivan Karp. 2006. Introduction to Karp, Katz, Szwaja, and Ybarra-Frausto 2006, 1–34.

Langer, Lawrence. 1998. *Preempting the Holocaust*. New Haven, CT: Yale University Press.

Levy, Daniel, and Natan Sznaider. 2006. *The Holocaust and Memory in the Global Age*. Translated by Assenka Oksiloff. Philadelphia: Temple University Press.

Linenthal, Edward. 1995. *Preserving Memory: The Struggle to Create America's Holocaust Museum*. New York: Columbia University Press.

Maas, Peter. 1996. *Love Thy Neighbor*. New York: Random House.

Moses, A. Dirk. 2012. "The Canadian Museum for Human Rights: The 'Uniqueness of the Holocaust' and the Question of Genocide." *Journal of Genocide Research* 14, no. 2: 215–38.

Novick, Peter. 1999. *The Holocaust in American Life*. Boston: Houghton Mifflin Harcourt.

President's Commission on the Holocaust. 1979. Report to the President. http://www.ushmm.org/research/library/faq/languages/en/06/01/commission/#principles.

Rancière, Jacques. 2004. "Who is the Subject of the Rights of Man?" *South Atlantic Quarterly* 103, no. 2/3: 297–310.

Rieff, David. 1996. *Slaughterhouse: Bosnia and the Failure of the West*. New York: Simon and Schuster.

Sandell, Richard. 2007. *Museums, Prejudice and the Reframing of Difference*. New York: Routledge.

Sikkink, Katherine, Thomas Risse, and Stephen Ropp, eds. 1999. *The Power of Human Rights*. Cambridge: Cambridge University Press.

Simon, Nina. 2010. *The Participatory Museum*. Santa Cruz: Museum 2.0. http://www.participatorymuseum.org/.

Spargo, R. Clifton, and Robert M. Ehrenreich, eds. 2011. *After Representation: The Holocaust, Literature, and Culture*. New Brunswick, NJ: Rutgers University Press.

Wiesel, Elie. 1993. Elie Wiesel's Remarks at the Dedication Ceremonies for the United States Holocaust Memorial Museum. April 22. http://www.ushmm .org/research/library/faq/languages/en/06/01/ceremony/?content=wiesel.

Williams, Paul. 2007. *The Global Rush to Commemorate Atrocities*. New York: Berg.

Witcomb, Andrea. 2003. *Re-Imagining the Museum: Beyond the Mausoleum*. London: Routledge.

Witz, Leslie. 2006. Transforming Museums on Postapartheid Tourist Routes. In Karp, Katz, Szwaja, and Ybarra-Frausto 2006, 107–34.

Young, James Edward. 1994. *The Texture of Memory: Holocaust Memorial and Meaning*. New Haven, CT: Yale University Press.

3

Civilian Agency in
Times of Crisis

Lessons from Burundi

MEGHAN FOSTER LYNCH

> Even in 1993 when Ndadaye was killed, people stayed calm. The situation here was normal, but in other places, people were taking revenge.
>
> Interview, Hutu husband and wife, Rumonge Commune, Bururi Province, May 2009

Introduction

In June 1993 Melchior Ndadaye was the first Hutu to be elected president of Burundi. In October he was assassinated by Tutsi soldiers. In the wake of Ndadaye's assassination, some Hutu civilians killed Tutsi civilians as an act of vengeance. In other areas, no ethnic violence occurred.

Why do civilians choose to promote peace or violence, and what are the consequences of their decisions? This chapter examines the different ways in which civilians respond to political crises, when their decisions are not constrained by the immediate presence of armed groups. With forty oral histories from civilian residents of Rumonge, Burundi, and their local civilian leaders, I re-create the processes of decision making in the immediate aftermath of the assassination of the newly elected Hutu president in 1993.[1] Although Rumonge had experienced severe ethnic violence in the past, and although the president's assassination triggered the killing of Tutsi civilians by Hutu civilians in many areas across Burundi, Rumonge remained peaceful during the initial years of the sixteen-year civil war in Burundi. I show that local peace was not a predetermined outcome but rather was highly contingent and threatened on multiple occasions.[2] However, local Hutu civilian leaders worked with their constituents and, later, with the largely Tutsi military, to prevent violence against Tutsi civilians.

In exercising their agency to promote peace, Hutu civilians successfully delayed the arrival of violence to Rumonge. Interestingly, this positive human rights outcome seems to have resulted not from a concern about human rights, in either an abstract or a concrete sense, but rather from a logic of preservation of self and community. According to my interviewees, it was the belief that preventing violence against others was the most effective way to prevent violence against themselves that motivated Hutu civilians to take action to maintain peace in their community. These findings underscore an important lesson for those who seek to reduce conflict violence: a belief in the universalism of human rights, while laudable in its own right, is not necessary to achieve a positive human rights outcome at the local level. Furthermore, particularly when decisions are made under conditions of danger and uncertainty, appealing to global human rights norms may be a less effective deterrent to violence than appealing to the desire for self-preservation.

A Brief Local History of Rumonge, Burundi

[After independence], people raised animals, farmed, and fished. There was enough to eat and there was peace. Afterwards, little by little, differences grew between ethnicities.

Interview, Hutu pastor, Rumonge Commune,
Bururi Province, May 2009

Burundi, a small country roughly the size of Maryland, nestles in the heart of sub-Saharan Africa, bordering Rwanda, Tanzania, and the Democratic Republic of Congo. The Tutsi minority, who make up about 15 percent of the population, dominated Burundi politically, economically, and militarily from independence until 1993. During this period, the country experienced several significant episodes of violent ethnic conflict between Hutus and Tutsis, in 1972, 1988, and 1991. The civil war began in 1993. That year, Melchior Ndadaye, a Hutu, became Burundi's first democratically elected president, but a mere three months after his inauguration, he was assassinated by disloyal factions of the still largely Tutsi army. While the most violent

Meghan Foster Lynch

periods of the war occurred between 1993 and 2003, the last rebel group demobilized only in 2009.

Rumonge is a long, thin commune bordering Lake Tanganyika in the southwest of Burundi.[3] It lies along the Imbo plains, a particularly fertile area. It is about twenty-five kilometers (15.5 mi) across the lake to reach the Congo, and a little over thirty kilometers (18.6 mi) from the southernmost point of the commune to the border with Tanzania. Its location made it an easy site for the Hutu rebels to attack in 1972.

On April 29, 1972, a group of Burundian Hutus, who had formed a small rebel group in exile, attacked and killed many Tutsis[4]—in large part police, politicians, and others in leaderships positions—in the southwest of Burundi, primarily in the communes of Nyanza-Lac and Rumonge.[5] By May 2, the acting head of the foreign ministry of Burundi, in a meeting with several foreign ambassadors, was calling the rebel attack a "genocide" motivated by "tribal hate," and ominously stated, "Thanks to the total confidence of the people the intruders have been neutralized" ("Burundi Foreign Ministry" 1972). The army and the government did indeed respond with extraordinary violence. In the areas where Tutsis had been killed, such as Rumonge Commune, men and older boys who did not flee in time to Tanzania or the Congo were hunted down and killed. Women, children, and the elderly sometimes were luckier, but many times were not.

The U.S. ambassador Thomas Melady wrote, less than a month after the beginning of the violence, "What began by a savage attack by organized bands in the south primarily directed against the Tutsis has turned into a vast blood-bath of Hutus. It is continuing. . . . We cannot at this time say how many people have died or how many more will die, but figures of 100,000 no longer make us incredulous" ("For Asst. Secretary" 1972). The Tutsi army targeted educated or wealthy Hutu men throughout the entire country, but violence in areas such as Rumonge was more indiscriminate: there are "reports from towns and missions in every corner of the country. In area after area, no educated male Hutu is believed to be alive. This [is] particularly true in the south where we have word from [a] growing number of villages that no Hutu males remain at all" ("Burundi: Numbers Game" 1972).

Interviewees in Rumonge likewise recounted extremely violent repercussions by the Tutsi military, often accompanied or aided by Tutsi civilians, after the brief rebel attack. Some people said that women and children were spared; others said that attacks were indiscriminate. The violence was clearly of a different nature than the violence that followed elsewhere in the country during later months. People were not selected based on any knowledge of who they were or what they did. Rather, any Hutu male above approximately age fourteen was targeted. One interviewee, who was sixteen at the time, described how he hid along the marshy shores of the lake for two weeks, before he was able to escape to Tanzania.[6] He told me that children hid in small groups and switched hiding places regularly, for fear of being discovered. At one point, the military arrived with dogs, to try to find people who were still hiding. Some boys managed to escape by wearing dresses, since girls were less likely to be targeted. My interviewees in Rumonge, including Tutsi witnesses, described a sustained campaign of violence during which Hutus faced extreme danger. Escaping one attack would buy only a short reprieve; the military systematically searched out and killed Hutus in hiding, as well as in traditional places of safety, like churches, where some had gathered, expecting protection.[7]

In Rumonge, the violence against Hutus in 1972 was a show of military force that demonstrated the Hutus' relative weakness. Despite their superior numbers, Hutus had been powerless to stop the military onslaught, and my interviewees recounted acute awareness of this powerlessness (Malkki 1995). Hutu civilians in Rumonge experienced the violent repercussions of the Hutu rebellion, which led to the development of the belief that Hutus could not win militarily in a fight against the Tutsis. They also knew that while the military had killed Hutus across the country, their area suffered the most and was particularly targeted because it was where the rebellion and the killing of Tutsi civilians originated. This experience led to a belief in reciprocity—a belief that, after the assassination of Ndadaye, the violence by the military would be most severe in areas where Tutsi civilians were killed, whereas violence would be comparatively limited in places that had remained peaceful. This belief in reciprocity, combined with the belief about their relative military weakness, formed a powerful incentive for Hutu civilians in Rumonge not to commit violence against Tutsi civilians in 1993.

After 1972, Hutus and Tutsis continued to live side by side in Rumonge. For the most part, the two groups got along, though some interviewees indicated that their good relations were only superficial. Children born after 1972, however, told me that ethnicity was not normally a salient divide during the late 1970s and the 1980s. The divisions were rather between the wealthy and powerful Tutsis and the poor Hutus and Tutsis. Political freedom was severely restricted, and the government kept close tabs on potential dissenters. Nonetheless, interviewees generally remember that period positively, as a time of relative plenty: "There was a lot to eat. Eighty percent or more of the people lived from agriculture. There were some small businessmen. In that period, the palm trees produced well."[8]

Toward the end of the 1980s, ethnicity again became more commonly discussed, particularly around the time of the violence in the northern communes of Ntega and Marangara. Hutu civilians in Rumonge found confirmation for their beliefs about low relative strength and reciprocity in the violent events of August 1988. At that time, violence against Hutu civilians by the Tutsi army was limited to Ntega and Marangara, where violence had been perpetrated by Hutu civilians (and allegedly Hutu rebels from Burundi and/or Rwanda) against Tutsi civilians. The absence of violence in Rumonge in 1988 reinforced the belief that the Tutsi military would reciprocate behavior. Violence against Hutus in 1988 was limited to the places where violence against Tutsis had taken place, just as the worst of the violence in 1972 took place where Tutsi civilians had been killed.

Starting in the early 1990s, faced with pressure from without and within, the ruling Tutsi government began to democratize. When the first democratic elections were held in Burundi in 1993, Melchior Ndadaye, a Hutu, was elected by a landslide, taking 65 percent of the popular vote. His party, the Front pour la Démocratie au Burundi (FRODEBU), also won a large majority in the legislature. This was a time of jubilation for most Hutus, who danced in the streets through the night and held numerous parades and celebrations. The Tutsis largely watched from the sidelines. To the surprise of many outside observers, the transition to democracy was peaceful, and Ndadaye was inaugurated as president in July 1993.

Civilian Reactions in Rumonge to Ndadaye's Assassination

In 1972, there was *a lot* of violence. In 1993, even if Hutus were mad, they didn't want to take revenge, to avoid repeating the events of 1972.

Interview, Hutu husband and wife, Rumonge Commune, Bururi Province, February 2009

The full story of the events of October 21, 1993, will probably never be known. What we do know is that a disloyal (Tutsi) faction of the military besieged the presidential palace, that Ndadaye and his family eventually surrendered, and that Ndadaye was tortured and then murdered in the military camp Muha that same evening (Guichaoua 1995; HRW 1994; Ntibantunganya 1999; Ntibazonkiza 1996; Parti Sahwanya-Frodebu 1994). Many other high-level FRODEBU politicians were assassinated the same evening or in the following days. By many accounts, the military did not foresee the uproar that the assassination would cause and simply buried Ndadaye unceremoniously on the camp grounds. That miscalculation led to more than a decade of violence and the deaths of an estimated three hundred thousand Burundians.[9]

Ndadaye's assassination devastated and enraged his supporters, and the coup was perceived, rightly, as an attempt by certain Tutsis to retake control of the government and military for the Tutsis. In many parts of the country, Hutus at the local level killed Tutsi neighbors in an attempt to avenge their president's murder and to protect their newfound political freedoms. In other places, such as Rumonge, the majority of Hutu civilians favored peace. Both Hutu and Tutsi interviewees in Rumonge agreed that the devastating violence committed by the Tutsi military against Hutu civilians in their commune in 1972 played a large role in Hutu civilians' decisions about how to react to Ndadaye's assassination. People feared a recurrence of the past:

You said that there was no violence here in 1993. Why was that?[10]
Here people had bad memories of 1972. The population didn't want to have the same problems.

You said that here, there was no trouble between Hutus and Tutsis in 1993. Why was it different here than in many other places?[11]
The violence of 1972 taught us something. We couldn't restart that situation.

I've heard that there wasn't much violence in Rumonge in 1993. Would you agree?[12]
That's true, there weren't any killings. It was only afterwards, when the rebellion started. They [the rebels] pillaged so that they could get food. They even killed. . . .
Why do you think there was no violence in Rumonge in 1993?
People saw what happened in 1972. The region experienced killings, and there were many refugees at that time. That's why they avoided violence.

You said that between 1993 and 1997, things were peaceful. Were people fighting to keep the peace or did this just happen?[13]
It's God who protected us. After Ndadaye's death, people here didn't do anything.

Local government archives contain contemporaneous reports that confirm that the population in Rumonge avoided violence.[14] According to a report from November 1993:

In general, the situation that has prevailed throughout the entire commune of Rumonge during all of this month of October 1993 has been good on the whole.

After the beginning of the sinister events of the night of October 20–21, 1993, which cost the life of his Excellence Mr. Melchior Ndadaye,

President of the Republic, and some of his close colleagues, all of the population was in despair due to this putsch and unexpected assassination.

Despite this horrible situation, the entire population maintained order and public security thanks to a committee of pacification composed of all political and social classes which was created immediately and which met to design together adequate strategies for pacification.

A message was written and transmitted to the population in all of the zones, and the pacification movement remains in effect during this period when the entire nation is in mourning. (Monthly Report 1993)

Another report discusses the "state of mind" of the population: "Despite the inhuman acts that happened here and there in our country, the population of Rumonge has remained calm, making their hearts peaceful" (Administrative Report 1994). Although "making their hearts peaceful" is likely too optimistic a turn of phrase, the report draws attention to the fact that ethnic violence had not occurred in Rumonge, contrary to the case in many other parts of the country.

Note that the explanations that my interviewees gave for the lack of violence following the assassination of Ndadaye do not center on moral reasoning about the ethicality of killing civilians. None of my interviewees said that Hutu civilians chose not to kill Tutsi civilians because they believed in universal human rights norms, nor because they were concerned that breaking international human rights law would lead to punishment. Indeed, I rarely heard an interviewee say that Hutu civilians chose not to kill Tutsi civilians because to do so would be wrong. Instead, interviewees focused on their belief that killing Tutsi civilians would be dangerous: as in 1972, it would bring the wrath of the army, whose strength civilians could not hope to contest.

It is perhaps surprising that my interviewees did not claim moral motivations. Interviewees often change their responses in order to make themselves more likeable to the interviewer. Furthermore, one might suspect that, over time, people might convince themselves that they had acted based on moral beliefs, even had they not done so, because people often retrospectively justify their decisions in ways that make them feel better about what they decided. The fact that my interviewees did not claim moral motivations suggests two points. First, it is unlikely that they were intentionally misrepresenting their motivations. It is difficult to construct a plausible scenario under which people would wish to claim motives of self-preservation when in fact they knew that they had been propelled by moral impulses. Second, if interviewees did not bring up human rights, in either a formal or informal sense, it suggests that human rights norms are even today not an obvious point of reference, a part of normal civilian discourse in Rumonge. And if that is true now, when branches of human rights organizations exist in Rumonge and discussions of human rights are common in the media, then it must have been true in 1993, when freedom of association and of speech were nascent in a Burundi emerging from decades of authoritarian government.

Although most Hutu civilians in Rumonge seem to have favored peace, primarily in order to avoid repercussions by the Tutsi military, there were of course groups who disagreed. If they had participated in violence against Tutsi civilians, the Tutsi military might have retaliated against all Hutu civilians in Rumonge. Because of the memories of 1972, those who favored peace did not merely favor it passively. They saw peace as a necessary measure of self-preservation, and many were thus ready to take action to prevent violence. In the following section, I describe five ways in which Hutu civilians in Rumonge prevented other Hutu civilians from attacking Tutsi civilians and successfully maintained peace in their community.

Threats to Peace in Rumonge and Local Responses

[After the assassination of Ndadaye], there was tension and there was going to be violence.

Interview, Hutu man, Rumonge Commune, Bururi Province, April 2009

On several occasions, groups of Hutu civilians threatened the peace in Rumonge. In some cases, they took up arms and were on the way to Tutsi households to kill Tutsi civilians when they were stopped. In other cases, they successfully engaged in threatening behavior, such as robbing Tutsi households during the night that had the potential to escalate to violence before others were able to intervene. However, through the vigilance and preventative action of those who preferred peace, no Tutsi was killed in Rumonge in the aftermath of Ndadaye's assassination.

Interviewees described five main ways by which local leaders among the Hutu civilian population maintained the peace: obedience, persuasion, coercion, prejudice reduction, and collaboration. I define local leaders as people who organized responses to potential violence. Many of these local leaders were in positions of leadership prior to Ndadaye's assassination. Some were local political leaders, who had been elected at the same time as Ndadaye and who thus had particular legitimacy in the eyes of the populace. Others were elders chosen by the community for their perceived wisdom. Others were men who held no official position but who argued publically for peace. These local leaders stepped up to enforce the preference for peace held by the majority of Hutus, and they succeeded in their mission.

Response 1: Peace via Obedience

On all of the hills, the *bashingantahe* got together and decided that there should be no violence.

Interview, Hutu husband and wife, Rumonge Commune, Bururi Province, February 2009

In some areas of Rumonge, there was disagreement among Hutu civilians about how to react to Ndadaye's assassination. Some favored killing Tutsi civilians, whom they viewed as complicit in the attempt to prevent Hutus from governing. Others argued for peace. In some of these places, people went to the *bashingantahe* for arbitration.[15] Elsewhere, the *bashingantahe* gathered people to inform them of the action to be taken. In still other areas, local political leaders took the lead in deciding what action the community should take. In Rumonge, the majority of the *bashingantahe* and the local political leaders supported peace, and in many places, their orders to remain peaceful were sufficient to dissuade those who were considering violence as an option. Peace was maintained via obedience. I define obedience here to mean that people accepted the guidance of the leaders because of their positions of authority, not because of logical arguments (persuasion) or threats (coercion) that the leaders made.

According to several interviewees, obedience to local leaders was key in maintaining peace:

Why wasn't there violence here in 1993 [after the assassination of Ndadaye]?[16]
There was tension and there was going to be violence, but with God's help, the local authorities took matters in hand.
Who were these authorities?
The Zone Leader.
How did the authorities tell people what to do?
There were meetings about remaining peaceful. I was at the meetings—you had to go. The Zone Leader assembled people and said, "We should live peacefully; no more of this nonsense about the Hutus of the plains and the Tutsis of the mountains." . . .
When were the meetings?
If people saw that things weren't going well, there were meetings. If there was a rumor, there were meetings. Usually about once a week, depending on the situation.

Both Hutu and Tutsi interviewees attributed the maintenance of peace in their area after Ndadaye's assassination to action taken by local leaders. One interviewee, when asked to explain the lack of violence, said simply that the authorities decided that there would be no violence:

> *What happened after the death of Ndadaye?*[17]
> On all of the hills, the *bashingantahe* got together and decided that there should be no violence.
> *Did they meet with the people about this, or just decide among themselves?*
> Among themselves.
> *How did the people know about their decision?*
> There was a priest who helped the population a lot. During Mass, he regularly asked people not to take revenge.
> *Were there Hutus and Tutsis at the same church when he preached about this?*
> Yes, Hutus and Tutsis.

Again, contemporaneous documents support the interviewees' accounts, describing how different leaders worked to maintain peace. Ndadaye was assassinated on October 21; shortly thereafter, the "peace meetings" described by my interviewees began:

> On November 6, 1993, a meeting [was held] which brought together the zone leaders, the public service leaders, the religious leaders, etc. It was presided over by the political councilor of the governor and had as its objective to provide advice on how to avoid the troubles that could arise and how to pass along the message of peace.
> On November 15, 1993, the meeting [was held] for pacification which brought together the commune's committee for pacification and all of the zone leaders, it was presided over by the interim administrator of Rumonge. The objective of the meeting was to evaluate the situation in all of the zones of the commune.
> On November 16, 1993, assemblies organized by the pacification committees [were held] in all of the zones so as to pass along the message of peace. . . .
> On November 18, 1993, the regular meeting of the commune's Commission for Pacification and Security [was held] and had as objective to find out the prevailing situation in all of the zones of the commune after the [peace] assemblies were held in all of the zones. It was presided over by the interim administrator of the commune of Rumonge.[18]

In some areas of Rumonge, directives by local leaders sufficed to keep the peace. In other areas, local leaders used different tactics, adapting to the different threats to the peace.

Meghan Foster Lynch

Response 2: Peace via Persuasion

They wanted to kill the Tutsis. With God's help, I tried to calm the population. . . . I explained to the population that they should stay united.
Interview, Hutu former local politician, Rumonge Commune, Bururi Province, April 2009

Hutus who had decided to kill Tutsis sometimes did not obey orders to avoid violence. In some of these cases, local leaders were nonetheless able to prevent violence by persuading those Hutus that violence was not the best course of action. Unlike in the earlier discussion of obedience, when I discuss persuasion I refer to instances when people would not have obeyed the leaders simply because of their position of authority but rather followed the leaders' advice because they were persuaded by the arguments that the local leaders provided.

The most successful persuasive arguments appealed to Hutus' memories of the violence of 1972. Instead of appealing to norms about human rights or morality and arguing that violence was wrong, leaders succeeded when they argued that violence was dangerous for those committing it and for all Hutus in the area:

> *What reasons did the leaders give for keeping the peace in 1993?*[19]
> They said, "If you get mixed up in this, you are the ones who are going to suffer." The population understood that it was the truth.

When news first came of Ndadaye's assassination, "the population was unhappy and angry. They destroyed bridges and they blocked roads, to prevent the intervention of the military."[20] This situation had the potential to escalate quickly. Indeed, several interviewees recounted the daring efforts of one local Hutu political leader to stop violence when a group had already decided to kill Tutsis, was armed, and was headed toward Tutsi houses. Once I located him, I asked him to tell me his story:

> I was the Chef de Zone. To protest, the Hutus blocked roads. They wanted to kill the Tutsis. With God's help, I tried to calm the population. . . . Trees had been cut.[21] Some people came to tell me, so I went, and I found at least fifty [armed] people [Hutu]. I told them that I was the Zone Leader. . . . I asked if they had confidence in me. They said yes. So I said, "Then don't kill the Tutsis. The Tutsis who killed the president were in Bujumbura. The Tutsis here stayed here. They didn't kill the president, so you shouldn't kill them." Afterwards, they went home. . . . If I had been indifferent, if I had let those Hutus kill the Tutsis—okay, the Tutsis would have been killed, but then the Hutus would also [subsequently] have been killed.[22]

He went on to describe how he reminded the armed men of what had happened in 1972 and told them that by killing Tutsis they would endanger their community, and for nothing, since local Tutsi civilians had no control over what was happening in the country. Local leaders like this zone leader prevented escalation by persuading those Hutus who did start to take up arms against Tutsi civilians to stand down.

Response 3: Peace via Coercion

If they don't stop, if they leave to go attack you, we'll call you in advance and tell you to be ready to attack them.

Interview, Tutsi man, Vyanda Commune [on the border with Rumonge], Bururi Province

In some places, neither obedience nor persuasion worked. Local leaders in one area thus turned to coercing peace. Ordinarily, we think of coercion as a negative force. In this situation, though, we see that coercion can be a powerful force for violence prevention.

Unknown assailants from Rumonge had been attacking Tutsi households in neighboring Vyanda at night. No violence had occurred, because Tutsis were concerned enough about the security situation that they were not spending the night in their houses but instead were hiding in banana groves. Tutsi property had been stolen, however, and after the attacks had been continuing for some time, the Tutsis decided that they could no longer tolerate the attacks. They planned an attack on the Hutus. An interviewee recounted that he had joined up with a group of men, and, during the day, they started heading toward Rumonge to attack. As they turned a corner, however, they came across a group of people, and they lost their nerve. They fled back home, and the group whom they had met, who were not among the assailants, was also scared and reported their encounter to the local authorities. Under the leadership of a local government official, elders and other important members of the community in Rumonge asked to meet with counterparts in Vyanda. At this meeting, the Rumongeans asked the Vyandans why they were attacking them. Startled, the Vyandans retorted that the Rumongeans had attacked first, and they were simply retaliating.

Through discussion, it came out that youth from Rumonge had initiated the attacks, without the support of the rest of their community. The representatives from Vyanda suggested that both sides cease the attacks. The leaders of Rumonge ordered their youths to stop the attacks, but the youths refused. The Rumongeans, acknowledging that they did not have sufficient control over their youth, then made an extraordinary offer. They publicly announced to the leaders of Vyanda that if the youths left Rumonge to attack Vyanda,

Meghan Foster Lynch

they would phone in a warning so that the Vyandans could set up an ambush. A nighttime ambush is deadly, so the youths relented and agreed to stop the attacks. The leaders of Rumonge in effect coerced peace, by threatening to harm members of their own ethnicity in order to prevent harm to the other.

Response 4: Peace via Prejudice Reduction

We increased contact with people from Rumonge. . . . We went to the market there, they came here, and the fear stopped.

Interview, Tutsi man, Vyanda Commune [on the border with Rumonge], Bururi Province

In another instance, the leaders of the same two communities described in the previous section then made another extraordinary decision. The two areas, while neighboring, are separated by a largely unpopulated steep hillside, so although some commerce took place, the two communities did not mix frequently. In some interviews, I had heard intriguing asides about how local authorities had come up with a plan to eliminate conflict by reducing prejudice through increased contact between two groups. And that is exactly what they did—they organized parties between the two areas to allow people to get to know one another and to decrease the mutual distrust:

I heard that the people of Rumonge had a party with the people of Vyanda. Do you know anything about that?[23]

Yes, I went to the party. Sometimes, the people from the Imbo [plains that include Rumonge] sent people here during the night to kill. . . . So we decided to have meetings to get the situation under control. . . . In Rumonge, we talked about everything. . . . Afterwards, we went back home. Then the people from Rumonge came here for a party. They were happy and drank. The people of Rumonge came here to see what the situation would be like and to see what kind of welcome they would receive. We welcomed them very warmly. Then they invited us to their place again [Rumonge]. They received us really well. I was told that, but I wasn't there the second time. And so what the youth had been doing was stopped. We increased contact with people from Rumonge, and violence ceased. We went to the market there, they came here, and the fear stopped. . . . When the people from Rumonge came here [for the party], there were a lot of them. They came in two trucks.

What happened next?

The people from Rumonge came here once, then we went there. When the people from Rumonge came here, they were proud because we gave them goats. When we went to Rumonge, they gave us a barrel of palm oil.[24]

Who organized the party? Who provided the goats?

The communal authorities.

Was there any kind of meeting here before the people from Rumonge came, to discuss how to behave?

Yes, there were meetings to tell us to avoid harassing people from Rumonge and instead to welcome them. They said that we needed to keep the commerce between us going so that we can increase our contact with one another.

Increasing contact has long been discussed by social psychologists as a measure to reduce prejudice. Though the hypothesis has received mixed experimental results, in Rumonge and Vyanda, leaders' efforts to get the two groups to be friends was successful. No ethnic violence occurred (Dovidio et al. 2003).

Response 5: Peace via Collaboration

The administration, the military, and the police all worked together for peace.

How did that work, practically speaking? What did they do?

The administration, accompanied by the military, would go into the field to raise the population's awareness and to tell them to keep peace and security.

Interview, Tutsi former soldier and former member of the intelligence services (Office de la Police Judiciare, OPJ), Rumonge Commune, Bururi Province, September 2009

In the initial period after Ndadaye's assassination, civilians were primarily on their own in deciding how to react. After a short period of time, however, the Tutsi military arrived in Rumonge. A new phase of violence prevention started. Since the Hutu civilians did not kill Tutsi civilians in Rumonge, when the military arrived it did not retaliate against Hutu civilians. According to one local Hutu political leader, "The commander said that we were lucky because we stayed calm, while in other places there were killings. . . . I told them that they shouldn't kill here because everyone stayed calm; that it was therefore in their interest to keep people calm."[25] Local leaders worked actively to build relationships with the military, and peace was maintained for the initial periods of the war:

So here there were no problems in 1993?[26]

No. They even gave a gift to the commander because there wasn't any violence in his region.

How did he prevent the violence?

He had meetings.

Were you at any of these meetings?

Yes.

What happened at the meetings?

He preached national unity. He asked the population to stay united.

When did he start having these meetings?

After the death of Ndadaye.

Long after or shortly after?

Almost immediately after.

Who were the meetings for?

For the zones, the hills, the commune.

Did many people attend the meetings?

Yes, there was a massive turnout.

What did the commander say at these meetings?

He invited the Hutus and Tutsis not to separate from each other.

Was it just he or was he with other people?

He was accompanied by the administrator and the zone leader.

There were times when the peace between the Hutu civilians and the Tutsi military was threatened, and local Hutu leaders had to step in to prevent violence:

> *How did the situation stay calm in 1993?*[27]
>
> The zone leader, [name removed], said we should stay united. It was thanks to the administrative authorities who helped. One day, the military grouped a lot of us together at the parish. We were forced to spend a night there. The zone leader stayed on the phone the whole time, alerting the higher authorities. He said the military had surrounded everyone and that this was not right. The next evening, the order came that everyone should be let go and should go home. . . .
>
> *Did the zone leader continue doing anything to keep the peace?*
>
> Yes, he had meetings twice a week on market days, on Wednesday and Sunday. People were scared because the military was there in great numbers on market days. There could be six military trucks sent there. But the situation changed progressively. Really, the zone leader did a lot to maintain our safety. He invited the population to cohabitate with the military despite the situation.

The local Hutu political authorities had developed good relations with the local members of the Tutsi military. After a time, however, the members of the military stationed in Rumonge were transferred to a different region. The new arrivals came from a violent region of Burundi. Within a short period of time, unprovoked, they massacred a group of Hutu civilians who were on their way to church. Some Hutus wanted to retaliate. Local Hutu leaders convinced them to wait. They then contacted the superiors of the members of the military stationed in Rumonge and made a formal complaint. They noted that the military was disrupting a peace that they had worked hard to maintain. In response, the offending members of the military were transferred, and no more violence occurred. An interviewee recounted the story:

So there was no violence during the whole period?[28]

Except in 1997. The military came in the morning and killed thirty-seven people. It was instigated by [name removed], the head of that military position. It was a Sunday.

How did you know about this?

We could hear it.

Where did this happen?

The colline [small hill] was [name removed]. They had prepared things so that when people went into church, they could kill them all, but there was a Hutu soldier who threw a grenade before the time of the attack to warn them. So, they were lucky because fewer people died. The military then telephoned to the base in Rumonge. They called to say they had been attacked by rebels. So, military trucks came to see what was going on and send reinforcements. They found dead civilians and not rebels. The commander came and asked, "If you killed rebels, where are their weapons?" They couldn't show any weapons, so the commander calmed the situation. They changed the head of the position and his men. They left here.

Even though the offending members of the military were merely transferred, this level of responsiveness to military crimes is surprising, given the high levels of impunity during the war in Burundi. Through close collaboration with the military, local Hutu leaders were able to prevent further violence against Hutu civilians, as well as to prevent retaliation by Hutu civilians against Tutsi civilians or members of the military.

The Limits of Civilian Agency

So how did the violence finally start [in 1995]?

The rebels and the military started attacking each other. . . . Then the military attacked the population to take vengeance.

Interview, Hutu husband and wife, Rumonge Commune,
Bururi Province, February 2009

Initial local variation in civilian-on-civilian violence had lasting effects on local-level violence against civilians by armed groups.[29] Where Hutu civilians did not participate in violence against Tutsi civilians, the Tutsi military was less likely to perpetrate violence against Hutu civilians, both because they needed their resources to fight elsewhere and because they were grateful that Tutsi civilians had been spared. This initial lack of violence by both sides led to the development of good relationships between civilians and the military. Surprisingly, given the history of Burundi and that of other conflicts in the region, Hutu civilians in these areas reported that the Tutsi military protected

Meghan Foster Lynch

them. These positive civilian-military relationships, in turn, delayed the arrival of the Hutu rebel groups (which were not supported by local Hutus), who had observed by this point that the presence of rebels in other communities had caused increased violence against both Hutu and Tutsi civilians.

Although Hutu civilians in Rumonge, in collaboration with the military, succeeded in maintaining peace in their community for a time, once Hutu rebel groups gained strength and could move into areas where they did not have civilian support, they entered Rumonge, which is in a strategic location. Their presence disrupted the relationships between the military and the Hutu civilians. Battles between the rebels and the military led to civilian casualties. Soon, the military suspected Hutu civilians of supporting the rebels, and the rebels suspected them of supporting the military. The benefits that they had gained by promoting peace fell away once civilian agency was constrained by the presence of armed groups:

> Because of the good relations that had developed, people hadn't been scared of the military. After the [military] ambush [against the rebels], the rebels attacked the military position at [name removed]. They killed many soldiers. The next day, I saw bodies. . . . After two weeks, the military attacked us. It was in the morning, at 7 a.m. They came; there were gunshots. They killed many people. It was the 15th of May, in 1997 or 1998.[30]

> *What was the most dangerous period in Rumonge?*[31]
> It started in 1995 with the beginning of the rebellion. The worst period was between 1995 and 2002.

> *At what points during the war were people in Rumonge scared?*[32]
> In those times, you couldn't *not* be scared. Even what happened in Rwanda in 1994 scared us, and it didn't even happen here. People were still scared in 1995, 1996. Starting then, there was violence between the army and the rebels. In 1997 and 1998, there was a lot of violence between the military and the rebels. They fought a lot among us.

The positive effects that occurred when Hutu civilians refrained from violence in the beginning of the war were eventually eroded once Hutu rebel groups became strong enough to coerce civilian cooperation and to maintain a simultaneous presence in more locations. At that point, rebels moved into areas that they had previously avoided, like Rumonge. Although their intent may, at least partially, have been to defend civilians of their ethnic group from violence, their presence rarely had a net protective effect for Hutu civilians. Instead, civilians were caught in the crossfire, were forced to provide material aid and support services to both sides, and constantly risked accusations of being on the "wrong side." The rebels' presence, and their conflicts with the military, increased violence against civilians in areas that had initially remained peaceful. The benefits that civilians had gained by promoting peace dropped off dramatically once civilian agency became tightly constrained.

Conclusion

When armies, militias, rebels, or guerrillas fight for political control, civilians often bear the brunt of the costs, both human and material. But civilians are not just acted upon; they, too, are actors, whose beliefs and decisions influence outcomes in and beyond their communities.

In Rumonge, Burundi, Hutu civilians' decisions not to attack Tutsi civilians after the assassination of President Melchior Ndadaye in 1993 allowed a period of peace when many other areas of Burundi were already at war. The majority of Hutu civilians in Rumonge seem to have favored peace, but that peace was threatened multiple times by those who were intent on revenge. When peace was threatened, local Hutu leaders reacted in a number of ways to try to prevent violence against Tutsi civilians. The five methods of violence prevention were described by my interviewees: obedience, persuasion, coercion, prejudice reduction, and collaboration. Using these different methods, leaders prevented violence or halted escalation.

As my interviewees attest, civilians can affect the trajectory of peace or violence in their communities in important ways. However, their ability to promote peace is limited when armed groups are present and promote violence. Even if civilians continue to refrain from violence, they are in a difficult position, one in which they can be accused of supporting the other side, forced to help an armed group, or end up caught in the crossfire.

Despite the limits of civilian agency, it will nonetheless be important to train local leaders in ways to keep the peace. If violence can be held off even temporarily, it is possible that the conflict will end before violence reaches the area. All five of the techniques used by local leaders in Rumonge can be taught, and there is reason to believe that they can be successful in a number of circumstances. In one program in the United States, preventing the escalation of violence via persuasion is taught to former gang members, who can then "interrupt" current gang members' violent intentions (Ritter 2009). Prejudice reduction and collaboration techniques are commonly used in schools and the workplace to attempt to reduce conflict between students and teachers or among colleagues (Paluck and Green 2009). Coercion through threat of violent sanction is the way law functions in many countries. Obedience to orders to *commit* violence is discussed more commonly in academic circles

(Blass 2002; Browning 1992; Kelman and Hamilton 1989), but commanders also regularly must find ways to make sure that combatants do *not* commit violence (Wood 2009). The example of Rumonge shows that local leaders can be powerful forces for peace.[33] If these tools can be shared with other leaders who are motivated to promote peace, communities will be better able to evaluate their options when faced with the possibility of violence.

My research highlights one of the paradoxes of human rights: if we are concerned with upholding the universality of human rights, appealing to those global norms—trying to persuade people not to participate in violence from either an ethical or a legal standpoint—may not be the most effective way to achieve that goal at the local level. In Rumonge, for the most part, my interviewees did not describe their decisions as resulting from a belief about what was right, nor from fear of noncompliance with international human rights laws or principles. Rather, in the moments when their decisions counted most—when uncertainty about what would happen and the risk of danger were extremely high—Hutu civilians focused on self-preservation. It so happened that their beliefs about the consequences of participating in violence against Tutsi civilians meant that upholding human rights was perceived by many to be the most likely path to self-preservation. But they did not consider international human rights law in their decision-making process. Paradoxically, these local actors upheld global human rights norms unintentionally. Some might say that they made the right decision for the wrong reason. In doing so they teach us a valuable lesson: if we are truly concerned about achieving positive human rights results, we would do well to focus on seeking the most effective, rather than the most normatively palatable, ways to do so.

Notes

For helpful discussions on topics addressed in this chapter, I thank Séverine Autesserre, Sam Foster Lynch, Neela Ghoshal, André Guichaoua, Stathis Kalyvas, Jana Krause, Philippe Rosen, Scott Straus, Elisabeth Wood, and my interviewees. For research assistance, I thank David Lynch, Bernard Ndayishimiye, Audifax Bigirimana, and Révocate Nzikibazanye. The fieldwork for this project was funded by a National Science Foundation Graduate Research Fellowship, a National Science Foundation Doctoral Dissertation Improvement Grant, and research grants from Yale's Institution for Social and Policy Studies, MacMillan Center for International and Area Studies, and Leitner Program in International and Comparative Political Economy. Any opinions and findings expressed in this chapter are those of the author and do not necessarily reflect the views of the funding organizations.

1. I conducted all interviews cited in this chapter, unless otherwise noted. Interviews were conducted in French if the interviewee spoke French or with the aid of a French-Kirundi interpreter if the interviewee did not speak French. All quotes are approximate, having been changed from Kirundi to French to English.

2. This chapter focuses on microlevel dynamics leading to an outcome of nonviolence or nonescalation of violence. Other works address a discussion of the meso- and macrolevel factors that can lead to these outcomes; see, e.g., Straus 2012.

3. Politico-administrative units in Burundi are, in decreasing order of size: province, commune, zone, and hill. There are 122 communes in Burundi.

4. The extent to which local Hutus participated in the violence is contested. In many places, it was reported that local Hutus fought against the rebels.

5. Some authors have said that all Tutsis were targeted (e.g., Chrétien and Dupaquier 2007).

6. Interview, Hutu man, Rumonge Commune, Bururi Province, April 2009.

7. Although some church leaders collaborated with the military, most of my interviewees said that most church leaders tried desperately to hold off the attacks and often initially succeeded. However, the military almost always returned shortly later and ignored the leaders' entreaties the second time.

8. Interview, Hutu man, Rumonge Commune, Bururi Province, May 2009.

9. No scientifically defensible estimates of conflict deaths in Burundi exist.

10. Interview, Hutu man, Rumonge Commune, Bururi Province, April 2009.

11. Interview, Tutsi man, Vyanda Commune (on the border with Rumonge), Bururi Province, April 2009.

12. Interview, Tutsi former soldier and former member of the intelligence services (Office de la Police Judiciare, OPJ), Rumonge Commune, Bururi Province, September 2009.

13. Interview, Hutu former rebel, Rumonge Commune, Bururi Province, June 2009.

14. Local government archives are primarily written in French. Quotations from these archives included in this chapter are my translations. I have tried to retain the style of writing, including awkward turns of phrases.

15. We would ordinarily translate *bashingantahe* as "elders," but the meaning is more precise. Literally "wise men," *bashingantahe* are a group of respected adult men (one cannot be a *mushingantahe* when young, but any male over the age of about forty can qualify) that the community selects based on a belief that they are wise and fair (powerful also plays into the equation). Their primary function is mediation and providing advice.

16. Interview, Hutu man, Rumonge Commune, Bururi Province, April 2009.

17. Interview, Hutu husband and wife, Rumonge Commune, Bururi Province, February 2009.

18. Administrative Report from the interim administrator of Rumonge to the governor of Bururi, Dec. 10, 1993, #531.0306.415.93.

Meghan Foster Lynch

19. Interview, Tutsi husband and wife, Rumonge Commune, Bururi Province, May 2009.

20. Interview, Tutsi former soldier, Rumonge Commune, Bururi Province, October 2009.

21. Trees are cut to create roadblocks. This measure has been used throughout Burundian history to prevent the army from entering or to prevent people from escaping in vehicles. To say that trees have been cut is literal, but it is also an expression of just how dire the situation is.

22. Interview, Hutu former local politician, Rumonge Commune, Bururi Province, April 2009.

23. Interview, Tutsi man, Vyanda Commune [on the border with Rumonge], Bururi Province.

24. Goats and palm oil are expensive and thus generous gestures.

25. Interview, Hutu former local politician, Rumonge Commune, Bururi Province, April 2009.

26. Interview, Tutsi husband and wife, Rumonge Commune, Bururi Province, May 2009.

27. Interview, Hutu husband and wife, Rumonge Commune, Bururi Province, May 2009.

28. Interview, Hutu husband and wife, Rumonge Commune, Bururi Province, May 2009.

29. For a more detailed discussion of how civilian choices lead to the escalation, de-escalation, or nonescalation of violence against civilians, see Lynch 2013.

30. Interview, Hutu man, Rumonge Commune, Bururi Province, April 2009.

31. Interview, Tutsi former soldier and former member of the intelligence services (Office de la Police Judiciare, OPJ), Rumonge Commune, Bururi Province, September 2009.

32. Interview, Hutu husband and wife, Rumonge Commune, Bururi Province, May 2009.

33. In a complementary finding about the importance of local dynamics, Autesserre 2010 shows that if local leaders are promoting violence, action by the international community to promote peace is unlikely to succeed.

References

Administrative Report from the interim administrator of Rumonge to the governor of Bururi. 1994. #531.0306/6/94. January 31.

Autesserre, Séverine. 2010. *The Trouble with the Congo: Local Violence and the Failure of International Peacebuilding.* New York: Cambridge University Press.

Blass, Thomas. 2002. "Perpetrator Behavior as Destructive Obedience: An Evaluation of Stanley Milgram's Perspective, the Most Influential Social-Psychological Approach to the Holocaust." In *Understanding Genocide: The Social Psychology of the Holocaust,* edited by L. S. Newman and Ralph Erber, 91–112. New York: Oxford University Press.

Browning, Christopher R. 1992. *Ordinary Men: Reserve Police Battalion 101 and the Final Solution in Poland.* New York: HarperCollins.

"Burundi Foreign Ministry Briefs Ambassadors in Insurrection, #402," 1972. *Messages Concerning the Burundi Massacres to and from American Embassy, Bujumbura, April 29 to August 29, 1972.* May 2.

"Burundi: The Numbers Game, #807." 1972. *Messages Concerning the Burundi Massacres.* June 6.

Chreìtien, Jean-Pierre, and Jean-François Dupaquier. 2007. *Burundi 1972, au bord des geìnocides.* Paris: Karthala.

Dovidio, John F., Samuel L. Gaertner, and Kerry Kawakami. 2003. "Intergroup Contact: The Past, Present, and the Future." *Group Processes and Intergroup Relations* 6, no. 1: 5–21.

"For Asst Secretary Newsom from AMB Melady, #641." 1972. *Messages Concerning the Burundi Massacres.* May 20.

Guichaoua, André, ed. 1995. *Les crises politiques au Burundi et au Rwanda (1993–1994).* Paris: Université de Lille 1.

Human Rights Watch, Fédération internationale des droits de l'homme, Ligue des droits de la personne dans la région des Grands Lacs, Organisation mondiale contre la torture, Centre national pour la coopération au développement, Nationaal centrum voor ontwikkelingssamenwerking, and NOVIB. 1994. *Commission Internationale d'enquête sur les violations des droits de l'homme au Burundi depuis le 21 Octobre 1993.* Unpublished document (copy in Lynch personal collection). July.

Kelman, Herbert C., and V. Lee Hamilton. 1989. *Crimes of Obedience: Toward a Social Psychology of Authority and Responsibility.* New Haven, CT: Yale University Press.

Lynch, Meghan Foster. 2013. "The Escalation of Mass Violence against Civilians." PhD diss., Yale University.

Malkki, Liisa H. 1995. *Purity and Exile: Violence, Memory, and National Cosmology among Hutu Refugees in Tanzania.* Chicago: University of Chicago Press.

Monthly Report from the interim administrator of Rumonge to the governor of Bururi. 1993. #531.0306/.405/93. November 23.

Ntibantunganya, Sylvestre. 1999. *Une démocratie pour tous les Burundais: De l'autonomie à Ndadaye 1956–1993.* Vol. 1. Paris: L'Harmattan.

Ntibazonkiza, Raphaël. 1996. *Biographie du président Melchior Ndadaye: L'homme et son destin.* Sofia: Bulgarian Helsinki Committee, 1996. Unpublished document (Lynch personal collection).

Paluck, Elizabeth Levy, and Donald P. Green. 2009. "Prejudice Reduction: What Works? A Review and Assessment of Research and Practice." *Annual Review of Psychology* 60:339–67.

Parti Sahwanya-Frodebu, Secrétariat Général. 1994. *La crise d'octobre 1993 ou l'aboutissement tragique du refus de la démocratie au Burundi.* Bujumbura: Editions Sahwanya-Frodebu.

Ritter, Nancy. 2009. "CeaseFire: A Public Health Approach to Reduce Shootings and Killings." *National Institute of Justice Journal* 264:20–25.

Straus, Scott. 2012. "Retreating from the Brink: Theorizing Mass Violence and the Dynamics of Restraint." *Perspectives on Politics* 10, no. 2: 343–62.

United States Embassy, Burundi (Ambassador Thomas Melady). 1972. *Messages Concerning the Burundi Massacres.*

Wood, Elisabeth Jean. 2009. "Armed Groups and Sexual Violence: When Is Wartime Rape Rare?" *Politics and Society* 37:131–61.

Part II

Interrogating
Classic Concepts

4

 Consulting Survivors

*Evidence from Cambodia,
Northern Uganda, and
Other Countries Affected
by Mass Violence*

PATRICK VINCK AND
PHUONG N. PHAM

Introduction

Over the last six decades, the modern international human
rights movement has told the story of hundreds of thousands of survivors of
heinous crimes, including mass killings, torture, rape, inhumane imprisonment, forced expulsion, and the destruction of their homes and villages.[1] Over
that period, the role of survivors during and after mass violence has significantly expanded, from that of a forgotten party (at best witness to the events)
to that of engaged civil society actors (Viano 1978). Victims of mass atrocities
have also become a central focus of transitional justice mechanisms established
to deal with a heritage of violence and human rights abuses, and they play an
increasingly active role in shaping the policies aimed at building a lasting
peace. In part, this shift simply reflects the broader emphasis on community
involvement and ownership as a core element of sustainable human development, but it is also the result of a unique need to rebuild broken institutions

from the ground up to prevent local conflicts from reigniting. In the process, the global demand for accountability and justice for victims has sometimes conflicted with the local contextualization and definition of victims' rights and expectations.

At the global level, the prevailing human rights principle regarding justice and accountability is that there can be no peace without justice, and that those responsible for serious crimes must be brought to justice (Bassiouni 1996). There is also a global consensus that efforts at pursuing international justice and enforcing international human rights norms and accountability after a repressive regime must be rooted in the local context, and that meaningful programming must be based on an extensive process of local consultation, including the consultation of survivors and families of victims (Kritz 1995; UN Secretary General 2004; Van Zyl 2000). Specifically, the practice of local consultation is seen as a participatory process to inform the design of accountability mechanisms that better reflect the population's needs and expectations. It helps shape the agenda and increase the sense of participation and ownership among affected communities. Consultations can be employed to discuss, for example, what form, if any, accountability mechanisms should take, what meaning trials hold, or if communities know about national and international justice efforts set up to serve them. Consultative processes can also be part of the monitoring and evaluation of the impact and legacy of international justice efforts, and inform "evidence-based transitional justice" (Pham and Vinck 2007).

In 1998 the signature of the Rome Statute instituting the International Criminal Court (ICC) marked further significant changes in how transitional justice mechanisms, and courts in particular, consider survivors of mass atrocities in their proceedings. The ICC provides unique access for victims of crimes and their families to express their views and concerns, and to claim reparation for the wrongs suffered. This is unlike previous international criminal courts (ICTY, ICTR) where victims were limited to a witness role. The ICC statute includes provisions that (1) allow victims to participate in the administration of justice in a variety of ways, including the opportunity to be heard at each stage of the proceedings, and (2) provide opportunity for reparations to victims, including restitutions, compensations, and rehabilitation (art. 75). In addition, article 79 of the Rome Statute (1998) calls for the creation of a Trust Fund for victims. Perhaps more importantly, the prosecutor must also take into account (1) the gravity of the crime, (2) the interests of the victims, and (3) the interest of justice, when initiating an investigation (art. 53 [c]) (UN 2002). At the Extraordinary Chambers in the Courts of Cambodia (ECCC) set up to put on trial senior leaders of the Khmer Rouge regime allegedly responsible for millions of deaths from 1975 to 1979, the role of victims has been extended

Patrick Vinck and Phuong N. Pham

to that of full civil parties (Pham et al. 2011). Both the ICC and the ECCC also have units specifically dedicated to outreach and victim participation.

Despite the global consensus governing local involvement in international justice, and the increased roles of victims in criminal prosecution, the process of consulting survivors and affected communities to gauge their opinions, perceptions, and attitudes is far from systematic. Scholars and practitioners from many disciplines (e.g., anthropology, public health, law, international justice, political science), as well as actors directly involved in conflict resolution and peacebuilding (e.g., governments, UN agencies, rebel groups), have only begun to engage in consultations with local populations. Courts and tribunals are ill equipped and insufficiently funded to conduct consultations in a systematic way. However, significant progresses have been made. Early on, the ad hoc tribunals for Rwanda and the former Yugoslavia did not have any form of outreach units and did not provide for victim participation. Most of the efforts continue to consider victims as a global concept, with a unified voice, failing to recognize the local heterogeneity of the concept of victims. As a result, consultation also frequently adopts methods, which by design are unable to represent this heterogeneity, for example by focusing consultation on a subset of victims with specific conflict experience and failing to engage the broader affected population.

Globally, victims are presented as an innocent or vulnerable party who collectively and individually deserve recognition and attention (Bouris 2007). Local experiences challenge this view as victims may be coerced into becoming perpetrators. Even when coercion is not part of the victimization experience, there is a wide range of experiences of violence among the high proportion of civilians who are victims in any given conflict, frequently as a result of deliberate and systematic violence against whole populations (Mani 2002; Swiss and Giller 1993). In places like Darfur, eastern Congo, Northern Uganda, or Rwanda, victims are counted in the hundreds of thousands or millions; they represent a large and diverse group of people. Local victims' organizations emerge within the civil society to defend the rights of specific groups of victims (e.g., women, children, etc.), to provide direct services, and to advocate on issues ranging from the need to fulfill basic needs for services and victim-oriented reparation to transitional justice mechanisms. Recognizing this variety of experiences and the role of victims as potential agents of change, the term "survivor" is generally preferred throughout this chapter.

Regardless of the complexity of their experiences, survivors' expectations are broadly assumed to be peace, a return to a normal life, and, arguably, reparation and justice. In developing countries, satisfaction of basic needs may be seen as the utmost priority. The possibility that what survivors want is a function of their patterns of exposure to trauma and subsequent psychological impact, and perhaps their own participation in violence, remain largely unexplored (Weinstein et al. 2010). Furthermore, most survivors remain a silent majority whose experience, needs, and expectations are poorly understood.

In this chapter, we discuss the importance of better understanding and localizing the concepts of survivors along with the tension with global efforts to strengthen victims as meaningful participants and possible beneficiaries in transitional justice mechanisms—with a focus on international criminal justice—and objectives such as restitution, reparation, redress, and reconciliation for survivors (Gibson 2004; Lillie 2005; Staub 2006). Specifically, we highlight the need for more methodical approaches to consultation and for international justice mechanisms to adapt and cope with the emerging norms on how to best engage with groups and communities affected by war in the process of redress. We build on lessons learned from several empirical research projects to capture the opinions and attitudes of survivors of mass violence in Cambodia, the Democratic Republic of Congo (DRC), Iraq, Northern Uganda, and Rwanda, and conclude by advancing some key guiding principles for consultations with communities victimized by war crimes.

Engaging Survivors

In Northern Uganda, after months of lobbying by civil society, consultation of survivors of the twenty-year-long conflict became an important part of the discussion on reconciliation and accountability during the 2007 peace negotiations between the infamous Lord's Resistance Army (LRA)—a group known for its brutality—and the government. In late 2007 a delegation of LRA envoys traveled to Northern Uganda, with funding from international donors, and organized several meetings in squalid camps for internally displaced people where civilians had been confined for much of the last decade. In one of those meetings, in front of a large crowd numbered in the hundreds, LRA envoys attempted to engage the public:

> I am from the LRA side, I ask for your forgiveness.
> Let's forgive all the crimes and rebuild our broken families.
> People of Koch, have you forgiven the LRA? (De Onis 2009)

In response to the question, hands were slowly raised; most appeared to be unsure about what to do. The LRA envoy spoke up again and said, "Please do me one more favor and raise your hand as a sign that you want the ICC warrants dropped and instead use the traditional means" (ibid.).

This second "favor" was questionable. For decades the LRA had preyed on civilians, abducting several tens of thousands of adults and children, and mutilating and killing countless others (Pham, Vinck, and Stover 2009). The setting and method of consultation by the LRA deterred survivors from speaking openly about their views and opinions. Rather the process appears to merely have sought to confirm and legitimize the LRA's political agenda (i.e., to drop the ICC's arrest warrants against four of its commanders, including its leader, Joseph Kony). Ultimately the peace process collapsed, but the consultation itself raised many questions about what constitutes meaningful ways of engaging in a dialogue with survivors, the validity of the various methods being used, what we can learn from such efforts, and the value of the information collected.

Efforts to consider survivors of mass violence in international justice vary in levels of engagement with affected communities. At the most basic level, survivors and communities can be informed by transitional justice institutions themselves before taking action, or as programs are being implemented. This is typically the top-down approach of outreach units within courts and tribunals.

The next level of engagement is to ask, or consult, survivors about their opinions on a range of issues related to the work of the courts. This is the majority of the work presented in this chapter, which is based on a series of open-ended surveys. However, this consultation remains one way (albeit bottom-up) and is only the beginning of a more complex form of engagement. A dialogue between survivors and the institutions set up to serve them allows for a true exchange, setting the basis for significant consultations on justice. These types of engagement are not common in transitional justice, but one example is a project that was conducted by an independent NGO in eastern DRC, Interactive Radio for Justice, which promoted such a dialogue. Outreach units within courts and tribunals are also increasingly responsive to questions and dialogue with affected communities.

Beyond one-way and two-way communications between survivors and the courts, survivors can become more or less involved in decision making. While local ownership may at first seem challenging in the context of international justice, there are numerous areas in which survivors can meaningfully be involved, for example with regards to reparation programs (what should be done, where, for whom, and by whom), or with regards to their own direct participation and representation in judicial proceedings.

Consultative processes may vary in objectives, respondents' characteristics, and methods. First, the objectives of consultations can be broadly categorized as (1) informative consultation, in which respondents are asked to present facts, views, opinions; or (2) deliberative consultation, in which respondents are given information and asked to discuss arguments in favor of, or against, proposed policies, sometimes seeking to build a consensus (Catt and Murphy 2003; Price and Neijens 1998). In informative consultation, the participants may or may not be informed about the policies considered. The advantage is that respondents provide unbiased information and opinions; the disadvantage is that they may not have sufficient knowledge of the issues at hand. In deliberative consultations, participants are provided with detailed information of the policies and decisions being made. Here, the advantage is that the participants are informed and may form opinions or make decisions based on the information provided; the disadvantage is that the participants may not be able to provide options other than the one presented to them, and that the type and manner in which they receive information may influence their opinions.

A second key question of consultative processes is to decide whom to consult. Any group can be consulted: politicians, elites, armed groups, interests groups, survivors' representatives, survivors themselves. Within those groups, respondents can be selected randomly, or they can be selected based on specific criteria (e.g., their knowledge, position in society, interest, experience). Alternatively, participants can also be self-selected (volunteers) or appointed by the communities to represent their voices. The key underlying question to consider is whom those consulted represent: Do their voices resonate with or represent a broader community, or are their opinions unique and based on their own individual experiences?

Consulting survivors is a common approach. However, who those survivors are is not well defined. One of the tensions between "global" victims and "local" survivors is that the former fails to recognize that they may be different groups altogether. For example, refugees are survivors in their own right, but their voices should not be the sole basis for consultation of survivors in a given conflict. The concept of survivor is broad and covers very different types of survivors. In mass violence, individuals may have had their property seized or destroyed, experienced displacement, imprisonment, physical violence, or lost financial resources. They may also more likely be firsthand witnesses to such crimes. Several empirical models have been used in the literature to define categories of victims, using physiological factors (e.g., injuries), sociological factors (e.g., level of disruption), economic factors (e.g., property loss), or measures of psychological impact of trauma, such as Post Traumatic Stress Disorder (PTSD). Depression and PTSD have been studied either as simple indicators of victimization or in relation to other factors (e.g., attitudes toward reconciliation) (de Jong et al. 2001; Pham, Weinstein, and Longman 2004; Mollica et al. 1998). Cumulative scales of exposure have also been used to define survivors in relation to attitudes toward justice and reconciliation (Pham,

Weinstein, and Longman 2004). Other classifications have been developed for the purpose of humanitarian assistance and care treatment.

Regardless of the normative approach used, the concept of victim is generally associated with a clear role alongside the perpetrator and, sometimes, the bystander (Stover 2005). Yet cases like the infamous LRA in Northern Uganda pose a challenge to such a dichotomous definition of victims (who suffer) and perpetrators (who inflict sufferance). The majority of the perpetrators of mass atrocities during the decades of conflict between the government of Uganda and the LRA have been abducted, forced to commit crimes, threatened with death, and in effect indoctrinated to become LRA fighters (Vinck et al. 2007). As a result, many LRA fighters are as much victims as perpetrators (Hovil and Lomo 2005). Similarly, in Iraq, talking about those who were forced to commit violence under the rule of Saddam Hussein, a doctor of Soulaymaniah (North) describes: "[I]t is difficult to say who is innocent, who is a good man, who is a bad man, who is criminal, who is not criminal, who was willing to do crimes, who was not willing" (ICTJ and HRC 2004).

Clearly, the local concept of victim is not a well-defined one. In Iraq, most people were forced to join the Ba'ath party and support the regime to access education and economic opportunities. Should they be considered less victims than others? What about LRA abductees who committed atrocities? As Fattah notes (2000), everyone establishes some kind of moral hierarchy of victims, based on individual systems of values and beliefs. The temptation is to distinguish between those survivors that we identify with as victims and who deserve assistance, and those unworthy victims who do not. Given the limited resources at hand in conflict-affected areas, and in order to avoid "ranking" the individual suffering to prioritize the needs and expectations, a local understanding of the concept of survivor is needed. This information is critical to evaluate the level of support for any transitional justice mechanism among various survivor groups. Justice may be seen as a priority for some, or inversely as secondary to other needs or even detrimental to sustainable peace by others.

The final issue to address is methodological. There is a range of mechanisms that can be used for consultation, including public forums, focus groups, key informant interviews, or surveys. Each method has advantages and limitations. Focus groups, for example, allow for in-depth discussions and understandings of the views and opinions of those consulted, but they are not appropriate to test hypotheses or draw conclusions for the broader population. The concept of consultation therefore regroups a variety of approaches with different objectives, respondents' characteristics and selection criteria, and consultation methods.

Our work focuses on surveys or large-population-based consultations similar to needs assessments or opinion polls. Applying this technique allows us to examine broad patterns of experiences, attitudes, and responses across geographic and socioeconomic boundaries. We use consultation as a means of bringing survivors' voices, advice, and information to decision makers. The method is meaningful, especially, because results can be compared across subgroups based on socioeconomic status, education, gender, ethnicity, or experience of violence, among other factors. The random selection of respondents allows us to minimize biases that may distort our understanding of survivors' views and opinions. Utilizing randomized survey methodology is limiting as it does not regularly allow for in-depth discussions of respondents' views. Therefore, to deepen our research and provide more informed conclusions, we triangulate survey findings through the application of multiple information-gathering techniques such as using key informant interviews and in-depth interviews with randomly selected participants to better understand and interpret survey results.

Our methodology follows traditional random survey methodology using large samples of individuals from populations in regions impacted by the crimes on trial. In Northern Uganda, for example, the sample was drawn from adult residents of the districts most affected by the conflicts. In the DRC, respondents were selected among individuals in the eastern part of the country (provinces of South Kivu, North Kivu, and district of Ituri). The sampling strategy is based on multistage systematic cluster random sample. First, we randomly select administrative units (e.g., villages), and then randomly select households within those units. The sample size is designed to provide statistically valid and representative results, often by regions or provinces. Once individuals are randomly selected within the households, teams of locally selected and trained interviewers administer a standard questionnaire. The questionnaire, translated in the local languages, is specific for each situation, adjusting for local characteristics of the conflicts and international justice processes. To establish better contact with respondents, we select interviewers who are representative of the ethnic groups in the area under study and who speak the local language. We also typically assign interviewers to same-sex respondents. However, conflict situations are challenging environments, sometimes requiring adaptation of the methodology. In eastern Congo, for example, some villages could not be accessed because of ongoing violence. In Iraq, ongoing violence meant that a true random selection of respondents was too dangerous. At the time of our study, though, we were able to move relatively freely and we organized more than eighty focus groups with representatives of various religious, ethnic, age, gender, and socioeconomic groups throughout the country.

The idea of using surveys to locally consult survivors of mass violence and wars is not new but rather a continuation of previous efforts to pursue populations' concepts and opinions on justice. As early as October 1945, the Intelligence Branch of the Office of the Director of Information Control, Office of Military Government for Germany (U.S.) set up an Opinion Survey Section to gather populations' perspectives about the reconstruction process in Germany, including perceptions of the Nuremberg trials (Merritt and Merritt 1970). Seventy-two surveys were conducted over a period of four years. Among other results, the surveys showed at first a strong popular interest in the trial among respondents in the American Zone of Occupation. Over time, however, interest in the proceedings declined as well as confidence in the completeness and reliability of the press coverage. While respondents appeared to be generally satisfied with the verdicts handed out in Nuremberg, perception of unfairness increased throughout the survey period (Merritt and Merritt 1970, 34–35).

Nearly half a century after the Nuremberg and Tokyo trials, a renewed focus on international justice prompted the international community to create tribunals to try and punish those responsible for war crimes, genocide, and crimes against humanity. Within this context, our surveys have sought to give a voice to the hundreds of thousands of survivors of heinous crimes, including mass killings, torture, rape, inhumane imprisonment, forced expulsion, and the destruction of homes and villages. Our objectives were to document their exposure to violence and its impact on their daily lives, and understand their priorities, needs, and attitudes and plans about social reconstruction. As part of this social reconstruction process, we consulted survivors about transitional justice mechanisms and international justice efforts, and the relationship between peace and justice.

Survivors' Views on International Justice and Reconstruction

Based upon the methodology just described, we conducted three separate surveys of the adult population in the conflict-affected areas of Northern Uganda to assess survivors' needs and wants regarding justice and accountability for crimes perpetrated against them and their communities. The first survey, held in April–May 2005, was conducted among 2,585 respondents at a time of ongoing violence with little prospect for peace. The second was conducted from May to June 2007 among 2,875 respondents at a time of physical peace (i.e., absence of violence) and strong prospects of a lasting peace. Both surveys were conducted in the northern Acholi districts and neighboring districts in the Lango and Teso areas. A third survey was conducted in 2010 in the northern Acholi districts only, among 2,498 adult residents.

The findings showed very high exposure to violence, reflecting the high toll paid by civilians in the conflict. In 2007, 95 percent of the respondents considered themselves victims of the war in Northern Uganda. Some events seemed to affect a large majority of the population, including displacement (86% of the respondents in 2007), and the loss of dwelling (86%) and productive assets (85%), while other events affect only a fraction of the population: 24 percent reported having been violently beaten and 37 percent reported being abducted (for various lengths of time); 3 percent reported having experienced sexual violence. Some respondents also were coerced into committing crimes and/or violence, such as looting (14%), beating (7%), or killing (3%). A larger proportion reported being forced to carry loads (29%). Experiences as a witness were among the most frequently reported exposures: 62 percent witnessed abduction, 47 percent witnessed killing, and 5 percent witnessed sexual violence. Studies conducted elsewhere confirm that witness experience is widespread and generally more frequent than direct experience of violence (Vinck and Pham 2009).

Regrouping individuals who experienced such a range of events under the term of victims, we are left with an accurate notion—virtually everyone experienced some level of violence, and most also assigned to themselves the status of victims—but which fails to recognize the specificity of individual victimization. The survey data from Uganda are illustrative of the challenging notion of victims. For nearly two decades, the LRA has waged a war against the people of Northern Uganda. The LRA, known for abducting civilians and children to serve as load carriers, soldiers, and sex slaves, is also known for its brutality, and for killing and mutilating civilians. According to the 2007 data for the Acholi districts only, as many as 49 percent of the respondents reported having been abducted at some point during the conflict; 28 percent reported having been abducted for at least a week. But what the data also show is that those who were abducted were more likely to be forced to commit violence, including beating and killing people. Overall, 39 percent of those who were abducted reported having been forced to loot, 20 percent were forced to beat someone, and 9 percent were forced to kill someone. But when considering only those who were abducted for at least a week, those frequencies increased to 59 percent, 33 percent, and 14 percent, respectively. As the length of abduction increased, the proportion of those forced to commit violence increased. Among those who were abducted by the LRA for at least a year, 90 percent were forced to loot, 74 percent were forced to beat someone, and 50 percent were forced to kill someone (Pham, Vinck, and Stover 2009).

Both 2005 and 2007 surveys suggested that peace and a return to "normal life" was a clear priority among the respondents, but this did not necessarily mean populations were ready to "forgive and forget" what had happened. In 2005 about three-quarters (76%) of the respondents said that those responsible for abuses should be held accountable for their actions. However, 71 percent stated that they would accept amnesty if it were the only road to peace. Given the choice, 54 percent would have preferred peace with trials over peace with amnesty (46%). By 2007 a larger number of respondents favored peace with amnesty (80%), which may be explained by the strong prospect for peace at the time of the survey and the prevailing message that trials would hinder peace. Similarly, in 2007 fewer respondents wanted to see LRA leaders be punished, face trial, and then imprisoned or killed compared to 2005. At the same time, awareness about the ICC had increased significantly.

The role of traditional ceremonies as an alternative to the ICC has long been debated in Northern Uganda. What our surveys showed was that not all respondents were familiar with such ceremonies, and not all believe them to be useful to deal with the LRA: in 2007, 49 percent of the respondents believed them to be useful to deal with the LRA. At the same time, two-thirds (67%) of the respondents believed it was necessary to chase away bad spirits to achieve peace. Non-Acholi respondents were especially skeptical of traditional ceremonies, which would address crimes committed only among Acholi. Overall, the results suggested that traditional ceremonies have a role to play in addressing the past crimes but that they should be part of a broader policy for accountability. It also highlighted the need to include non-Acholi survivors of the violence in the discussion on accountability. Acholi and non-Acholi respondents varied greatly in the mechanisms they identified to achieve peace, the latter favoring violent means, such as waging war or killing the LRA. They also varied in their support for various transitional justice policy options: non-Acholi respondents were more likely to support trials.

In addition, our survey shows that the various patterns of exposure result in different expectations and sometimes competing needs. Analysis of the 2005 survey data showed that respondents reporting symptoms of PTSD and depression were more likely to favor violent over nonviolent means to end the conflict. The odds of having PTSD and depression significantly increased among those who had been abducted and/or threatened with death. We also found that that those with PTSD were less likely to support amnesty, and those with depression were less likely to support traditional justice/ceremonies (Vinck, Pham, Weinstein, and Stover 2007). These results show that attitudes and needs toward peace and justice, specifically the type of means proposed to end the conflict as well as proposed accountability mechanisms, vary widely among survivors and are associated with patterns of exposure to trauma and subsequent symptoms of psychological stress.

In the DRC, we surveyed 2,620 adults randomly selected in the provinces of North Kivu and South Kivu and in the district of Ituri in late 2007. As in Uganda, the results showed that virtually everyone in eastern Congo has been exposed to violence. Many respondents were interrogated or persecuted by armed groups (55%), forced to work or enslaved (53%), beaten by armed groups (46%), threatened with death (46%), or had been abducted for at least a week (34%). In eastern DRC, 23 percent witnessed an act of sexual violence, and 16 percent reported having experienced sexual violence.

When asked what should happen to those who committed crimes, respondents most frequently said they should be punished (69%), put in jail (34%), face trial (25%), or be killed (20%). Respondents showed high expectations that many actors would be punished. When asked about justice, and given the choice, most respondents would favor national trials (45%) or international trials in DRC (40%). Few chose international trials abroad (7%) or no trials at all (8%). Only one-fourth of the respondents had some level of awareness about the work of the International Criminal Court (27%) and the trial against Thomas Lubanga (27%).

In Cambodia, we conducted a national survey among a sample of one thousand adult residents from September to October 2008. Over one year after the adoption of the internal rules setting up the ECCC, 39 percent of the respondents said they had no knowledge of the court and 46 percent had only very little knowledge about it. Respondents also had little knowledge about the Khmer Rouge regime: 81 percent of those who did not live under the Khmer Rouge regime described their knowledge of that period as poor or very poor, in part due to the lack of formal education in school on that period. Although the ECCC judged crimes committed thirty years ago, most respondents still harbored feelings of hatred toward former members of the Khmer Rouge regime, and most wanted to see them held accountable. Respondents further showed little confidence in the national judicial system.

Lessons Learned and Best Practices

Ill-conceived international justice efforts not only cost millions of dollars but they also fail to meet survivors' needs and expectations; they may also be a source of renewed violence in situations of fragile peace (Stover and Weinstein 2005, 326). The call for increased consultation, participation, and local ownership is an answer to these criticisms. At the same time, there may be tension between local participation and ownership in the process of designing and implementing international justice, and a strict normative approach that would require prosecution of at least those who bear primary responsibility for atrocious crimes (Orentlicher 2007). In other words, if a majority supports amnesty, then should it be the norm? Opposing survivors' views with international norms fails to recognize that survivors are not a homogeneous group; they have competing and sometimes opposing demands. By uncovering those opinions and factors that shape them, consultation enables a dialogue that gives important legitimacy and public accountability to the international justice processes, at the same time addressing the basic human right of the individuals to redress in cases of heinous and criminal activity enacted upon them.

Based on our experience collecting and examining the data from each survey, we can draw some preliminary conclusions about what can be learned from local survivors' consultation and ways to make the global work of international courts and tribunals more meaningful. First, consultations provide unique information about the level of knowledge and perception about the courts. Our work suggests that few respondents are aware of the work of the courts, and those who are aware typically expect courts to bring about peace, arrest perpetrators, hold those responsible accountable, and provide reparations. This suggests that one of the main challenges for courts is to manage the high expectations attached to their efforts. Perception of impartiality and corruption are equally important to address. Unmet expectations and disenchantment will ultimately undermine the legitimacy of the courts in the eyes of the survivors. Managing expectations and perception should therefore be central to the outreach message. This must be done locally and in direct response to local consultations as expectations range widely among survivors.

Second, most respondents expect the court to uncover the truth about what happened and why it happened. Courts, however, are set up mainly to examine factual truth about specific charges and hence may fall short in providing in-depth insights into the abuses and the motives behind it at the local level. Nonetheless, it is important for courts to make sure that their findings contribute to establishing a broader narrative about past abuses and mass violence.

Third, even where crimes were committed decades prior to the criminal proceedings, our surveys indicate that courts operate in environments plagued with social tensions and often ongoing violence. Surveys help us understand the nature of insecurity that potentially hinders survivors' willingness to talk openly about their experience or participate in proceedings (Stover, Sisson,

Pham, and Vinck 2008). Surveys may also help gauge possible reactions to court decisions that may be perceived as controversial.

Fourth, justice must be local. Respondents in the DRC showed strong preference for proceedings held in the country. Elsewhere, national judicial systems and traditional practices have a role to play in addressing past violations. International courts and tribunals must be part of a broader local process and work toward capacity building of local actors and the local judicial system. Consultation may help inform the arrangements between the international and local institutions.

Fifth, international justice efforts must establish principles and procedures relating to reparations, as is the case for the ICC (McCarthy 2009). The politics of reparation is emerging as a new challenge for international courts, debating the type of reparations that should be provided (e.g., financial or symbolic), who should receive reparation (e.g., individuals or communities), and who should pay for it (e.g., governments, international community). Surveys may uniquely contribute to answering those questions and ensure that reparation programs address the needs of survivors.

Finally, international justice efforts are relatively recent. The ICC has yet to complete the prosecution of its first case, and much of its principles and procedures remain to be defined (e.g., on reparation). Consultation is essential in assessing the impact of international justice and ensuring that lessons learned contribute to improving the work of the courts. As several ad hoc tribunals and hybrid courts complete their work, much needs to be done to understand the legacy of those institutions.

Survivors' consultations are a valuable tool to inform the design of accountability policies and international justice efforts. However, meaningful consultation about international/ized criminal institutions will require identifying key guiding principles based on lessons learned from the fields of monitoring and evaluation research, and participatory theory and practice (Lundy and McGovern 2008). Various methods are available, including public forums, focus groups, key informant interviews, or population surveys. All these methods of consultation have strengths and limitations, and it is essential for those conducting the consultation to understand and explicitly acknowledge them. Regardless of the method chosen, our studies and field experience suggest that consultation processes about international justice must meet four conditions in order to yield meaningful results.

First, the consultation must be conducted in an environment that is culturally appropriate and that guarantees the security of those interviewed, allowing survivors to speak openly about their views and opinions. In ongoing conflicts or in situations where various armed groups still hold a significant amount of power and influence, those interviewed may not feel comfortable expressing their views. They may eventually be put at risk if they were to voice their opinions. Similarly, family background, education, religion, belief system, or sociopolitical outlook must be taken into account to develop a culturally sensitive consultation process (Benson 2006). Public meetings especially must be used with caution, and additional care should be taken to guarantee the confidentiality and eventual anonymity of interviewees.

Second, the consultation process must be seen as legitimate and impartial, and guarantee that the views and opinions expressed by those consulted will be heard and acted upon. While consultation by parties involved in conflicts (such as those conducted by the LRA and the government in Uganda) may be genuine, it is possible that respondents will not feel free to express their opinions, and that perceived partiality will undermine the outcome of the consultation. Furthermore, beyond the consultation, decision makers should engage in a dialogue with individuals and communities that are consulted to explain and discuss decisions resulting from the consultation processes.

Third, the consultation effort must be inclusive and systematic. Consultations tend to focus on individuals and groups that are considered most victimized, or that hold specific knowledge or positions in the communities (e.g., traditional and religious leaders, civil society representatives). This approach may leave out less organized groups or ones that are considered as only marginally exposed. In Uganda, for example, although the brunt of the conflict took place in the Acholi districts, other areas were affected as well. Our results show significant differences in perceptions and attitudes between these communities.

Finally, the consultation must prevent or mitigate the retraumatization of respondents. Emotional responses are expected when respondents are asked to relive traumatic events or to answer questions that remind them of those events. Indeed, the organization and individuals implementing the consultation process must make sure that proper referrals or care are provided.

Note

1. As Aryeh Neier puts it, "[T]he international human right movement is made up of men and women who gather information on rights abuses, lawyers and others who advocate for the protection of rights, medical personnel who specialize in the treatment and care of victims, and the much larger number of persons who support these efforts financially and, often, by such means as circulating human rights information, writing letters, taking part in demonstrations, and forming, joining, and managing rights organizations." The movement is rooted

in the principles recognized in the Charter of the United Nations, the Universal Declaration of Human Rights, and global and regional treaties (Neier 2012).

References

Bassiouni, M. Cherif. 1996. "Searching for Peace and Achieving Justice: The Need for Accountability." *Law and Contemporary Problems* 59, no. 4: 9–28.

Benson, Jill. 2006. "A Culturally Sensitive Consultation Model." *Advances in Mental Health* 5, no. 2: 97–104.

Bouris, Erica. 2007. *Complex Political Victims*. Bloomfield, CT: Kumarian Press.

Catt, Helen, and Michael Murphy. 2003. "What Voice for the People? Categorising Methods of Public Consultation." *Australian Journal of Political Science* 38, no. 3: 407–21.

De Jong, Joop, Ivan H. Komproe, and Man Van Ommeren, et al. 2001. "Lifetime Events and Posttraumatic Stress Disorder in 4 Postconflict Settings." *Journal of the American Medical Association* 286, no. 5: 555–62.

De Onis, Paco (Producer), and Pamela Yates (Director). 2009. *The Reckoning: The Epic Story of the Battle for the International Criminal Court*. United States. Skylight Pictures.

Fattah, Ezzat A. 2000. "Victimology: Past, Present and Future." *Criminologie* 33, no. 1: 17–46.

Gibson, James. 2004. "Does Truth Lead to Reconciliation? Testing the Causal Assumptions of the South African Truth and Reconciliation Process." *American Journal of Political Science* 48, no. 2: 201–17.

Hovil, Lucy, and Zachary Lomo. 2005. "Whose Justice? Perceptions of Uganda's Amnesty Act 2000: The Potential for Conflict Resolution and Long-Term Reconciliation." *Refugee Law Project*. Working Paper 15. February.

ICTJ and HRC. 2004. "Iraqi Voices: Attitudes toward Peace and Justice." Occasional Paper Series. Human Rights Center, University of California–Berkeley, and International Center for Transitional Justice. May.

Kritz, Neil. 1995. *Transitional Justice: How Emerging Democracies Reckon with Former Regimes*. Washington, DC: United States Institute of Peace.

Lillie, Christine. 2005. "Women Survivors' Experience of Justice in Rwanda." Poster presentation at the Meetings of the International Society for Political Psychology. Toronto. July.

Lundy, Patricia, and Mark McGovern. 2008. "Whose Justice? Rethinking Transitional Justice from the Bottom Up." *Journal of Law and Society* 35, no. 22: 265–92.

Mani, Rama. 2002. *Beyond Retribution: Seeking Justice in the Shadows of War*. Cambridge: Polity Press.

McCarthy Conor. 2009. "Reparations under the Rome Statute of the International Criminal Court and Reparative Justice Theory." *International Journal of Transitional Justice* 3, no. 2: 250–71.

Merritt, Anna J., and Richard L. Merritt. 1970. *Public Opinion in Occupied Germany: The OMGUS Surveys, 1945–1949.* Urbana: University of Illinois Press.

Mollica, Richard, Keith McInnes, Thang Pham, Mary Catherine Smith Fawzi, Elizabeth Murphy, and Lein Lin. 1998. "The Dose-Effect Relationships between Torture and Psychiatric Symptoms in Vietnamese Ex-Political Detainees and a Comparison Group." *Journal of Nervous and Mental Disease* 186, no. 9: 543–53.

Neier, Aryeh. 2012. *The International Human Rights Movement: A History.* Princeton, NJ: Princeton University Press.

Orentlicher, Diane. 2007. "'Settling Accounts' Revisited: Reconciling Global Norms with Local Agency." *International Journal of Transitional Justice* 1:10–22.

Pham, Phuong N., Harvey M. Weinstein, and Timothy Longman. 2004. "Trauma and PTSD Symptoms in Rwanda: Implications for Attitudes toward Justice and Reconciliation." *Journal of the American Medical Association* 292, no. 5: 602–12.

Pham, Phuong, and Patrick Vinck. 2007. "Empirical Research and the Development and Assessment of Transitional Justice Mechanisms." *International Journal of Transitional Justice* 1, no. 2: 231–48.

Pham, Phuong N., Patrick Vinck, and Eric Stover. 2009. "Returning Home: Forced Conscription, Reintegration, and Mental Health Status of Former Abductees of the Lord's Resistance Army in Northern Uganda." *BMC Psychiatry* 9, no. 1: 23.

Pham, Phuong, Patrick Vinck, Mychelle Balthazard, Michelle Arévalo-Carpenter, and Sokhom Hean. 2011. "Dealing with the Khmer Rouge Heritage." *Peace Review: A Journal of Social Justice* 23, no. 4: 456–61.

Price, Vincent, and Peter Neijens. 1998. "Deliberative Polls: Toward Improved Measure of 'Informed' Public Opinions." *International Journal of Public Opinion Research* 10, no. 2: 145–76.

Staub, Ervin. 2006. "Reconciliation after Genocide, Mass Killing, or Intractable Conflict: Understanding the Roots of Violence, Psychological Recovery, and Steps toward a General Theory." *Journal of Political Psychology* 27, no. 6: 867–94.

Stover, Eric. 2005. *The Witnesses, War Crimes and the Promise of Justice in The Hague.* Philadelphia: University of Pennsylvania Press.

Stover, Eric, Miranda Sisson, Phuong Pham, and Patrick Vinck. 2008. "Justice on Hold: Accountability and Social Reconstruction in Iraq." *International Review of the Red Cross* 90, no. 869: 5–28.

Stover, Eric, and Harvey M. Weinstein. 2005. "Conclusion: A Common Objective, a Universe of Alternatives." In *My Neighbor, My Enemy: Justice and Community in the Aftermath of Mass Atrocity*, edited by Eric Stover and Harvey M. Weinstein, 323–42. Cambridge: Cambridge University Press.

Swiss, Shana, and Joan E. Giller. 1993. "Rape as a Crime of War: A Medical Perspective." *Journal of the American Medical Association* 270, no. 5: 612–15.

United Nations. 2002. "Rome Statute of the International Criminal Court." UN Docs A/CONF.183/9. http://www.un.org/law/icc/index.html.

UN Secretary General. 2004. *The Rule of Law and Transitional Justice in Conflict and Post-conflict Societies, Report of the Secretary General.* S/2004/616. United Nations Security Council.

Van Zyl, Paul. 2000. Promoting Transitional Justice in Post-Conflict Societies. In *Security Governance in Post-Conflict Peacebuilding,* edited by Alan Bryden and Heiner Hänggi, 209–31. Geneva Centre for the Democratic Control of Armed Forces.

Viano, Emilio. 1978. "Victims, Offenders and the Criminal Justice System: Is Restitution an Answer?" In *Offender Restitution Theory and Action,* edited by Burt Galaway and Joe Hudson, 91–100. Lexington, MA: Lexington Books.

Vinck, Patrick, and Phuong N. Pham. 2009. "Peace-Building and Displacement in Northern Uganda: A Cross-Sectional Study of Intentions to Move and Attitudes towards Former Combatants." *Refugee Survey Quarterly* 28, no. 1: 59–77.

Vinck, Patrick, Phuong N. Pham, Harvey M. Weinstein, and Eric Stover. 2007. "Exposure to War Crimes and its Implications for Peace Building in Northern Uganda." *Journal of the American Medical Association (JAMA)* 298, no 5: 543–54.

Weinstein, Harvey M., Laurel E. Fletcher, Patrick Vinck, and Phuong N. Pham. 2010. "Stay the Hand of Justice: Whose Priorities Take Priority?" In *Localizing Transitional Justice: Justice Interventions and Local Priorities after Mass Violence,* edited by R. Shaw, L. Waldorf, and P. Hazan, 27–48. Stanford: Stanford University Press.

5

"Memoria, Verdad y Justicia"

The Terrain of Post-Dictatorship Social Reconstruction and the Struggle for Human Rights in Argentina

NOA VAISMAN

Introduction

In Argentina the collective cry "Memory, Truth, and Justice" (Memoria, Verdad y Justicia) has occupied a central place in public discourse. In the long aftermath of the military dictatorship (1976–83) and in the context of ongoing processes of social reconstruction, this demand has been heard in places as varied as courtrooms and street demonstrations to private conversations and public debates in the national media. At first glance the request seems simple enough: to learn the truth about what happened while the junta was in power, to construct a clear memory of the events, and to see that justice is carried out. Nevertheless, over the years these three terms have yielded a wide array of interpretations. What should be remembered? Who decides what is to be commemorated and how? What kind of justice should be carried out and in what context? Who must be tried and who should be absolved? How can the truth be discovered? And what kind of truth are the people willing to hear? All these questions reflect the complex nature of the three terms, and provide a lens through which to understand the varied social and political processes they have given rise to.[1] In this chapter I focus on one term—truth—and explore its use and significance in some ethnographic detail. Through an examination of three events, I show that the meaning of this classic category within the human rights and transitional justice literatures shifts and transforms as a result of local forces and changing sociopolitical circumstances. Moreover, by exposing the tensions that exist between local notions of human rights and the universalizing force of human rights discourse, I consider the role of human agency in shaping human rights struggles and the desire for truth more specifically. My broader aim is to contribute to a nuanced and grounded analysis of human rights that embraces the paradoxical nature of the field that is always, as Stern and Straus point out in the introduction to this volume, local, political, and historical simultaneously.

The three scenarios analyzed center on the work of the human rights organization H.I.J.O.S. (Sons and Daughters for Identity and Justice against Oblivion and Silence [Hijos e Hijas por la Identidad y la Justicia contra el Olvido y el Silencio]). In examining the group's particular interpretations of "truth," I ask what that term and its application might tell about the long process of social reconstruction following mass human rights violations. I have chosen to focus on H.I.J.O.S. for a number of reasons: the group represents a new generation within the human rights camp in Argentina, and in that capacity it has offered new visions and targets for the local struggle for truth about the past and its consequences. Moreover, particularly between the late 1990s and early 2000s, this group had played an important role in shaping local demands for post-dictatorship justice and in propelling civil society into action. But their use of the term "truth" also enfolds many tensions and contradictions that exist both within the group and between the group and other social and political organizations. Exploring these tensions can contribute to a richer interpretation of the grounded nature of human rights in a particular local.

Much like the package of measures discussed by transitional justice scholars and activists (Elster 2006; Hayer 2001; Hinton 2011; Shaw and Waldorf 2010; Teitel 2003), which include truth commissions, judicial prosecutions, commemorative projects, and reparations, the three terms—truth, justice, memory—develop through reciprocal processes. That is, all three terms evolve in relation to one another and are consequently hard to disentangle. Moreover, the exact direction and particular form that each term has taken is in

Noa Vaisman

large part an outcome of complex social and historical processes, ongoing negotiations between human rights organizations and the state, and debates between different groups within civil society.[2]

Within transitional justice processes truth has occupied a special place. First, the creation and proliferation of truth (and reconciliation) commissions in many different parts of the world has established the institution as well as the term as key components in the transitional justice "toolkit" (Shaw and Waldorf 2010, 3). Second, academic works on truth commissions have pointed to the different interpretations the term has received, highlighting in the process the complex relations that exist between the meaning of the term and the historical events under consideration (Chapman and Ball 2001; Wilson 2001).[3] Thus, as Naomi Roht-Arriaza notes, in the context of Latin American dictatorships, the demand for truth has a particularity unmatched by other human rights struggles (Roht-Arriaza 2006, 3–4; see also Crenzel 2008a). Specifically, forced disappearances—the method of repression used by the military regime in Argentina, as in other parts of the Southern Cone—is secretive in nature. It involved the abduction, imprisonment in clandestine detention centers, torture, and eventually assassination of thousands; it was also vehemently denied by the perpetrators of the crime throughout the period of state terrorism and even years later (Robben 2011). In other words, the demand for truth (as for justice and memory) has been set against an overarching and dominant discourse of denial and lies spread by the dictatorial rule both during and following the fall of the regime.

My goals in examining the meaning of truth in the Argentine context are two. First, I will demonstrate the complexity of this key term and the changes it has undergone since the return to democratic rule. Because many years have passed since the initial transition, an examination of the country's historical struggle for truth can afford insight into the meaning of the term, its use, and the transformations it has undergone. Moreover, changes in the demand for truth reflect a generational transition, a point I elaborate on by focusing my analysis on the children of the disappeared's vision of the term. Second, I am interested in exploring the locally inflected meanings of truth in the early to mid-2000s in Argentina. By focusing on the human rights activists' work I explore the obstacles they faced and the paths they chose to follow in their struggles to confront and come to terms with the country's past. In this way I also reflect on the way human rights discourse and activism are embedded in local politics and always imagined within a particular set of historical and social circumstances. In the conclusion to this chapter, I highlight the significance of exploring the social and cultural circumstances that shape complex terms such as truth, memory, and justice.

Transition and the Demand for Truth

Argentina has been hailed by activists and scholars alike as an example of a pathbreaking transition. Following the fiasco of the Malvinas/Falkland Islands War, dramatic social pressures, a broad legitimacy crisis, and a declining economic situation, the military regime that took over the country on March 24, 1976, was forced to step down. The first democratically elected leader, Raúl Alfonsín, faced the daunting task of dealing with the legacy of human rights violations committed by the previous regime, namely, the forced disappearance of perhaps thirty thousand individuals. Thus, he had to not only confront the military's attempt to absolve itself from future accusations but also provide a reasonable response to the human rights organizations' (HROs) demand to put on trial the perpetrators of the crimes and to learn of the final fate of each and every disappeared.[4] The military regime had issued a final document, which asserted that the disappeared were guerilla fighters who went into exile; some had been killed in an unconventional war and buried in unidentified graves, and the rest should be considered dead for legal purposes. A few months later the military also issued amnesty for all acts committed during its time in power (Brysk 1994, 60–62). To tackle these (inaccurate) declarations and the legacy of the repression, Alfonsín chose a double route: by an executive decree he created a national investigation committee, the CONADEP (National Commission on the Disappearance of Persons [Comisión Nacional sobre la Desaparición de Personas]), and he gave the highest military court, the Supreme Military Council, the role of sentencing the leaders of the regime. These acts resulted in the production of the *Nunca Más* report, which meticulously documented and then disseminated information about the repression and the disappeared, and, after some delay, the trial of the leaders of the three juntas that ruled Argentina between 1976 and 1983 by a civilian court (el juicio a las Juntas) (Brysk 1994; Crenzel 2008b; Sikkink and Booth Walling 2006).[5] But both measures had their limits for the production of truth. The CONADEP was established for a fixed period and a clearly defined purpose, and did not succeed in investigating all cases of repression. And the trial of the juntas, which has been considered by many a pathbreaking event in the history of transitional justice in Latin America, was peculiar in the sense that while information about the trial and its development was disseminated mainly through a daily newspaper dedicated to the theme, the broadcast of its audio-visual recordings was quite restricted—three minutes daily but without sound (Feld 2002). Consequently, *Nunca Más*, which became an instant best seller, allowed Argentines to read about the repression in an official report, but the live and shocking testimonies produced by the trial did not reach the majority of the Argentine population in audio or visual form until much later, in 1998. In this way the truth about the repression and its reach was shaped and restricted in various ways by the format and the limits of the mediums and of its dissemination.

The initial measures taken by the government to produce truth and justice were halted by two laws: the Final Stop Law (Ley de Punto Final) and the Due Obedience Law (Ley de Obediencia Debida) passed in 1986 and 1987, respectively. These laws, dubbed by the HROs as the impunity laws, put a final date on the possibility of prosecution and a limit on who was to be prosecuted and for what crimes, as it was argued that most perpetrators were "just following orders" (Brysk 1994; Robben 2005). While these laws were partly a reflection of the political position of the government and partly a reaction to the adverse situation created by the armed forces at the time (i.e., a few attempted coups), they had difficult implications for the human rights struggle. Specifically, the impunity laws blocked almost every path toward discovering the truth about the disappeared and their final whereabouts, uncovering and documenting the repression, and identifying all the perpetrators of the crimes. They also ushered in a period of silence about the past.

By the end of the 1980s the social and political climate, and the economic conditions in the country, had changed. Hyperinflation and dramatic social unrest led to Alfonsín's resignation and to the election of Carlos Saúl Menem as the new president of Argentina. This second phase of the transition, and particularly Menem's first term, is characterized by oblivion and impunity (Crenzel 2011, 5). Thus, early in his presidency (1989 and 1990), Menem offered pardons to the junta leaders and to those who had been sentenced by Alfonsín's government. As he explained it: "[T]he past has nothing more to teach us . . . we must look ahead, with our eyes fixed on the future" (Feitlowitz 1998, xi). In effect, Menem was trying to expunge the past or, at the very least, silence it.

Around the mid-1990s the beginning of some social stirrings were felt on the streets. This was a time when a new demand for truth was being heard. Again a combination of elements, processes, and events brought new social forces to the fore, including the retired navy captain Adolfo Scilingo's confession of his participation in the "death flights," which was followed by confessions from other perpetrators of crimes.[6] The testimonies produced some new evidence, and they also brought the truth about the brutality of the repression straight into the homes of all Argentines as Scilingo gave an interview on a popular television show. While Menem attempted to discredit Scilingo and his confessions, General Martín Balza, head of the armed forces, recognized that during the military dictatorship mass human rights violations were carried out

(Roniger and Sznajder 2005, 152–53), thus providing for the first time an official admission by the armed forces of the violations committed. Other factors contributing to the change were the beginning of a growing presence of testimonies and accounts by ex-detained-disappeared persons and by former exiled and political prisoners about their experiences during the dictatorial rule (van Drunen 2010, 165–208). These came in the form of books, documentary films, and media reports.[7] Moreover, beginning in 1998 the search for the truth was officially recognized through the institutionalization of the "truth trials" (Sikkink 2008, 12). These trials, which aimed to find information about the disappeared and gather data about the repressive mechanisms used by the armed forces, were initiated at a time when impunity was still widespread. Although the trials could not lead to the sentencing of perpetrators for their crimes, their significance lies in the recognition of the relatives' and Argentine society's "right to truth."

Another significant element that contributed to the changes was the coming of age of the generation of the children of the disappeared who began asking about their familial and collective past. In 1996, when thousands went out to the streets to commemorate the twentieth anniversary of the military coup, H.I.J.O.S.—the human rights organization made up of the children of the disappeared, the exiled, and the political prisoners—made one of its first public appearances. During the event members of the organization walked under the banner carrying their name (which in Spanish has a double meaning—children of—and an acronym for Sons and Daughters for Identity and Justice against Oblivion and Silence) into the Plaza de Mayo, symbolically asserting their place in one of the most significant spaces in the struggle for human rights in Argentina.

Since the mid-1990s H.I.J.O.S. specifically, and the generation of the children of the disappeared more broadly—those born just before or after the military coup of March 24, 1976—have become a central force in the social demand for truth and justice in post-dictatorship Argentina. Thus, when H.I.J.O.S. was first founded it defined its goals through a number of demands that included (1) the individual and collective reconstruction of the past, (2) the identification and return of all the children appropriated during the military rule, (3) claiming the spirit of the struggle of their parents, and (4) calling for official juridical justice through social condemnation (H.I.J.O.S. 2012a). In the years since its founding, the organization has carried out many different demonstrations and public events aimed at revealing the truth about the past, making that truth present in the public sphere, and revealing the identity of the perpetrators of human rights crimes through what they define as acts of social condemnation (Kaiser 2002; Siedel 2011; Taylor 2002). These acts—

Noa Vaisman

the *escraches*—emerged and developed as a result of the impunity that reigned in the country at the time. The organization has also been active in promoting other human rights issues, participating in events that repudiate present human rights violations and injustices, and engaging with the needs of the community in which their house was located (Bonaldi 2006).

Kathryn Sikkink (2008) has argued that human rights groups in Argentina have been particularly creative in propelling and supporting new forms of justice and truth telling in the post-dictatorship period. In developing her argument she suggests that a number of factors have contributed to the novel nature of human rights activists' work in the country, among them the type of transition to democracy, the financial and social support networks of the HROs, and the history of political activism in Argentina. Sikkink's analysis provides the foundation for my claims in this chapter. Specifically, I investigate further her general observation regarding the creativity of human rights activists on the ground by analyzing the innovative nature of H.I.J.O.S.'s interpretations of the term "truth" in the context of the last dictatorial rule. The group's attempt to define the term and to create spaces for its articulation is one aspect of their mission, which is broadly defined as the reconstitution of the social fabric destroyed by the military dictatorship. According to the group, mending the social fabric depends in large part on civil society finding out about the human rights violations committed during the time of the dictatorship and understanding the events that preceded the rise of the military rule. Learning the truth, they expect, would open a number of different paths for post-dictatorship social reconstruction. First, it would create a strong movement of social condemnation of the perpetrators; this force would work against the widespread impunity instated by the different democratically elected leaders. Second, it would allow Argentines to retake hold of their history, an act that—according to H.I.J.O.S. and other HROs—is essential for the health of Argentine democracy. Third, Argentines would be able to imagine a different kind of future for the country, maybe one that is similar to the future the disappeared themselves had fought for.

The three following events, which took place during my fieldwork, between 2004 and 2006, reflect the specific moment and particular circumstances in Argentina at the time.[8] In May 2003 Néstor Kirchner, until then the somewhat anonymous governor of the southern province of Santa Cruz, was elected president. While his election served to stabilize the political arena that was still experiencing the ripple effects of the 2001 socioeconomic crisis, it did not produce any great expectations among the vast majority of the population. One of Kirchner's first acts was to align himself with the historic HROs and their struggle. He declared himself a member of the generation of the disappeared and a son of the Madres (here referring to the Madres de Plaza de Mayo and specifically to their internationally recognized struggle for truth and justice since the time of the dictatorial rule).[9] While integrating the discourse of the HROs into his own political discourse Kirchner also propelled a number of important changes in the area of collective memory and justice seeking. For example, he presided over the transformation of the Navy Mechanics School (ESMA, Escuela de Mecánica de la Armada)—an emblematic torture and detention center during the dictatorship—into a "Space for Memory and for the Promotion and Defense of Human Rights," and he publically declared that he would support the annulment of the Full Stop and Due Obedience laws, a statement that propelled members of the Chamber of Deputies to present a proposal for annulment that was approved in August 2003, thus revoking both laws (van Drunen 2010, 215). He also initiated a reform in the Supreme Court; in June 2005, with the new judges in place, the Final Stop and Due Obedience laws were finally declared unconstitutional by the Supreme Court of Argentina. These steps opened the way to new trials and judicial accountability more broadly, a process that has picked up since 2006. These trials have become key instruments in the production of truth in this historic moment.

However, the struggle for justice and truth has not been smooth. For example, while the impunity laws were declared unconstitutional and the cases against the perpetrators of the crimes reopened, the oral trials were not reinaugurated until much later. In fact, in 2006 and even a few years later, the sense among HROs was that the justice system was "pulling them along," purposely delaying the investigations that would allow the trials to be elevated to the oral and public stage of deliberation (see the *escrache* against the judicial system described in the following section).[10] Moreover, while Kirchner's declarations and acts did contribute to the growing social engagement with the past, this process began before his presidency and continued with some vigor during his and later his wife's, Cristina Fernández de Kirchner, presidency.[11]

Escrache a Videla: Telling It Like It Was

March 24, 2006, was the thirty-year anniversary of the military coup. The event was marked across the city of Buenos Aires in myriad commemorative acts, demonstrations, and public discussions. Among these the *escrache* against Jorge Rafael Videla was key. *Escrachar* means to make evident, "to make apparent the face of a person who attempts to go unnoticed" (H.I.J.O.S. 2012b). The word has been used as both noun and verb to define the demonstrations organized by H.I.J.O.S. to out the perpetrators of crimes that took place during the dictatorship. Because of the impunity laws (Final Stop and Due Obedience laws) these perpetrators were living as regular citizens, sometimes quite anonymously, in the midst of the population. But for the social fabric to mend, claimed H.I.J.O.S., people need to know about the past and expel these perpetrators from the social body. The assumption here is that if people know about the crimes and are able to recognize their neighbor, or the person they serve in the café or work with in the clinic, they might refuse to share their everyday world with them. In this way the perpetrators would become social outcasts, and at least some measure of justice would be served. This form of justice—social condemnation (*condena social*)—was particularly crucial during the period when almost all judicial recourse was closed off to the victims.

While the practice of the *escrache* has developed and evolved over the years, the *escrache* against Videla was conducted according to an early format: posters were hung around the city and a call went out to gather at a specific time and place for the march that would culminate in front of the home of the perpetrator—Jorge Rafael Videla, the leader of the first junta, who was serving house arrest at his home at Avenue Cabildo 639.[12] Many social and political organizations were also contacted prior to the event; their representatives attended planning meetings with members of H.I.J.O.S. several times prior to the *escrache*.[13] On the day of the event, thousands assembled behind the large H.I.J.O.S. banner.

Around four in the afternoon, the official time of the *escrache*, the crossroad of Santa Fe Avenue and Fitz Roy Street was still only sparsely dotted by protesters. The ground, on the other hand, was already covered with the leaflets announcing the *escrache*, and the large open truck that was to lead the way was parked a block or so ahead of us on the path we were to take only a short while later. About an hour later the street had completely transformed, as thousands gathered behind the large banner of H.I.J.O.S. and the *murga* band that was leading the procession.[14] Members of other HROs, such as Madres de Plaza de Mayo—Línea Fundadora (Madres LF), and social and political movements marched behind them, hoisting their own large banners. Leading the procession from the back of the open truck were two members of H.I.J.O.S. singing and shouting into a small microphone. Inciting the demonstrators, they chanted, "One must jump, one must jump, he who does not jump is a military man."[15] We made our way down Luis María Ocampo Avenue and reached the large gates of the Military Hospital (Hospital Militar). Here the truck stopped and blocked the road. Joining the representatives of H.I.J.O.S. on the truck were three children of the disappeared who were abducted as infants and raised without knowledge about their past and their real biological parents. Each told the story of abduction and identity restitution, generating strong emotional reactions in the crowd. The location of these testimonies was symbolic for two reasons. First, during the dictatorship a small section within the Military Hospital served as a clandestine maternity ward for pregnant disappeared women. Many of the women held here underwent cesarean sections and shortly after were transported to their death. Second, Videla, who had enjoyed some freedom after the amnesties, was first put on house arrest in 1998 when he was tried and accused of participating in the forced disappearance of infants during the dictatorial rule. This was one of the only crimes not covered by the impunity laws. During and after the testimonies provided by these recovered individuals, members of H.I.J.O.S. sprayed graffiti on the walls and gates of the notorious hospital: "Where are our brothers?" referring to the close to five hundred individuals who were abducted when infants under military rule.

Following the emotive testimonies, the *escrache* continued toward its destination—the home of Jorge Rafael Videla, an apartment on the fourth floor of a nondescript building on the wide Cabildo Avenue. The building entrance was guarded by a high fence, and a line of police officers in bright orange jackets stood blocking the door.[16] Slowly many of the close to twelve thousand people who attended the demonstration congregated on the wide avenue. The truck was parked in the middle of the street, serving again as an open stage from which the representatives of the HROs could give their speeches; perpendicular to the truck was a car that held a small crane. The Madres LF spoke first, followed by a member of the HRO Abuelas de Plaza de Mayo, and then H.I.J.O.S. began to speak.[17] The group's speech began by noting the void, both personal and collective, that was created with the disappearance of thirty thousand individuals. It was not only that the disappeared were missing from the family picture but, as the group stated in the speech: their "projects, ideas, dreams, the happiness of being together and of struggling together for a better country" were lost with them. Furthermore, the group stated, with their disappearance the meaning of being a young person had changed:

> When our fathers and mothers were young, being young was to get involved in everything, to want to be part of every decision, it was to want to change the direction of the world and to want to play an active part and [a] mobilizing [force in] this change. Later, being young had become different kinds of carelessness [thoughtlessness] and the "don't get involved." It is because of this that to condemn the coup is also to restore a form of youth . . . we have to do politics, with our hands and feet we have to build our country, the world in which we want to live.

The group noted that to repudiate the coup is not only to repudiate the military but to repudiate those who participated actively in the repression, those who created and implemented the economic and social conditions that went hand in hand with the coup, and to condemn the religious, legal, and medical personnel who supported and took part in the repression.

A little later the group stated:

> Because memory is much more than remembering a few events or dates. Memory is the attempt to understand the past, to take a political position about what happened, it is to try to learn who preceded us and it is to create with all this tools that in this, our time, can help us in advancing towards a better world, a just world, with solidarity. Memory is also not to disappear our disappeared. It is to give them back their identity, each one, with his history, his likes, his ways. It is to give back to each one his political identity and to remember that only thirty years ago, in this country, there existed many organizations . . .

This statement was followed by a long list of names of the different guerilla groups and social and political organizations that existed during the period before and at the beginning of the dictatorial rule.

While the speech thus far had been read aloud from the truck, it was now time for the crane to take center stage. Naming the crimes Videla had committed and was convicted of, and the judicial processes against him, a member of H.I.J.O.S. standing on the crane called out that now they were going to visit him "because we want to talk to you face to face. Because we know that you must [should] be in your house, but we are uncertain if you are complying with your house arrest. It is you, filthy rat, we have come to *escrachar*!" While naming the crimes—the murders, torture, disappearances—Videla committed, the crane lifted up to the fourth floor, carrying with it a long fabric on which were attached the pictures of the disappeared. Reaching toward the skies the faces of the disappeared towered above the crowd staring directly at the building where Videla resides. Directing the accusations toward the shut blinds, the H.I.J.O.S. representative called out that they will visit not only him but the rest of the perpetrators of the crimes of the dictatorship, those who were complicit with the military rule, the ideologists and those who commit crimes today. Then the representative threw half a dozen or so paint balls at the building, marking its fourth floor with large red splashes.[18]

The event I described contains a number of elements that highlight the particular ways in which H.I.J.O.S. views truth. First, a central aspect of the organization's work has been the recovery of the past, particularly the social and political events that took place prior to the military rule. To this end, naming the guerilla organizations, political groups, and social organizations that existed prior to the coup is one form of truth telling and a way to bring them back to people's awareness. It is also a way to signal to the crowds and to those who view the event on television or hear about it on the radio that the dictatorship did not happen in a vacuum; it was a planned and well-orchestrated reaction to a different political path that the country could have taken, had the military been stopped.[19] Second, while not unique to the events organized by H.I.J.O.S., the appearance of the photos of the disappeared at the center of the demonstration gives these enigmatic figures a material existence. It is no longer the thirty thousand disappeared who seem to have no face or body that can attest to their having once existed; instead, each person is identifiable and visible in the public sphere. This is a form of truth telling that works against the dictatorial regime's use of the term "disappeared" to connote those abducted and assassinated during the period of state terrorism. A third element H.I.J.O.S. highlights in the speech is a different view of politics and specifically of what being a youth might mean in this era. No longer the indifferent ones who characterized the recent past, the youth are now called upon to imagine and work together to reconstitute their country and society. And, in the process of this collective struggle to mend the social fabric, the youth need to recount the past and learn or even recuperate that which was lost by acts of repression and disappearance.

In this context, truth is set against the project of the military rule. But it is not only the silenced voices of the disappeared and the alternative political paths that were destroyed with the disappearances that the work of H.I.J.O.S. attempts to recuperate. It is also a project to rewrite history by bringing into public discourse the complex political and social conditions that preceded the coup. Moreover, it is a project that combats the outcomes of the transition or, more specifically, the impunity that was instituted by the successive elected leaders. Thus, it is a project aimed at changing the present moment as much as it is about the past, and as H.I.J.O.S. states clearly in the speech: "as long as they [the *genocidas*] are not condemned we will be living in a state of impunity . . . impunity ruins the social values.[20] . . . The impunity gives continuity to the set of values imposed by the dictatorship." By demanding that truth about the past be revealed and justice be served—in this case, if not by the state then at least by the people—the group is calling to establish a social world based on a different set of values where truth occupies a central place.

It should be noted that in other parts of H.I.J.O.S.'s speech, this demand for justice and truth is also extended to the present state of repression and to current human rights abuses, specifically, repression by police, the "easy trigger"

Noa Vaisman

(*Gatillo fácil*) policy that is the cause of death of many young people in Argentina today. It is important to note that the question of the relation between the past and the present, between the struggles to remember and tell the truth about the past, and the condemnation of present human rights abuses is not clear-cut. In fact, this has been the very source of the contention between the different HROs as well as between HROs and other political and social movements in the past few years, leading, in 2006, to a difficult and yet unresolved rupture between the groups and within H.I.J.O.S. itself. Specifically, under the Kirchners' governments, which have aligned themselves with the struggle for human rights and its attendant calls for justice and truth, the denunciation of current human rights abuses has become so entangled with the struggle to recognize past abuses that HROs end up on opposing sides of the political fence.

"Tomar el Pelo"[21]

On a hot day at the end of summer 2005, I arrived at the plaza in front of *Tribunales* in the late morning and watched as members of different HROs slowly gathered in front of the large old building.[22] The Palace of Justice is located in a central spot in Buenos Aires, very close to 9 de Julio Avenue and to the Colón Theater. The large old stone building with its six thick columns and wide stairs overlooks a medium-size plaza covered with grass and palm trees. The building has, for some time now, been surrounded by a high fence, which in this case served the participants of the event as a place to hang their banners. These included the banner of the Association of Ex-Detained Disappeared (Asociación de Ex-Detenidos Desaparecidos) and posters announcing the large demonstration that was to take place a few days later to mark the anniversary of the military coup.[23] Members of H.I.J.O.S., who arrived around midday, set up their large banner right on the street in front of the large building, and underneath they positioned three plastic chairs. Holding another banner with the demand "trial and punishment [to the *genocidas*]" ("*Juicio y Castigo*"), they announced that the symbolic act they were carrying out was aimed at calling the people's and the justice system's attention to the situation of the trials against the generals. "We are cutting our hair so they will not be able to fool us any longer [*para que no nos toman más el pelo*] . . . it is over twenty years that the *genocidas* are walking free . . . we demand justice now." The activists then turned to the actual ceremony. First, a number of Madres and Abuelas had locks of their hair cut and placed in a see-through bag,[24] then members of H.I.J.O.S. sat on the chairs and had their heads shaved. Very quickly the large bag was filled with hair that threatened to spill out, at the bottom locks of gray and white hair and on top dark brown and black hair, marking the layers of generational history.

After the haircuts were completed, those present began singing one of the chants commonly heard in large demonstrations: "Olé olé, olé olá, olé olé, olé olá, like the Nazis it will happen to you, wherever you go we will look [for you]."[25] The chant was followed by a short declaration: "We are calling for a common and perpetual imprisonment for all the *genocidas*, they have to be in an ordinary prison and not in their own homes. We demand justice for the thirty thousand disappeared. . . . The Madres started this struggle and we the Hijos [here they are playing on the term *hijos* (children of) and H.I.J.O.S. (the name of their organization)] are continuing it. Trial and punishment to the *genocidas*."[26] As is customary at the end of this kind of event, they called out: "Thirty thousand detained-disappeared" and the crowed answered them in unison: "Present!" This call was repeated three times, followed by the shout "Now" while the crowd answered "and forever." After a few more chants H.I.J.O.S. announced on the megaphone that they were going to try and enter *Tribunales* in order to hand over the hair. Carrying the large transparent plastic bag, they walked up the wide flight of stairs and three (with the bag) managed to get past the guard at the entrance. The symbolic act was complete when, some twenty minutes later, the three representatives returned to report that although at first no one wanted to take the hair, they eventually handed it over to an officer of the court.

This event was organized by H.I.J.O.S. but attended by many members of other HROs, among them Madres LF, Abuelas, Asociación de Ex-Detenidos Desaparecidos, and Familiares de Desaparecidos y Detenidos por Razones Políticas, and covered by a number of media venues (the newspaper *Crónica*, the television newsgroup Telefe, and Radio Mitre). If in the previously described event H.I.J.O.S. enacted their vision of history and truth by reading aloud the names of many armed groups and political and social organizations that existed before the last military coup, in *this* event they were demanding a different kind of truth. This truth was about the present. In calling for the courts to refrain from "fooling" or deceiving them (here referring both to themselves and the people [*el pueblo*] more broadly), H.I.J.O.S. was demanding accountability and transparency in present legal processes about the past. In other words, they called for truth about why the investigations were taking so long, allowing the perpetrators to die of old age or to enjoy their freedom rather than to be held in common prisons like other criminals. On the other hand, another form of truth was sought out in this event: this was the truth about the past that would be revealed in public and oral trials against the *genocidas*.

Thus, the event brought together past human rights violations and present obstructions of justice.

The Decision to Find Out the Truth about the Past (and the Present)

In March 2004, as part of the events marking the anniversary of the military coup, the Navy Mechanics School (ESMA) was declared a Space for Memory and for the Promotion and Defense of Human Rights (Espacio para la Memoria y para la Promoción y Defensa de los Derechos Humanos). This event, which affirmed the transformation of the former clandestine torture camp into a Space for Memory, was moving for all present and for members of H.I.J.O.S. in particular. During the ceremony the gates of the large establishment were opened, and members of the organization, some of whose parents had passed through the torture center, were able to cross the lawn and enter the central white building. Accompanying them as they entered this emblematic space was another individual—Victoria Donda.

As she later found out, Victoria is a child of disappeared, born in the ESMA during her mother's forced disappearance. She was appropriated by Juan Antonio Azic, a member of the taskforce that operated in the ESMA and that disappeared and tortured thousands. She had grown up most of her life with no knowledge about her origins or the history of her biological family. Only a few months before this dramatic event, Victoria had found out that the people she thought were her parents were not her genetic parents but rather her appropriators. She is one of the close to five hundred children disappeared during the dictatorship and raised by the perpetrators of the crime and their accomplices. The event at the ESMA came at a very poignant time for her: during the months prior to the event she was struggling to decide whether to undergo a DNA test that could reveal her biological origins. While her desire to learn who her genetic parents were was rather strong, she was also afraid that going through the test would implicate the people who raised her in the crimes of appropriation and identity alteration. That is, not going through with the test would help her protect those whom she considered to be her parents. The conflicting desires—to know her genetic origins and to protect the people who raised her—created great tensions for Victoria, and it was the visit to the ESMA during this dramatic event that eventually resolved the conflict.[27]

As she describes in her book *My Name Is Victoria* (*Mi nombre es Victoria*), and as I was told in a number of interviews with members of H.I.J.O.S., she had walked into the building with members of the committee Hermanos (brothers/sisters) who within H.I.J.O.S. are responsible for investigating and contacting individuals whom they suspect might be among the five hundred disappeared children. In the case of Victoria they had presented her with their suspicions about her origins only after the official demand for extradition against the person who raised her was made public and he had attempted to commit suicide. It was in light of these events that the visit at the ESMA became a transformative moment. The moment is described in her book:

> [B]eside [Victoria] was Paula, an activist in H.I.J.O.S. whom she had already known and who was five months pregnant. [Victoria] drew her hand close to the budding belly, and she could no longer contain her tears. She must not have been much bigger than the small baby that Paula had in her [belly] when her mother was brought to the ESMA. (Donda 2009, 22)

This realization, along with knowing how brave her mother had to be to withstand the torture and inhumane conditions in the clandestine camp (ibid., 23–25), gave Victoria the courage to undergo the DNA test that would uncover and restore a truth that had been hidden for years. A short time after the event at the ESMA, Victoria discovered that she is in fact the child of María Hilda Pérez and José María Laureano Donda, both disappeared by the military regime.

While H.I.J.O.S. was not the main protagonist in this event, it was the group's vision of truth and justice that was in part acted on.[28] The group claims that a "society that does not try to learn the truth about its own past is destined to fail."[29] This truth is not limited to the collective realm but extends to an individual's past as well—in this case the hidden histories of those who were forcibly disappeared and appropriated by the military regime. To that end, the work of the committee Hermanos within H.I.J.O.S. is aimed at uncovering these disturbing histories and helping the individuals in question reach the decision to undergo a DNA identity test. Similar to the two previous scenarios, here again truth is entangled with both memory and justice, and all three must be uncovered, learned, and embodied by the individual as well as the collective.

But truth is not simply the identification of biological relations broken off and eliminated through disappearance, nor is it just the repudiation of familial relations constructed by the military regime; rather truth is the unveiling of the secrets and lies instated by the regime and the uncovering of the dictatorial contriving of a social world. The reconstitution of truth will not only create a better foundation for the individual's identity and future development but will also mend the Argentine social fabric. The underlying assumption then is that truth is the total and complete transparency of the past in the present. And only by gaining full and detailed knowledge about the past can memory be constructed and justice reached. While in the *escrache* and in the event performed in front of the Palace of Justice truth was located at the collective level, in the case of those identified as disappeared through DNA identity tests truth is located primarily at the individual level.[30] In this latter case, the individual must take responsibility for the collective, because "as long as there is [even] one sole identity changed a whole generation might have doubts about his origins."[31]

Conclusion: *"No Perdonamos, No Olvidamos, No Nos Reconciliamos"*

This statement—we do not forgive, do not forget, do not reconcile—appears at the conclusion of many of H.I.J.O.S.'s documents and speeches, such as the one read aloud at the *escrache* against Videla. The position has led the organization to invent new practices when searching for truth, applying justice, and creating memory. At the same time, while the statement depicts an uncompromising position vis-à-vis the human rights violations committed by the dictatorial rule, it has, in the work of H.I.J.O.S., been complemented by a critical reading of the historical context that gave rise to the dictatorship. The group's interpretation of the past reveals another truth about this historical period—one that was not often discussed prior to the mid-1990s. Specifically, H.I.J.O.S. as a group and others of their generation (as well as survivors of disappearances, those exiled, and political prisoners) have worked to recuperate the history of the period both prior to and during the dictatorship, to uncover the complex historical events that led to the coup, and to reveal the extent and the organized nature of the repression. In the reconstruction of the past the group has, on the one hand, expressed a critical stance toward some of the choices made by their parents and their generation; on the other hand, it has attempted to rescue from oblivion the projects and aspirations that that generation had for Argentine society. Vindicating their parents' struggles for a just and more egalitarian society has meant that their work is framed in relation to these older projects that the authoritarian rule tried to erase. In this way the group is, in effect, bringing back into the public sphere the ideologies and political futures that were silenced by the dictatorial rule and by impunity.

During its tenth anniversary the HRO stated: "[W]e were born in our parents' struggle and they live on in ours." According to the group, only by creating a memory of the past, by having official justice executed, and by revealing the truth about the events that took place during the dictatorship can the social fabric of Argentine society be mended. While their aim is recuperating the past, they have not neglected the present: their work reveals the continuities between human rights of the past and human rights of the present. In this way they have broadened the scope of what truth (as well as memory and justice) may mean in the context of a long transition from authoritarian rule.

Notes

Fieldwork was supported by a scholarship from Cornell University Graduate School and a small grant from the Tinker Foundation. The writing of this chapter was supported by a postdoctoral fellowship at the Hebrew University in Jerusalem.

1. The meaning of each of the terms—memory, truth, and justice—and what they may entail has produced numerous ruptures and disagreements between the different human rights organizations in Argentina. These conflicts have, of course, added and given shape to the terms and their use.

2. While there have been attempts to find recourse in international forums, as Elizabeth Jelin notes (2007, 141), in the Southern Cone and in Argentina specifically, international agencies and NGOs did not play a significant role in the struggles to settle the accounts with the past as they had in other Latin American countries.

3. The TRC had identified four types of truth, which it aimed to elucidate and uncover in its investigations: scientific or forensic truth, narrative truth, social or dialogue truth, and restorative truth.

4. HROs that emerged during the dictatorship (e.g., Madres de Plaza de Mayo and Abuelas de Plaza de Mayo, among others) are composed predominantly by family members of the disappeared.

5. There was controversy surrounding the commission and the trials, particularly as most HROs rejected both the structure of the commission and the relatively limited scope of the original judicial proceedings. But as Crenzel (2008b) describes in some detail, the initial limited scope of CONADEP's investigations was expanded on the ground as a result not only of the social dynamics and personal ties that developed both within and around the commission but also as a consequence of the testimonies and evidence collected during the investigation.

6. During these flights, drugged and naked disappeared persons were thrown alive from airplanes into the Río de la Plata.

7. The movies produced at the time mark the beginning of a documentary film boom, which brought vivid testimonies and archival material into the present (Amado 2009).

8. This was the period of sustained fieldwork for my dissertation; since that time I have returned annually or twice a year to conduct additional fieldwork.

Noa Vaisman

9. This public positioning of the head of state, and the acts and pronouncements that followed, opened up new opportunities for HROs and their struggle for truth and justice. However, they also brought to the surface new and old tensions. Specifically, the new political constellation raised a core dilemma: Should HROs function as critical voices outside of state-led institutions or should they be integrated into the state apparatus? Different HROs held different positions on the subject, and the relationship to the state became a core tension that was the cause for a new split, which took place in 2006 within the HROs and between the HROs and numerous social and political movements on the Left. Within H.I.J.O.S. this split was triggered by the March 2006 events but it had its origins in deep tensions and contradictory views within the group (Vaisman 2008; van Drunen 2010).

10. According to Valeria Barbuto, who works in CELS (Center for Legal and Social Studies [Centro de Estudios Legales y Sociales]), since 1992 in Argentina the legal process has two stages. The first is the written stage, which is closed to the public. During this time the investigation is conducted, and evidence and testimonies are collected. The second stage is the public and oral stage, when the case is deliberated and the same elements are brought forth to argue the case (IDES 2011).

11. Some of the processes were generated by HROs, social and political groups, and artists; they included commemoration events, artistic representations, and public debates where the past was confronted directly. These events were initiated around the mid-1990s, and while there was growing grassroots support for them they gained force, in part after Kirchner first made a number of political statements and symbolic acts. Broadly stated, the Kirchners's leadership created a new and very favorable constellation for the struggle for truth, memory, and justice in Argentina.

12. During the first phase of this practice *escraches* were similar to other demonstrations in that they consisted of a loud gathering, but unlike other such events held in central plazas these were held in front of the perpetrator's home or work place. They also consisted of short performances, dances, and newly invented chants. The practice later evolved and included work with members of the neighborhood where the *escrache* was to take place. Artistic performances in the neighborhood's plaza, public discussions, and collective work centering on the country's past all contributed to the event's preparations. Following a few months of intensive work in the neighborhood the *escrache* would be carried out. The idea was that if people knew more about the past, their commitment to the cause of justice and truth would be greater.

13. I attended one of these meetings and observed as the representatives discussed with H.I.J.O.S. the plans for the *escrache*, the order the demonstrators would march in, and the events that would take place.

14. *Murga* is the dance and music associated with the carnival in the region of the Río de la Plata. The music is characterized by dramatic and repeated drumming,

and the dance by jumps and turns. The dancers are usually dressed in colorful and shiny cloths, lending a sense of lightness and rebellion to the scene.

15. *Hay que saltar, hay que saltar, el que no salta es militar.* Here and throughout the chapter all translations from Spanish are my own.

16. Later the PFA—the Federal Police Force—appeared, dressed ready for combat as is customary now in riots all around the world. In Argentina these police officers are called *Tortugas*, meaning "turtles," a term that refers to the shields they hold and the colors of their uniform.

17. Here I provide only a portion of this powerful speech.

18. Paint balls are balloons filled with paint that are thrown on locations such as homes or work places of perpetrators during an *escrache*. While this event was exhilarating in both its magnitude and its symbolic statement, it ended on a rather different note. During the time that representatives of H.I.J.O.S. were reading the speech, members of a number of political organizations and social movements began pushing each other, causing a strong wave of compression along the avenue. At the same time, other activists began throwing objects, such as garbage and a large garbage can, at the police who were standing behind the fence. Members of H.I.J.O.S. who had watched the events develop from the truck made a rapid decision to stop the *escrache* midway and, contrary to the original plan, encouraged people to disperse. As a few of them explained to me later, they saw the situation and decided it would be wiser to stop the event than to allow it to develop and become violent, a situation that, in all likelihood, would provoke a tear gas attack as the PFA were already feeling threatened. The fighting between the groups, they explained, had originated a number of days earlier and had very little if anything to do with the *escrache*.

19. The decision not to discuss the political affiliation of the disappeared can be traced to the CONADEP, where it was "feared that this would provide public opinion with a justification for the violations" (Crenzel 2008b, 189).

20. In Argentina among HROs and in the popular media, the perpetrators of the crimes committed during the military rule are sometimes referred to as *genocidas*—those who committed genocide.

21. The meaning of this proverb is: to fool or to cheat someone, to pull their leg. The play on words (*pelo*=hair) is important for understanding the act carried out by the group.

22. The event took place on March 21, 2005. It was part of the numerous events that took place around the day commemorating the rise of the dictatorship (March 24). An announcement of the event was given the night before, during a demonstration in the neighborhood of San Telmo to commemorate residents of that neighborhood who were disappeared by the dictatorship.

23. The association is made up of survivors of the various detention centers and others who share their position and goals to achieve justice, and to construct the memory of the era before the dictatorship and the period of the dictatorial

rule. For further information please see http://www.exdesaparecidos.org.ar/aedd/quienesomos.php.

24. These are members of the HROs Madres LF and Abuelas de Plaza de Mayo.

25. *Olé olé, olé olá, olé olé, olé olá, como a los Nazis les va a pasar; a donde vayan los iremos a buscar.*

26. Until recently perpetrators of crimes who were seventy years old or older could serve their sentences under house arrest instead of in a regular or military prison.

27. Victoria Donda was one of the three individuals who spoke in front of the clandestine maternity ward during the *escrache* against Videla almost two years after the event at the ESMA.

28. That said, members of the HRO presented the group's demands and vision about the past in the event that took place that morning after the signing of the agreement between the national and the city governments regarding the future of the ESMA.

29. See www.hijos-capital.org.ar under the section Hermanos, accessed April 18, 2007.

30. However, some of these individuals have come forward and testified in court and have presented their story in the mass media.

31. See www.hijos-capital.org.ar under the section Hermanos, accessed April 18, 2007.

References

Amado, Ana. 2009. *La imagen justa: Cine argentino y política (1980–2007)*. Buenos Aires: Colihue.

Bonaldi, Pablo. 2006. "Hijos de desaparecidos: Entre la construcción de la política y la construcción de la memoria." In *El pasado en el futuro: Los movimientos juveniles*, edited by Elizabeth Jelin and Diego Sempol, 143–84. Madrid: Siglo XXI.

Brysk, Alison. 1994. *The Politics of Human Rights in Argentina: Protest, Change and Democratization*. Stanford, CA: Stanford University Press.

Chapman, Audrey R., and Patrick Ball. 2001. "The Truth of Truth Commissions: Comparative Lessons from Haiti, South Africa and Guatemala." *Human Rights Quarterly* 23:1–43.

Crenzel, Emilio. 2008a. "Argentina's National Commission on the Disappearance of Persons: Contributions to Transitional Justice." *International Journal of Transitional Justice* 2:173–91.

———. 2008b. *La historia política del Nunca Más: La memoria de las desapariciones en la Argentina*. Buenos Aires: Siglo Veintiuno.

———. 2011. "Introduction. Present Pasts: Memory(ies) of State Terrorism in the Southern Cone of Latin America." In *The Memory of State Terrorism in the Southern Cone: Argentina, Chile, and Uruguay,* edited by Francesca Lessa and Vincent Druliolle, 1–13. New York: Palgrave Macmillan.

Donda, Victoria. 2009. *Mi nombre es Victoria: Una lucha por la identidad.* Buenos Aires: Sudamericana.

Elster, Jon. 2006. *Retribution and Reparation in the Transition to Democracy.* Cambridge: Cambridge University Press.

Feitlowitz, Marguerite. 1998. *A Lexicon of Terror: Argentina and the Legacies of Torture.* Oxford: Oxford University Press.

Feld, Claudia. 2002. *Del estrado a la pantalla: Las imágenes del juicio a los ex comandantes en Argentina.* Madrid: Siglo Veintiuno.

Hayner, Priscilla. 2001. *Unspeakable Truths: Transitional Justice and the Challenge of Truth Commissions.* New York: Routledge.

H.I.J.O.S. 2012a. "Historia." http://www.hijos-capital.org.ar/index.php?option=com_content&view=article&id=19&Itemid=400.

H.I.J.O.S. 2012b. "Comisión Escrache." http://www.hijos-capital.org.ar/index.php?option=com_content&view=section&layout=blog&id=7&Itemid=407.

Hinton, Alexander Laban, ed. 2011. *Transitional Justice: Global Mechanisms and Local Realities after Genocide and Mass Violence.* New Brunswick, NJ: Rutgers University Press.

IDES (Instituto de Desarrollo Económico y Social). 2011. "Los crímenes de lesa humanidad en la Argentina: Estado de situación, preguntas y desafíos. Primera reunión de actualización para investigadores." May 20.

Jelin, Elizabeth. 2007. "Public Memorialization in Perspective: Truth, Justice and Memory of Past Repression in the Southern Cone of South America." *International Journal of Transitional Justice* 1:138–56.

Kaiser, Susana. 2002. "Escraches: Demonstrations, Communication and Political Memory in Post-Dictatorial Argentina." *Media, Culture and Society* 24:499–516.

Robben, Antonius C. G. M. 2005. *Political Violence and Trauma in Argentina.* Philadelphia: University of Pennsylvania Press.

———. 2011. "Testimonies, Truths and Transition of Justice in Argentina and Chile." In Hinton 2011, 179–205.

Roht-Arriaza, Naomi. 2006. "The New Landscape of Transitional Justice." In *Transitional Justice in the Twenty-First Century: Beyond Truth versus Justice,* edited by Naomi Roht-Arriaza and Javier Mariezcurrena, 1–16. Cambridge: Cambridge University Press.

Roniger, Luis, and Mario Sznajder. 2005. *El legado de las violaciones de los derechos humanos en el Cono Sur: Argentina, Chile y Uruguay.* La Plata: Ediciones Al Margen.

Seidel, Katja. 2011. "'The Impossible only Takes a Little Longer,' or What May Be Learned from the Argentine Experience of Justice." *Social Anthropology* 19, no. 3: 305–12.

Shaw, Rosalind, and Lars Waldorf. 2010. "Introduction: Localizing Transitional Justice." In *Localizing Transitional Justice: Interventions and Priorities after Mass Violence*, edited by Rosalind Shaw and Lars Waldorf, with Pierre Hazan, 3–26. Stanford, CA: Stanford University Press.

Sikkink, Kathryn. 2008. "From Pariah State to Global Protagonist: Argentina and the Struggle for International Human Rights." *Latin American Politics and Society* 50, no. 1: 1–29.

Sikkink, Kathryn, and Carrie Booth Walling. 2006. "Argentina's Contribution to Global Trends in Transitional Justice." In *Transitional Justice in the Twenty-First Century: Beyond Truth versus Justice*, edited by Naomi Roht-Arriaza and Javier Mariezcurrena, 301–24. Cambridge: Cambridge University Press.

———. 2007. "The Impact of Human Rights Trials in Latin America." *Journal of Peace Research* 44, no. 4: 427–45.

Taylor, Diana. 2002. "'You Are Here': The DNA of Performance." *Drama Review* 46, no. 1: 149–69.

Teitel, Ruti. 2003. "Transitional Justice Genealogy." *Harvard Human Rights Journal* 16:69–94.

Vaisman, Noa. 2008. "Talk, Dreamwork and Specters: (Re)Constructing Patterns of Truth, Self and Society in Present-day Buenos Aires." PhD diss., Cornell University.

van Drunen, Saskia. 2010. *Struggling with the Past: The Human Rights Movement and the Politics of Memory in Post-Dictatorship Argentina (1983–2006)*. Amsterdam: Rozenberg Publishers.

Wilson, Richard. 2001. *The Politics of Truth and Reconciliation in South Africa: Legitimizing the Post-Apartheid State*. Cambridge: Cambridge University Press.

6

The Paradoxes
of Accountability

Transitional Justice
in Peru

JO-MARIE BURT

In April 2009 a special chamber of the Peruvian Supreme
Court found former president Alberto Fujimori guilty of
crimes against humanity and sentenced him to twenty-five years in prison, the
maximum sentence allowed by law (Burt 2009). Another Supreme Court tribunal upheld the conviction later that year. The Fujimori trial and conviction
were widely viewed as a watershed in domestic efforts to obtain truth and justice for state-sponsored crimes committed in the context of Peru's internal
armed conflict (1980–2000). Prior to the Fujimori conviction a specially constituted court, the Sala Penal Nacional (Special Criminal Court), had handed
down a number of convictions in other emblematic cases of human rights
violations from this period, including convictions for the 1990 disappearance
of the university student Ernesto Castillo Paez, the 1988 assassination of the
journalist Hugo Bustíos Saavedra, and the forced disappearances of several
municipal authorities from the Andean community of Chuschi in 1991. The
Fujimori conviction appeared to consolidate this emerging system to investigate and prosecute human rights crimes. The transparency of the process,
the affirmation of the rule of law that it entailed, and the visibility and impact

of the guilty verdict were seen by human rights activists, victims, and judicial operators alike as a major precedent that would validate and strengthen their efforts to promote accountability for other grave violations of human rights committed during Peru's internal conflict.

Indeed, Peru's successful prosecution of a former head of state for grave violations of human rights has come to represent an important precedent in global justice efforts. The "justice cascade" notwithstanding, it is still rare to see criminal prosecutions of former government officials for human rights violations, and it is even rarer for such prosecutions to be conducted by domestic tribunals.[1] (More commonly such prosecutions are conducted by international tribunals, such as the international criminal tribunals for the former Yugoslavia and Rwanda, the International Criminal Court [ICC], or by hybrid tribunals, such as the Special Court for Sierra Leone or the Extraordinary Chambers in the Courts of Cambodia.) In a 2012 *New York Times* op-ed piece, Jim Goldston, the president of the Open Society Justice Initiative and a former ICC prosecutor, argued that greater efforts should be expended to strengthen domestic justice systems rather than international justice mechanisms. Prosecution of human rights violations and crimes against humanity in local courts with local judges was far more effective, he argued, than international tribunals could ever be. His first example of a successful domestic prosecution was the Fujimori trial (Goldston 2012).

Three years after the conclusion of the Fujimori trial, however, empirical research into Peru's domestic human rights prosecutions reveals a dramatic inversion of past successes in its transitional justice process. Indeed, in recent years, high-ranking government officials, retired military officers, and conservative politicians have launched vicious campaigns against human rights lawyers, NGOs, and judicial operators involved in human rights prosecutions, accusing them of "persecuting" the armed forces, politicizing justice, and manipulating victims for political or financial ends. There have been renewed efforts to impose amnesty laws and shut down criminal prosecutions. Beyond this vociferous campaign against the judicialization process, this chapter documents concrete backsliding in Peru's human rights prosecutions efforts, measured in closed cases, investigations that have yet to come to fruition after more than a decade, a minuscule number of cases brought to open trial, and high rates of acquittal of former state agents charged with human rights crimes based on what human rights lawyers charge are legally suspect arguments.

This chapter also identifies and interrogates the paradox at the heart of Peru's transitional justice process. It explores the factors that allowed for the successful and watershed prosecution of a former head of state for grave violations of human rights—the "Peruvian precedent"—while at the same time problematizing Peru's transitional justice process in recent years as conservative forces and other factors have regrouped, in large part in response to these very successes, and have sought to undermine the accountability agenda. The backtracking has been so dramatic, it is argued here, that rather than speak of the "Peruvian precedent" it is more accurate to speak of the "Peruvian paradox." I provide empirical evidence of this paradox—the slow but steady backtracking that has occurred in Peru's transitional justice process, particularly as it relates to criminal trials for human rights violations—and I offer some preliminary explanations for it, using a grounded analysis approach based on data collection, participant observation, interviews with relevant actors, and historical analysis of events.

Background: The Peruvian Precedent

In 1980, as Peru made a transition to democratic government after more than a decade of military rule, the Shining Path launched a rural insurgency designed to topple the state and impose Communist rule. Government forces deployed massive and often arbitrary violence to combat the insurgents, resulting in massive violations of human rights. A second insurgent group, the Túpac Amaru Revolutionary Movement (MRTA), became active in the mid-1980s. An estimated 69,000 Peruvians perished in the conflict, including some 15,000 disappeared.[2] Hundreds of thousands were displaced and orphaned (Burt 2007; Degregori 1991; Gorriti Ellenbogen 1999; Stern 1998). The government of Alberto Fujimori (1990–2000) came to power by election in the midst of massive economic crisis and spiraling violence, carrying out a self-coup and suspension of Congress in 1992 with the backing of the armed forces and instituting authoritarian rule marked by a decline in political violence but a systematic campaign of repression and human rights abuses against perceived government opponents.

During the conflict period, human rights organizations (HROs) and survivors and relatives of victims pressed tirelessly and in the face of great danger to bring to justice those responsible for human rights abuses (Youngers 2003). They documented specific cases of rights abuses, presented writs of habeas corpus, litigated human rights cases, and defended victims, but the norm was impunity for violations committed by state agents.[3] After the collapse of the Fujimori regime in late 2000, the human rights community lobbied forcefully for a truth commission to investigate the causes and consequences of the violence. In June 2001 the interim government of Valentín Paniagua (2000–2001) created the Peruvian Truth Commission, which was renamed the Truth and

Reconciliation Commission by Alejandro Toledo after winning the presidency in 2001 (Degregori 1991; González Cueva 2006; Laplante and Theidon 2007).

The Peruvian human rights movement played a crucial role in pressing for a truth commission that would adopt an integral vision of transitional justice, meaning that it would not simply investigate the horrors of the past but also attempt to identify those responsible and hold them accountable, as well as to propose individual and collective reparations to victims and their family members. This was a critical departure from standard practice in the design and practice of truth commissions in the region, at least since the Chilean truth commission, known also as the Rettig Commission, created in 1990, which sidestepped the quest for retributive justice in human rights cases based on the argument that political constraints made trials impossible (Zalaquett 2003). Aside from the Peruvian Truth and Reconciliation Commission (CVR), the only other truth commission in the region to date to link truth and justice was the very first one to successfully culminate its work, Argentina's National Commission on the Disappeared (CONADEP), created in 1983 after the collapse of the military dictatorship in that country (CONADEP 1984). However, a series of military uprisings prompted the transitional government to adopt new laws that effectively ended criminal prosecutions in Argentina. In the wake of the Argentine experience, other countries in the region adopted truth commissions like the Chilean Rettig Commission, which proposed to investigate the nature and extent of human rights violations committed by repressive military regimes but stopped short of holding any individuals accountable for these crimes. Trials, it was argued, were destabilizing for the new and fragile democracies taking hold, and they were seen as undermining rather than contributing to national reconciliation (Teitel 2000).[4]

Beyond the lobbying efforts of human rights groups and civil society organizations, other factors, both domestic and international, played a crucial role in shaping the mandate of the Peruvian truth commission. While the Peruvian government engaged civil society groups in a dialogue about the contours of a possible truth commission, the Inter-American Court of Human Rights handed down a sentence in March 2001 in the Barrios Altos massacre case that fundamentally shaped the possibilities of justice in postwar Peru. Not only did the Court determine that the Peruvian State was responsible for the 1991 massacre and ordered it to investigate, prosecute, and punish those responsible, but it also established that the amnesty laws passed by the pro-Fujimori Congress in 1995, which until then had shielded human rights abusers from criminal prosecution, violated Peru's obligations under the American Convention on Human Rights and declared that the law lacked legal standing (Barrios Altos Case 2001). Shortly thereafter, a judge reopened the

Barrios Altos case, issuing indictments of several alleged members of the Colina Group, the military death squad responsible for this and other atrocities during the Fujimori era. The Peruvian Constitutional Tribunal later upheld the Inter-American Court ruling in the Barrios Altos case, thus removing a key legal obstacle to criminal prosecutions for human rights violations in postwar Peru.

Timing was important here. The Barrios Altos ruling came shortly after the Paniagua government had requested that Peru be allowed to return to the contentious jurisdiction of the Inter-American Court of Human Rights. In 1999, angered by several rulings of the Court that questioned its antiterrorism legislation and use of military courts, the Fujimori government had withdrawn Peru from the Court's jurisdiction. Returning Peru to the Inter-American system was one of the measures adopted by the Paniagua administration to restore credibility to Peru's new democracy after a decade of authoritarian, corrupt, and abusive rule. In restoring Peru's acceptance of the jurisdiction of the Inter-American Court, Paniagua agreed that the Peruvian state would abide by the Court's rulings and a series of friendly settlements in more than 150 cases, a significant number of them involving human rights violations, from the Fujimori era. Barrios Altos was one of these cases. Aside from this, however, investigating the crimes of the Colina Group and the Fujijmori government more broadly coincided with the efforts of the Paniagua administration to eradicate corrupt elements from government institutions and establish a more solid ground for democratic governance.

Domestic power politics also played an important if surprising role in the debate about the truth commission's mandate. A month after the Barrios Altos ruling, a videotape from 1999 was made public of the top military brass, led by none other than Fujimori's infamous security advisor, Vladimiro Montesinos, eliciting the signatures of hundreds of military officers in support of the 1992 coup d'état and the 1995 self-amnesty laws. The videotape launched yet another scandal, not only because it revealed the deep politicization and manipulation of the military during Fujimori's rule but also because the current military chiefs of the army, navy, and air force were among those in the video signing the so-called letter of subjugation to Fujimori's coup and what amounted to an impunity pact. Immediate demands for their removal and a major overhaul of the armed forces followed. The military leaders offered their resignations, and the armed forces issued a public statement apologizing for its past support of the Fujimori regime and pronouncing its support for the creation of a truth commission. In a message to the nation on April 17, 2001, Paniagua accepted the resignations and announced that he would create a truth commission to promote national unity and reconciliation. Thanks in large part to this episode, the armed forces lacked the political capital to impose conditions of any kind on Peru's truth commission as it took shape in the following months, particularly with regard to the issue of criminal prosecutions of past human rights violations (Burt 2009).

With these antecedents in mind, we can better understand why, nearly two decades after the creation of the CONADEP, the Peruvian CVR adopted an integral view of transitional justice. International courts had determined that amnesty laws could not continue to prevent prosecutions, and those most likely to mobilize to prevent prosecutions—the armed forces—were unable to do so in light of the "letter of subjugation" video. In these circumstances, the view put forth by human rights organizations prevailed: prosecutions were considered to be not an obstacle to, but an essential component of, national reconciliation.

For the CVR, justice consisted of at least two key elements: accountability for perpetrators of grave human rights violations, on the one hand, and meaningful reparations for victims, on the other. In pursuit of accountability, the CVR created a special legal unit that was tasked with investigating specific cases of grave violations of human rights. (Other units were established to investigate the more historical and anthropological dimensions of the political violence, including in-depth regional studies of violence in specific areas of the country [Gonzalez Cueva 2006].) In its Final Report, presented to President Toledo on August 29, 2003, the CVR made a series of recommendations that the Peruvian State should pursue in order to achieve its stated objective of national reconciliation. One of these recommendations was to prosecute grave human rights violations. To that end, CVR investigators handed forty-seven cases to the Public Ministry and Judiciary for criminal prosecution. Since the majority of Shining Path crimes had already been adjudicated (or those responsible killed in combat or otherwise), most of these cases involve state agents who enjoyed virtually total impunity during the two decades of the conflict.[5] However, the Peruvian state, in an effort to uphold rulings by the Inter-American Court that determined that military courts used to try cases of terrorism and treason during the Fujimori regime denied due process, held new trials for hundreds of individuals accused on terrorism charges, including top leaders of the Shining Path. The CVR also recommended the creation of a specialized legal system to investigate and prosecute human rights cases.

It took a while, but by late 2004 and early 2005 the Peruvian state followed through with that recommendation. Special units were set up in the Public Ministry to investigate human rights cases, while the Sala Penal del Terrorismo (National Terrorism Court) was reconstituted as the National Criminal Court (Sala Penal Nacional) and charged with adjudicating cases of human rights violations, crimes against humanity, and terrorism. The National Criminal Court handed down its first conviction against state agents for human rights violations in 2006, when four police officers were sentenced to fifteen to sixteen years for the forced disappearance of the Catholic University student Ernesto Castillo Páez, who was abducted on October 21, 1990, by government forces and whose body remains missing.[6] The ruling was significant because the Court accepted the CVR's findings that crimes of forced disappearance were not isolated incidents but part of a systematic and widespread pattern of human rights violations in Peru during the internal armed conflict. The Court also determined that this and similar crimes in which the body has not yet been found constitute ongoing crimes and hence are not subject to statutes of limitations, reaffirming jurisprudence that has been developed and applied elsewhere in the region (Rivera Paz 2006; Sala Pena Nacional 2006).

A number of other cases have been successfully prosecuted since 2006 (Rivera and Burt, forthcoming). In 2007 three sentences were handed down in cases investigated by the CVR: in February two army officers were convicted of the forced disappearance of the mayor and other municipal authorities of the Andean district of Chuschi; in April two army officers were convicted of the forced disappearances of Efraín Aponte Ortiz in 1991; and in October two army officers were convicted for the murder of the journalist Hugo Bustíos, who was investigating human rights violations when he and a colleague were shot in 1988. In 2008 the former head of the National Intelligence Service (SIN) and army general Julio Salazar Monroe was convicted in the disappearance and murder of nine students and a professor from La Cantuta University, as were eleven other army officers who had participated in those crimes as members of the Colina Group. A handful of other convictions were handed down that year as well. The trial of former president Alberto Fujimori, which started in December 2007, culminated in April 2009 with a guilty verdict. In October 2010 nineteen members of the Colina Group, including close Fujimori allies Gen. (ret.) Nicolás Hermoza Ríos, the former army chief, and Vladimiro Montesinos, his security advisor, were sentenced to fifteen to twenty-five years for the Barrios Altos massacre.

These achievements reflected the highly effective and well-organized activism of Peruvian civil society, as well as a favorable political environment that facilitated the judicialization process. While the Toledo government did not actively promote or support the criminal prosecution of human rights violations, it allowed the process to move forward and did not interfere with the judiciary. At the level of the judiciary, initial reform efforts also facilitated this process, as did an institutional desire to promote a new image of a reformed judiciary after years of political subordination to the Fujimori regime. It was this particular confluence of factors, then—a political transition in which new democratic leaders sought to eradicate corruption through criminal prosecutions; legal authorities determined to restore credibility to judicial institutions; persistent demands and activism by civil society actors, especially human rights organizations and victims associations, for truth and justice for human rights violations; and the influence of international rulings and agreements in the context of Peru's transition—that generated a favorable political context for criminal prosecutions of perpetrators of human rights violations. These factors contributed to the creation of a coalition of actors favoring an accountability agenda (Burt 2011). The existence of this coalition in 2005, when Alberto Fujimori made his ill-fated trip to Chile, fundamentally shaped the way the Peruvian state responded to the news that Alberto Fujimori had left his safe haven in Japan, where he had lived since fleeing Peru in November 2000, for neighboring Chile.

The Extradition and Trial of Alberto Fujimori

Both the Paniagua and the Toledo governments sought Fujimori's extradition from Japan, to no avail.[7] When Fujimori fled to Japan, the birthplace of his emigrant parents, the government recognized his Japanese citizenship and essentially ignored the requests of two different Peruvian administrations to extradite Fujimori. Most observers assumed that Fujimori would remain in Japan indefinitely to elude justice.

But Fujimori was an ambitious man. In November 2005 he left Japan by plane for Chile, where he presumably planned to launch his political comeback by running for president in Peru's 2006 elections. Within a few hours of his arrival, Chilean authorities placed Fujimori under arrest. The Toledo government announced it would seek Fujimori's extradition from Chile to face charges in Peru for human rights violations, usurpation of authority, and corruption.

Peru's human rights community mobilized to support the extradition process, organizing visits to Chile to speak with the press and meet with government and judicial authorities to plead their case. International human rights organizations, including Amnesty International, Human Rights Watch, and the International Federation of Human Rights (FIDH), also played a central role by providing legal arguments supporting the extradition request and lobbying the Chilean government and legal officials (Amnesty International 2007; HRW 2005; IFHR 2007). In November 2006 the Inter-American Court of Human Rights rendered a judgment in the La Cantuta case—one of the key cases for which Fujimori's extradition was being sought. The Court found that the Peruvian state had not only violated the right to life of the victims but also the right to a fair trial and to judicial protection of the relatives of the victims. The Court noted that the disappearances and extrajudicial executions in the La Cantuta case amounted to a crime against humanity and, asserting that that all states have the duty to cooperate to eradicate impunity, urged cooperation on the part of all states toward that end (La Cantuta Case 2006). This was seen as a direct call to Chile to collaborate with Peru's extradition request, which was approved by the Chilean Supreme Court in September 2007.[8] Within hours of the extradition ruling, Fujimori was returned to Peru.

It is important to note that the political will to see through the extradition process was closely tied to the nature of the transitional governments in power. The interim governments of both Valentín Paniagua (November 2000–July 2001) and Alejandro Toledo (2001–6) empowered legal authorities to prosecute criminal activities during the prior regime (though admittedly these initial prosecutions focused primarily on economic and political crimes rather than human rights violations), hence the political will to actively pursue extradition in the Fujimori case existed and in the end was successful. It is not difficult to imagine that had a different president been in office when Fujimori arrived in Chile, the outcome could have been quite different. This highlights the important weight of the political in legal outcomes, a theme to which we will return later in the chapter.

The Special Criminal Court, a chamber of three Supreme Court justices, was specially created to hear all the cases against Fujimori. The Special Criminal Court determined that there would be three different public trials against Fujimori, with one charge to be heard in a summary trial. The first public trial, focusing on human rights violations, started on December 10, 2007.

The human rights trial against Fujimori centered on four key cases: the Barrios Altos massacre, which took place on November 3, 1991, in which fifteen people, including an eight-year-old child, were killed while attending a neighborhood barbecue, and four others were gravely wounded; the disappearance and later killing of nine students and a professor from La Cantuta University on July 18, 1992;[9] and the kidnappings of the journalist Gustavo Gorriti and the businessman Samuel Dyer in the aftermath of the April 5, 1992 coup d'état. The Barrios Altos massacre and the La Cantuta disappearances were both carried out by the Colina Group, a clandestine unit of military officials associated with the army and National Intelligence Service, whose purpose was to eliminate suspected insurgent sympathizers.

Fujimori's political allies charged that the trial was politically motivated, a vendetta by Fujimori's enemies designed to destroy his reputation and his political organization. However, charges that this was a show trial seem unsubstantiated. In the immediate aftermath of Fujimori's flight to Japan, several of his former associates were arrested, prosecuted, and convicted on corruption and related charges. This was not a politically motivated trial against Fujimori per se, but rather the culmination of an effort on the part of two successive democratically elected governments to sanction criminal acts committed during his regime and lay the foundation for a more transparent and democratic system. Moreover, the trial was widely viewed as an exemplary process that set a new standard for the Peruvian courts as well as a critical precedent for global justice efforts worldwide (Ambos 2011; Méndez 2010). Throughout the trial, the Supreme Court justices upheld international standards for a fair, independent, and impartial trial that adhered to guidelines and procedures outlined in Peruvian criminal law and fully upheld Fujimori's due process rights (HRW 2009; Méndez 2010).

The Special Criminal Court emitted its sentence in the Fujimori case on April 7, 2009. The Court found that Fujimori was the person who had ultimate control and power of decision (*autoría mediata*) over the illegal state apparatus that committed the crimes of aggravated homicide, assault, and kidnapping in the four cases mentioned above and sentenced him to twenty-five years in prison (Sala Penal Especial 2009).[10] The Court considered that the prosecution had fully proven that the former president, as commander in chief of the armed forces, had direct control over the Colina Group, a military unit that operated from within the army intelligence services and engaged in a number of extralegal killings, forced disappearances, and torture, including the Barrios Altos and La Cantuta massacres. The Court also determined Fujimori's responsibility in ordering the illegal kidnappings of Gustavo Gorriti and Samuel Dyer. According to the Court, these crimes took place in a context of systematic human rights violations, and as such constitute crimes against humanity in international law. The verdict was widely hailed by domestic and international legal experts as exceptionally thorough and analytically sound (Ambos 2011; HRW 2009; Méndez 2010). On December 30, 2009, a second panel of five Supreme Court justices unanimously upheld the twenty-five-year sentence against Fujimori.[11]

The Fujimori verdict generated expectations that there would be a sort of ripple effect in the justice system in favor of human rights accountability. This was not an isolated prosecution, as noted earlier; there had been a number of convictions handed down since the 2006 ruling in the Castillo Páez case, which seemed to indicate a favorable trend in the realm of truth recovery and justice seeking. The Fujimori trial and conviction had established an important precedent. Over the course of nearly a year and a half, the proceedings in the Fujimori trial had been in plain view of the public through the daily broadcasts of the hearings on national TV and radio. All of the participants in the process, including Mr. Fujimori and his legal team, treated the proceedings in a respectful way, dignifying the court and the legal process itself, an important example in a country that had a historically weak and corrupt judiciary and in which the rich and powerful were generally seen as being above the law. The verdict was impeccably argued, and it stood the test of time, having withstood an appeal as well as several habeas corpus petitions designed to overturn the Fujimori sentence, as well as political campaigns to have Fujimori freed via a presidential or humanitarian pardon. "I now know that there is justice for the poor," said Raida Cóndor, the mother of Armando Amaro Cóndor, one of the missing students from La Cantuta, an affirmation of the notion that in a democracy the powerful are not above the law. The expectation, then, that this process would strengthen efforts to obtain truth and justice in cases of grave human rights violations seemed well founded.

Beyond Fujimori: Human Rights Prosecutions in Peru

The afterglow of the Fujimori trial notwithstanding, fundamental shifts were already underway that were at work to undercut Peru's transitional justice process. There were, indeed, mundane problems that made the justice process slow and inefficient, a problem that is not unsurprising in a country such as Peru, where the legal system has not been known for its celerity or efficacy. Beyond this, however, it soon became evident that the successful prosecutions of former state agents to date had unleashed a backlash among sectors of the armed forces and conservative politicians and elites who sought to bring the accountability agenda to a standstill.

Human Rights Prosecutions in Peru: Progress and Setbacks

In response to an observed gap in knowledge and understanding of the status of human rights prosecutions in Peru, the author, in close collaboration with local Peruvian human rights organizations, endeavored to collect data about ongoing cases in order to better grasp the scope and extent of human rights trials in postconflict Peru. Working with the Coordinadora Nacional de Derechos Humanos, the umbrella organization of Peru's principal human rights organizations, the "Human Rights Trials in Peru Project" has sought to develop actionable information about human rights investigations and prosecutions in Peru.[12] After several months of data collection, the project developed a registry of 250 cases that are being litigated by human rights organizations throughout Peru. The project has collected information about sentences, number of convictions and acquittals, as well as information about cases currently in public trial or that are close to reaching that stage. The project has also collected data from the Public Ministry on the number of denunciations of human rights violations it has received since 2001.[13]

The data collected reveals a disturbing picture. The Public Ministry is charged with investigating crimes and issuing indictments. Only a fraction of cases under investigation by the Public Ministry have led to formal indictments and public trials. Of the 2,880 denunciations before the Public Ministry, investigations have been closed in nearly half (1,374, or 48 percent) of cases. According to state prosecutors interviewed in the context of this research, this is due to lack of evidence (most of the cases are between twenty and thirty years old) or to the inability of prosecutors to obtain official information from military and other government offices that would help them identify the perpetrators. A significant number of the cases on file—1,349, or 47 percent— remain in the preliminary and intermediate phases of investigation, where they have languished for years. Only a miniscule percentage of cases—less than 1 percent—have moved forward to public trial.

Another level of concern focuses on the comportment of the Judiciary, which is charged with the adjudication of human rights cases. One concern is efficiency. We have documented several instances in which there have been long delays in bringing cases in which indictments have been issued to public trial. For example, in the case of the Cabitos 1983—one of the forty-seven cases investigated by the CVR, involving the arbitrary detention, torture, forced disappearance, and/or extrajudicial execution of more than fifty Peruvians at the Los Cabitos military base in Huamanga, Ayacucho—it took more than two years from the original indictment, issued in May 2009, to the opening of the trial in May 2011.[14] Once in public trial, hearings are scheduled intermittently and only for a few hours at a time, resulting in extended trial periods. The Cabitos case, for example, is still ongoing, two years after its start date.

One key reason for this is that since 2008, the mandate of special system to investigate and prosecute human rights violations has been expanded such that judges have increasingly less time and resources to focus on human rights cases. Set up in 2004 and 2005 to allow state prosecutors and judges to focus exclusively on cases of terrorism, human rights violations, and crimes against humanity, the special human rights system's mandate has expanded, since

2008, to include cases of narcotrafficking, money laundering, kidnapping, and freedom of speech, among others. This has effectively undermined the specialized nature of the human rights system and diluted its effectiveness. Today, human rights cases now constitute less than 10 percent of the caseload of the National Criminal Court. As a result, those few cases that reach the public trial stage are assigned sessions that last only two or three hours a week, resulting in unnecessarily long trials. The judges have suspended hearings on multiple occasions, sometimes because the defendants' lawyers are not present or because the judges, who are involved in multiple cases, have conflicts. In the Accomarca case, a massacre that occurred just weeks after Alan Garcia became president in 1985 in which sixty-nine peasants were killed by army forces, the public trial began in November 2010 and as of September 2013 is still ongoing. The lack of celerity in these cases is perceived by survivors and relatives of victims, who have already waited two or more decades for their cases to be heard before the courts, as another violation of their human rights and undermines their confidence in the justice system.

Rights advocates have also denounced a dramatic shift in sentencing patterns, especially by the National Criminal Court (Rivera Paz 2009, 2011). To provide context to such claims, the Human Rights Trials in Peru project has endeavored to collect information about sentences emitted in human rights cases. As of December 2012, the project had documented forty-eight sentences in human rights cases. These represent thirty-seven unique cases or episodes of violence, since some cases have been fragmented into two or more legal processes, while in others the first-instance verdict was overturned and a new trial held, resulting in a second and sometimes a third sentence in a single case. The majority of these cases involve the crimes of forced disappearance or extrajudicial execution (Human Rights Trials in Peru 2013).

The convictions to date have included some very high-profile cases (aside from the Fujimori verdict), several of which have been upheld on appeal by the Peruvian Supreme Court. This includes the 2008 guilty verdict for the retired general Julio Salazar Monroe for the disappearance of the students and professor from La Cantuta University, which resulted in a sentence of twenty-five years in prison. In October 2010 the Barrios Altos case culminated—after a public trial that lasted five years!—in a guilty verdict for nineteen of the thirty-two defendants, with sentences ranging between fifteen and twenty-five years (Primera Sala Penal Especial 2010). Those found guilty include Fujimori's powerful advisor, Vladimiro Montesinos; former head of the armed forces retired army general Nicolás Hermoza Ríos; two other army generals; and the operative heads of the Colina Group, Army Major Santiago Martin Rivas and Carlos Pichilingue. This is the first conviction for human rights abuses for Montesinos and Hermoza Ríos, considered to be the two strong-men who ruled with Fujimori for the better part of his ten-year rule.

At the same time, however, the overall acquittal rate is very high and has gotten worse in recent years. Looking at the human rights sentences in more detail, we see that of these forty-eight sentences, one or more defendants have been found guilty and sentenced to prison in twenty cases. In twenty-eight cases, all of the defendants have been acquitted. In 58 percent of sentences emitted, then, all the defendants have been acquitted.

Looking at the numbers of individuals convicted or acquitted, the numbers are even more dramatic. A total of 187 state agents have been prosecuted since 2006. Of those, 66 have been convicted, while 121 have been acquitted.[15] In other words, 35 percent of those prosecuted have been convicted, while 65 percent have been acquitted. Peruvian courts are twice as likely to acquit than to convict in human rights cases. On their own, these numbers are surprising, but even more so if we consider them comparatively. In Argentina, which restarted human rights prosecutions after the amnesty laws were declared un-constitutional in 2005 by the Supreme Court, 89 sentences were handed down between 2006 and 2012; during the same time period 354 defendants were convicted, while 35 were acquitted. Twice as many sentences were handed down in Argentina as in Peru during the same period, involving the prosecu-tion of nearly two times more individuals. More significantly, the conviction rate in Argentina is 90 percent, compared to Peru's 35 percent conviction rate.[16]

If we examine the sentencing patterns of the National Criminal Court (SPN) alone, which is warranted since it is the primary national-level judicial body charged with prosecuting human rights cases, the numbers are even more problematic. In the thirty-six sentences handed down by the SPN between 2005 and 2012, of a total of 122 defendants, the SPN has acquitted 97 and found 25 guilty.[17] This represents a conviction rate of 24 percent. In other words, defendants are four times more likely, overall, to be acquitted than convicted by the SPN.

It is important to note that to date, the Supreme Court has nullified or partially nullified fourteen sentences in which one or more state agents were acquitted and in virtually all cases has ordered a full or partial retrial. This suggests a level of contention within the Peruvian Judiciary about the norms and concepts being applied in these cases, although further study is required to fully understand the dynamics at work. In at least two cases, the retrial also resulted in acquittals of all defendants, and at least two cases have gone to a third retrial.

A more detailed analysis of sentencing patterns is currently in progress. It is conceivable that the high rate of acquittals reflects merely that due process is at work and prosecutors are not successfully proving their cases. However, our preliminary research suggests that in many cases, sentences acquitting defendants diverge from jurisprudence outlined in earlier sentences of the SPN itself and other Peruvian courts as well as standards and norms established in international law. For example, in recent sentences the SPN has insisted on the need for direct evidence to demonstrate culpability in human rights violations. This contradicts the jurisprudence established in the Fujimori (and other) sentences establishing that in cases of grave human rights violations, in which direct evidence may not exist because of the context in which they occur, circumstantial evidence can be used to establish individual culpability. In recent sentences the Court has refused to acknowledge that superior orders to commit human rights violations may be verbal and clandestine, requiring instead documentary evidence establishing the existence of superior orders in order to demonstrate intellectual authorship. The Court has failed to analyze the role of the military as an organization in the implementation of superior orders. In addition, the Court has in some cases disqualified the testimony of family members, who are often the only witnesses to crimes particularly in the case of forced disappearances, arguing that their testimony is biased. As a result, the Court has prioritized the responsibility of the material authors, primarily low-ranking officers and soldiers, belying a now-robust international jurisprudence emphasizing the need to hold accountable those who impart orders. While in early sentences the Court refers to several cases of human rights violations as crimes against humanity, in more recent sentences it obviates such references and refers to these cases as "excesses" committed by the armed forces in the context of the counterinsurgency war. Such arguments mark a departure not only from the Court's earlier sentences but also from the findings of the CVR, and thus they open the door to legal arguments that such crimes are subject to statutes of limitations (Rivera and Burt, forthcoming). They also contract several rulings handed down by Peru's Constitutional Tribunal, which establish that international law must be considered by Peruvian courts when adjudicating human rights cases.

In cases of forced disappearance, early sentences emitted by the SPN, for example in the Castillo Páez and the Chuschi cases, established that these constituted crimes against humanity. However, in a number of recent sentences, judges have ignored these precedents or revised them in such ways that result in the acquittal of alleged perpetrators. For example, in the 2009 ruling in the Los Laureles case, the SPN obviated the doctrine, which it itself had earlier accepted, that forced disappearance is an ongoing and permanent crime that cannot be the subject of statutes of limitation (Rivera Paz 2009).[18] In recent years, the Court has adopted a binding accord, which states that if the person charged with committing the crime of forced disappearance is no longer a member of the armed forces, they cannot then be held accountable for the crime, a juridical aberration that has been challenged by international jurists but remains technically still on the books in Peru (V Pleno Jurisdiccional de las Salas Penales Permanente y Transitoria 2009).[19]

The question then is why the same Court that produced important and substantive sentences in 2006, 2007, and 2008 began to adopt different criteria in recent years, which have resulted in such a high rate of acquittals. While further research is needed, our preliminary investigation suggests that shifting political winds have narrowed the space for accountability efforts. At the same time, pressure is being applied to judicial operators to apply narrow criteria to these cases. This raises important questions about the independence of the judiciary vis-à-vis other powerful actors, primarily the Executive and the armed forces.

The Impunity Bloc

It is perhaps not surprising that Peru's judicialization process is plagued by a series of capacity issues that undermine the efficient and swift resolution of such a large number of complex human rights cases. These are well documented in our research through interviews with judicial operators as well as human rights lawyers and activists. But these capacity issues only tell part of the story. They do not reveal the profound political shifts that may be behind some of these trends. Only through a grounded analysis of Peru's transitional justice process, and an understanding of the political factors at play, can we unpack these shifts and their impact on accountability efforts in Peru.

The shifts arguably began with the election of Alan García to a second term in the presidency (2006–11). Garcia has not been successfully indicted on human rights charges to date. Nonetheless, the fact that massive human rights abuses occurred during his first term in office (1985–90) has led to speculation that he could at some point be put on the dock for direct involvement in some cases or for a failure to act or to investigate other cases. Surely this was foremost in Garcia's mind when he selected the former navy admiral Luis Giampetri to be his vice presidential candidate. Giampetri is a hard-line military officer who led naval forces in the 1986 Fronton prison uprising, when combined military forces used "excessive military force" to regain control of the prisons and then summarily executed more than one hundred inmates who had surrendered (El Fronton Case 2003). He has vigorously and consistently defended the armed forces, and with as much vigor has criticized human rights activists and judicial operators for engaging in a witch hunt against the military. He has even charged one of the human rights lawyers involved in the Fronton case, Carlos Rivera of the Institute of Legal Defense (IDL), of being a Shining Path sympathizer.

The Garcia government also adopted a new policy establishing that the state would pay for the defense lawyers of any military or police officer accused of human rights violations. In 2008 this policy was modified so that the Ministry of Defense and Interior would coordinate the selection of defense lawyers for active and former state agents accused of human rights abuses and assume all associated costs. This was challenged by the Ombudsman's Office and human rights groups alike; according to the Ombudsman's Office, 74 percent of victims lack legal representation in their cases (Defensoría del Pueblo 2008, 167–69). Taking into account that the majority of victims—more than 75 percent, according to the CVR—are poor, indigenous rural people who have difficulty accessing the justice system, this policy would seem to create an uneven playing field and may be a decisive factor in the high number of acquittals since 2008.

During Garcia's rule, the neutrality of the Executive toward the judicialization process gave way to active interventionism. Garcia, Giampetri, and successive ministers of defense–the most vocal being Rafael Rey Rey, a former ally of the Fujimori regime—have made pointed, sometimes vitriolic statements against the judicialization process and those responsible for carrying it forward, including prosecutors, judges, and especially human rights lawyers. An exhaustive discourse analysis is not possible in this chapter, but a brief analysis of the discourse deployed during the Garcia government with regards to the judicialization process should suffice to reveal the hostility deployed against the process and those who participate in it. It is important to note that this discourse was sustained, meaning it was reiterated frequently over time; consistent, in that it almost always attacked human rights defenders and judicial operators; and high profile, since it was conveyed by a variety of top government officials, including the president, the vice president, and ministers of defense, among others.

The key points of the official discourse were as follows: the armed forces saved Peru from terrorism; there was never any systematic violation of human rights (as documented by the CVR) by state security forces; efforts to prosecute individual members of the military for human rights violations amounted to political persecution against the entire military institution; and such efforts must cease, via an amnesty law or other such mechanism, in order for Peru to achieve any real peace. For example, in 2006 Vice President Giampetri stated, "Ungratefully, many men in uniform who fulfilled their patriotic duty are the object of unjust persecution through legal processes that are provoked by interests whose true interests are far from true justice."[20]

Or consider these words, spoken by then President Alan Garcia in 2008, in the context of the anniversary of the creation of the Peruvian Navy, in which he adopts the language of the military when referring to human rights trials as persecution by the courts:

> How long will those who saved Peru from terrorism continue to be persecuted? If [Peruvian hero Miguel] Grau were alive would they have persecuted him too? [Will they continue to persecute] those who wrote a page of glory for Peru in the twentieth century, having eliminated the largest threat our country has faced, the threat of death, the beheading of innocents?[21]

Not only are individual officers or soldiers who are under investigation or indicted considered to be victims of the "persecution"—the entire military institution is being persecuted. This of course serves to reinforce the veritable military "wall of silence" surrounding human rights violations. To wit, the 2010 statement of then Defense Minister Rafael Rey Rey, in reference to the criminal investigations against two generals accused of grave human rights violations:

> Today, when we remember the sacrifice of our heroes of the Morro de Arica, I ask out loud what millions of Peruvians of good faith are asking: How much longer, how much longer will there be so much injustice, so many irregularities, so much abuse? . . . Honor and glory to the Peruvians who offered their lives to give us freedom and peace and to those who offer their lives now to give us order and security![22]

Such statements were giving expression to a deep-seated anxiety among high-ranking and some midlevel military officers as criminal trials in human rights cases moved forward. That resistance to the trials was articulated by top government officials reveals that the pro-impunity alliance was supported at the highest levels of power. Such statements were followed by vociferous demands for an amnesty law or some other kind of "political solution" that would bring an end to the trials. In 2008 two bills were proposed in Congress, one by Mercedes Cabanillas, a member of Garcia's political party, APRA. Neither of these bills prospered, most likely because with the Fujimori trial in full swing and international eyes on Peru, it was evident to lawmakers that such a move would be internationally condemned. In 2010, though, Alan Garcia passed a series of executive decrees, one of which—Decree Law 1097—was a veiled amnesty law that would not only effectively end criminal prosecutions for human rights violations but would also free those already convicted of such crimes, including perhaps Fujimori himself. The decree law elicited such reprobation domestically and internationally that Garcia was obliged to revoke it (Burt 2010).

It is no surprise that military and government officials refuse to collaborate with criminal investigations so as to help clarify the circumstances surrounding different cases of human rights abuses (especially the fifteen thousand forcibly disappeared, of whom less than one thousand have been identified in the ten years since the CVR's Final Report) or help identify those individuals responsible for specific abuses, whether as material or intellectual authors. Many cases cannot move forward due to insufficient information about perpetrators, who often used only pseudonyms while engaging in counterinsurgency operations. The armed forces have steadfastly refused to provide information to facilitate the identifying alleged perpetrators, backed by the discourse of high government officials who accuse human rights NGOs and the legal system of "persecuting" the armed forces and promoting a "terrorist agenda."

Interviews with judicial operators and human rights activists reveal that these key actors in Peru's judicialization process perceive and are sensitive to the government's hostility to the accountability agenda, and some have modified their behavior accordingly. Prosecutors and judges have admitted in off-the-record interviews that they have received visits from unnamed emissaries who transmit "concern" about the "politicization" of the judiciary and urge caution. There have been less tactful messages as well, as in the charges brought by then President Garcia against the Ayacucho state prosecutor Cristina Olazabal, accusing her of misuse of her legal authority. Olazabal had issued an indictment in the Accomarca case, which included an accusation against Garcia for the crime of genocide. Olazabal nearly lost her job (she was defended by the human rights community), but the Public Ministry dropped the charges against García, who is now simply a witness in the case. Olazabal was demoted to assistant prosecutor. She soon left the Public Ministry and retired to private life. In yet another example, in 2010 state prosecutors in the human rights system were obliged to participate in a two-day symposium co-organized by the Public Ministry and the armed forces. One prosecutor told me that on the first day of the event, which took place at the Public Ministry, a military officer who was a defendant in one of the cases she was investigating was slated to deliver a lecture about how to investigate human rights cases. On the second day, the symposium took place in the "Pentagonito," the headquarters of the armed forces, and the day's proceedings were followed by display of military skills at a firing range. Another prosecutor told me he felt that the entire enterprise was intended to intimidate judicial operators like him who were engaged in human rights investigations.

Political interference in the judicial process reflects not merely the fact that still powerful political elites in Peru could potentially be put on trial for human rights violations. It also reflects the recomposition of deeply conservative sectors of the armed forces and the political right in Peru that refuse to acknowledge any wrongdoing on the part of the military in Peru's internal armed conflict, and that continue to perceive any attempt to hold accountable individual members of the armed forces (or former presidents such as Fujimori) as a belligerent act. These same sectors frequently attack the CVR as biased, and they outright reject its conclusions, falsely claiming that it does not condemn Shining Path and MRTA abuses and focuses only on military violations of human rights. Prosecutors and judges have reported that they have received pressure from emissaries of both the Executive and the armed forces to desist in their criminal investigations. Thus, despite significant advances in Peru's efforts to achieve accountability for the terrible crimes of the past, impunity in Peru is still quite robust.

These concerns remain as real as ever. In the context of the newly elected government of Ollanta Humala, there appears to be little impetus to supporting victims seeking truth and justice for crimes of the past. Of course, it is well known that Humala is a former army captain who was formally charged as being responsible for the forced disappearance of several people when he was in charge of a military base in Madre Mía, in the Upper Huallaga Valley, during the early 1990s. During the 2005–6 presidential campaign, witnesses came forth identifying Humala as "Captain Carlos" (who was identified as such in the CVR's Final Report) and charged him with a variety of human rights crimes. Prosecutors opened a case against him but ultimately dismissed the case when the witnesses retracted their testimony. While Humala's supporters point to this as proof of his innocence, Humala has never frontally addressed the accusations against him and hence doubts linger in the minds of many about his role in Peru's internal armed conflict. While the Humala government has not been as aggressive in its stance vis-à-vis the judicialization process, nor has there been any progress in providing government documents that would help clarify human rights investigations, and government support of military officers accused of human rights violations remains steadfast. The attitude seems to be to avoid confrontation (perhaps to avoid showdowns with those sectors of the Left still supporting his administration) but to do nothing to fulfill this aspect of the CVR's mandate. There has been some support, however, for paying out economic reparations, which had been sorely neglected by previous governments—a nod perhaps to Humala's more left-wing supporters that is less politically charged.

Conclusion: Politics and Transitional Justice

The Peruvian case raises a number of questions for the theory and practice of transitional justice. On the face of it, Peru raises profound questions about the viability and practicality of criminal prosecutions of grave human rights violations. The "Peruvian precedent" of the Fujimori (and other important) human rights prosecutions notwithstanding, this chapter has revealed a serious paradox at the heart of Peru's transitional justice process, which I imagine is not terribly different from that experienced elsewhere.

I have examined the tensions between the universal demand for justice embedded in human rights and transitional justice discourse, and the local realities of contentious legal and political practice in postconflict Peru. I have examined how, in the context of a transition from two decades of internal armed conflict and authoritarian rule, a coalition of organizations, institutions, and individuals coalesced to propose an integral approach to transitional justice that incorporated the key elements of a universal human rights discourse: the right to truth, justice, reparation, and guarantees of nonrepetition. In this context, existing amnesty laws were overturned, special investigative units and courts set up to prosecute human rights cases, and efforts to extradite fugitives pursued, including against the former president Alberto Fujimori. This is the backstory to the 2007 extradition and 2009 conviction of Fujimori, a historic and precedent-setting event for global justice efforts.

But analysis of transitional justice in Peru since the Fujimori verdict reveals a reconfiguration of local power in which powerful elites, both civilian and military, have joined forces in an attempt to derail transitional justice efforts, especially trials, in Peru. The second half of this chapter revealed some of the underlying difficulties of an ordinary justice system grappling with human rights crimes, which are extremely complex cases to prove in a court of law, not least because they often took place years or even decades earlier and evidence and witnesses may be difficult to gather. Beyond these essential but mundane capacity issues, I have documented the constellation of conservative forces that have (re)emerged to challenge the legitimacy of criminal prosecutions; question the motives of human rights activists, victims, and judicial operators involved in these processes; and assert a discourse portraying the military as victims of "political persecution." Indeed, this new constellation of forces has contributed to undermining Peru's judicialization efforts.

The coalition of forces supporting an accountability agenda in Peru has not been routed completely. The pro-accountability coalition has rallied at key moments, for example in a massive national and international effort to nullify Garcia's 2010 amnesty law, or to challenge a Supreme Court sentence in 2012 overturning key provisions in the 2010 Barrios Altos sentence (Burt 2012). However, in the context of the reconfigurations of power outlined here, and the high-powered support the impunity bloc has been able to mobilize since 2006, their ability to achieve any further progress in achieving accountability for past human rights violations has been severely compromised. The result is a judicialization process that has been emasculated, with cases choking in an overburdened prosecutors' office, long-delayed trials giving real meaning to the axiom that "justice delayed is justice denied," and courts handing down highly questionable sentences. This may be impunity by another name.

This brings us back full circle to the question of the role of politics in transitional justice. Powerful forces seem to have conspired to prevent justice, perhaps indefinitely. I don't think this is necessarily the case, though. No theorist of transitional justice predicted that more than fifteen years later, Argentina would declare its amnesty laws unconstitutional and begin prosecuting state agents in 2005—twenty years after the transition to democracy—or that Uruguay, where total impunity ruled after its transition in 1985, would prosecute a former president and a former military dictator for human rights violations, even as it grapples with sharp discrepancies over whether to uphold or overturn its 1986 amnesty law. Or that Guatemala, that terrifying beautiful land of impunity, would some day put former de facto president Efraín Ríos Montt on trial for genocide. Perhaps this is real challenge for transitional justice theory: rather than the current focus on understanding the "impact" of transitional justice on "democracy" or "human rights" in an abstract way, we need to better understand, through grounded contextual and historical analysis, how politics fundamentally shapes the terrain upon which those seeking truth and justice think and act and struggle to achieve those objectives, and how others, sometimes successfully, and sometimes not, seek to obliterate it.

Notes

1. On the justice cascade, see Sikkink 2011. On trials against former heads of state, see Lutz and Reiger 2009.

2. According to the Truth and Reconciliation Commission, the Shining Path insurgent movement was responsible for the largest percentage of deaths due to violence (54%), while state security forces were responsible for approximately 34 percent of all deaths.

3. During the period of conflict, virtually all cases of human rights violations brought before the Peruvian courts were transferred to military courts, where those implicated were set free or given minimal administrative sanctions.

4. See for example the Commission for Historical Clarification in Guatemala, which published its final report "Guatemala: Memory of Silence" in 1999; and the Commission on the Truth for El Salvador, which presented its report "From Madness to Hope: The 12-Year War in El Salvador: Report of the Commission on Truth for El Salvador" in 1993. Kathryn Sikkink and Carrie Booth Walling challenge these arguments in their journal article (Sikkink and Walling 2007).

5. Many of the cases against Shining Path leaders prosecuted during the Fujimori era had to be retried, since they were found to have violated due process procedures.

6. The Inter-American Court had ruled on this case in 1997, ordering the Peruvian state to investigate, prosecute, and punish those responsible, but the 1995 amnesty law shielded the presumed perpetrators from prosecution. The case was reopened in Peru under the aegis of the special human rights system. The 2006 verdict was upheld on appeal in 2008.

7. This section draws on a previous article of mine (Burt 2009).

8. This was the second ruling in the extradition request. The first ruling, handed down by Judge Orlando Álvarez in July 2007, was overturned on appeal. Extradition was granted for four cases of human rights violations and five other cases involving usurpation of authority, corruption, and related charges, a small number compared to the sixty cases for which extradition was sought by the Peruvian government. By the rules of the extradition treaty between Peru and Chile, Fujimori can be prosecuted only for the cases for which extradition was approved. For any new charges to be filed and prosecuted in a court of law, the Peruvian government would have to request approval by the Chilean Supreme Court. To date, only one additional case—the use of state funds to purchase the editorial lines of the tabloid press (*prensa chicha*)—has extradition been sought and approved. "Fujimori a juicio por financiar 'prensa chica' con fondos públicos," *La República*, November 14, 2012.

9. The remains of the body of one student, Luis Enrique Ortiz Perea, and the partial remains of four others, were located one year later. The other five bodies remain missing.

10. In Peruvian law, *autoría mediata* is attributed to those who have dominion over an "organized power apparatus" and thus have the power to order and direct the individual members of that apparatus to commit crimes or, in this case, human rights violations. There is no equivalent to *autoría mediata* in English-speaking legal systems. It is sometimes translated as "perpetration by means" of an organized apparatus of power or other instrument (Ambos 2011; Burt 2009).

11. Fujimori was found guilty in all the other cases brought against him. However, by Peruvian law criminal sentences are not cumulative; Fujimori must serve the longest prison sentence of twenty-five years. According to Peruvian law,

Jo-Marie Burt

those convicted of aggravated kidnapping cannot apply for normal reductions in prison terms and could be considered for such a reduction only after serving three-quarters of their term, nor can they receive the benefit of a presidential pardon.

12. Six key organizations litigate human rights cases in Peru and have contributed to the collection and analysis of data for the Human Rights Trials in Peru project: the Asociación Pro-Derechos Humanos (APRODEH); the Instituto de Defensa Legal (IDL); the Comisión de Derechos Humanos (COMISEDH); Paz y Esperanza, the Comisión Episcopal de Acción Social (CEAS); the Federación Ecuménica para la Paz (FEDEPAZ); and the Women's Rights Defense Group (DEMUS). The project was launched with the generous support of the Latin American Studies Association "Otros Saberes" Initiative and the Latin American Program of the Open Society Foundation. A website featuring the project's findings and publications can be viewed at http://rightsperu.net/.

13. The trial mapping project in Peru, which developed in close association with similar projects in neighboring Argentina and Chile, is described more fully in Collins, Balardini, and Burt 2012.

14. Interviews with Public Prosecutor Luz del Carmen Ibañez, Lima, June 2010, and Dr. Gloria Cano, a human rights lawyer representing the victims in this case, Washington, D.C., March 28, 2011.

15. The majority of these are members of the Peruvian security forces. A handful of those convicted are civilians, including former president Alberto Fujimori, his security advisor Vladimiro Montesinos (though he was a military officer in the 1970s), and ten members of the self-defense committees, which were civilian militias that operated under the legal control of the armed forces.

16. Argentina statistics are from Centro de Estudios Legales y Sociales 2013; Peru statistics are from Human Rights Trials in Peru 2013.

17. Ten of those found guilty were members of self-defense committees, civil militias formed by peasants seeking to protect their communities from Shining Path incursions, who came under the legal control of the Peruvian armed forces during the Fujimori government.

18. In one important case, however, the Court ruled in the case of Los Laureles that forced disappearances is a permanent, ongoing crime, presenting a challenge to the Plenary Agreement mentioned earlier. This contradiction has not yet been resolved in Peruvian jurisprudence (Rivera Paz 2011).

19. International human rights organizations questioned the validity of this argument; see the letter presented to the Peruvian Supreme Court by Human Rights Watch and signed by several international law experts, available at http://derechoshumanos.pe/2010/06/organizaciones-internacionales-presentan-analisis-sobre-la-interpretacion-vinculante-del-delito-de-desaparicion-forzada-realizada-por-la-corte-suprema/.

20. *Perú.21*, October 9, 2006.

21. *Perú.21*, October 8, 2008.

22. *La Razón*, June 13, 2010.

References

Ambos, Kai. 2011. "The Fujimori Judgment: A President's Responsibility for Crimes Against Humanity." *Journal of International Criminal Justice* 9:137–58.

Amnesty International. 2007. "Fujimori Case: The Supreme Court of Justice Must Comply with Obligations of International Law Contracted by Chile." AI Index: AMR 22/006/2007. August.

———. 2009. "Peru: The Conviction of Fujimori—A Milestone in the Fight for Justice." April 7.

Barrios Altos Case. 2001. Inter-American Court. Judgment of March 14. Ser. C. No. 83. http://www1.umn.edu/humanrts/iachr/C/75-ing.html.

Burt, Jo-Marie. 2007. *Political Violence and the Authoritarian State in Peru: Silencing Civil Society*. New York: Palgrave McMillan.

———. 2009. "Guilty as Charged: The Trial of Former Peruvian President Alberto Fujimori for Grave Violations of Human Rights." *International Journal of Transitional Justice* 3, no. 3: 384–405.

———. 2010. "1097: La nueva cara de la impunidad." *NoticiasSER*, September 9. http://www.noticiasser.pe/08/09/2010/contracorriente/en-edicion.

———. 2011. "Challenging Impunity in Domestic Courts: Human Rights Prosecutions in Latin America." In *The Transitional Justice Handbook for Latin America*, edited by Felix Reategui, 285–311. Brasília: The Brazilian Amnesty Commission, the Brazilian Ministry of Justice, and the International Center for Transitional Justice.

———. 2012. "Impunity Returns to Peru." Open Democracy, July 31. http://www.opendemocracy.net/jo-marie-burt/impunity-returns-to-peru.

Centro de Estudios Legales y Sociales. 2013. *CELS Juicios: Proceso de justicia por crimenes de lesa humanidad. Estadísticas*. April 29. http://www.cels.org.ar/blogs/estadisticas/.

Collins, Cath, Lorena Balardini, and Jo-Marie Burt. 2012. "Mapping Perpetrator Prosecutions in Latin America." *International Journal of Transitional Justice*, 1–21.

Comisión Nacional sobre la desaparición de Personas (CONADEP) National Commission on the Disappearance of Persons. 1984. "Nunca Más [Never Again]." September 20.

Defensoría del Pueblo. 2008. Informe Defensorial N 139. *A cinco años de los procesos de raparación y justicia en el Perú: Balance y desafíos de una tarea pendiente*.

Degregori, Carlos Iván. 1991. "How Difficult It Is to Be God." *Critique of Anthropology* 11, no. 3: 233–50.

El Fronton Case. 2003. "Las ejecuciones extrajudiciales en El Frontón y Lurigancho (1986)." In the Final Report of the Peruvian Truth and Reconciliation Commission. Vol. 7, 2.67.

Goldston, James. 2012. "International Justice Must Start at Home." *New York Times*, July 17.

González Cueva, Eduardo. 2006. "The Peruvian Truth and Reconciliation Commission and the Challenge of Impunity." In *Transitional Justice in the Twenty-First Century: Beyond Truth versus Justice*, edited by Naomi Roht-Arriaza and Javier Mariezcurrena, 70–93. New York: Cambridge University Press.

Gorriti Ellenbogen, Gustavo. 1999. *The Shining Path: The Millenarian War in Peru*. Chapel Hill: University of North Carolina Press.

Human Rights Trials in Peru. 2013. *Estadísticas y Gráficos sobre las sentencias en casos de graves violaciones de derechos humanos*. April 29. http://www.rightsperu.net.

Human Rights Watch (HRW). 2005. "Chile: Flawed Decision Not to Extradite Fujimori: Judge's Ruling Ignores Key Evidence." July 11.

———. 2009. "Peru: Fujimori Verdict a Rights Victory." April 7.

International Federation for Human Rights (IFHR). 2007. "Fujimori: Extradition to Peru or Trial in Chile."

La Cantuta Case. 2006. Inter-American Court of Human Rights. Judgment of November 29, 2006. http://www.corteidh.or.cr/docs/casos/articulos/seriec_162_ing.pdf.

Laplante, Lisa, and Kimberly Theidon. 2007. "Truth with Consequences: Justice and Reparations in Post-Truth Commission Peru." *Human Rights Quarterly* 29, no. 1: 228–50.

La República. 2009. "Sentencia reivindica también la memoria de víctimas de Fujimori." April 11.

Lutz, Ellen, and Caitlin Reiger, eds. 2009. *Prosecuting Heads of State*. London: Cambridge University Press.

Méndez, Juan E. 2010. "Significance of the Fujimori Trial." *American University International Law Review* 25, no. 4: 649–56.

Perú.21. 2006. "Giampetri insiste: Militares son perseguidos por la justicia." October 8.

Rivera Paz, Carlos. 2006. *Una Sentencia Histórica: La desaparición forzada de Ernesto Castillo Páez*. Lima: Instituto de Defensa Legal.

———. 2009. "Del delito permanente a la 'doctrina Hanke Velasco': La desaparición forzada en las sentencias de la Sala Penal Nacional." *Instituto de Defensa Legal*, October 29.

———. 2011. "La desaparación forzada es un delito permanente." *Instituto de Defensa Legal*, October 5. http://lamula.pe/2011/05/10/la-desaparicion-forzada-es-un-crimen-permanente/carlosrivera.

Rivera Paz, Carlos, and Jo-Marie Burt. Forthcoming. *El proceso de justicia frente a crímenes contra los derechos humanos en el Perú*. Lima: Instituto de Defensa Legal and George Mason University.

Primera Sala Penal Especial. 2010. Corte Superior de Justicia de Lima, Sentencia en el caso Barrios Altos-Santa-Pedro Yauri. Exp. 28-2001. October.

Sala Penal Especial. 2009. Corte Suprema de Justicia, Exp. No. AV-19-2001. Sentencia Alberto Fujimori Fujimori. April 7.

Sala Penal Nacional. 2006. Corte Suprema de la República del Perú, Sentencia Caso Ernesto Castillo Páez, March 20. Exp. 111-04.

Sikkink, Kathryn. 2011. *The Justice Cascade. How Human Rights Prosecutions are Changing World Politics.* New York: W. W. Norton.

Sikkink, Kathryn, and Carrie Booth Walling. 2007. "The Impact of Human Rights Trials in Latin America." *Journal of Peace Research* 44, no. 4: 427–45.

Stern, Steve, ed. 1998. *Shining and Other Paths: War and Society in Peru, 1980–1995.* Durham, NC: Duke University Press.

Teitel, Ruti. 2000. *Transitional Justice.* London: Oxford University Press, 2002.

V Pleno Jurisdiccional de las Salas Penales Permanentes y Transitorias. 2009. *Acuerdo Plenario No. 9-2009/CJ-116 Concordancia Jurisprudencial. Asunto: Desaparación Forzada.* November 13.

Youngers, Coletta. 2003. *Violencia política y la sociedad civil en el Perú.* Lima: Instituto de Estudios Peruanos.

Zalaquett, José. 1993. "Introduction." In *The Report of the Chilean National Commission on Truth and Reconciliation*, 6–17. Notre Dame, IN: University of Notre Dame Press.

Part III

New Horizons

7

The Aporias of New Technologies for Human Rights Activism

FUYUKI KURASAWA

Introduction

In the arena of human rights politics, we are currently witnessing the confluence of two major developments. On the one hand, global civil society is continuing to expand and thicken across the world, an essential component of which are the webs of social movements and nongovernmental organizations (NGOs) increasingly utilizing discourses of human rights or explicitly identifying as human rights based institutions. Hence, advocacy grounded in the denunciation of the specific, local manifestations of injustices and mass violations of universal socioeconomic and civil-political rights, or yet again, in struggles to protect and locally realize universal notions of global justice, has become a defining characteristic of civil societies at the national and transnational scales (Falk 2000; Keck and Sikkink 1998; Kurasawa 2007; LSE 2001).[1] On the other hand, the consolidation of the Internet and, more specifically, the emergence and ubiquity of Web 2.0 and mobile technologies—namely, so-called social media such as Twitter, Facebook, and YouTube accessed via computers and smartphones—have contributed to redefining how human rights activism is practiced today, above all because of the distinctively and properly *social* features of social media: their interactivity and dialogical character (which contrasts with the top-down, unidirectional structure of the conventional

broadcast paradigm); their user-generated content; their institutional configuration as decentralized and frequently self-organized networks; the instanta-
neity of the circulation of information among users, due to their digital and
even viral nature; and their integration into portable devices, which are themselves employed as tools mediating social interactions (Burgess and Green
2009; Shirky 2008; Surman and Reilly 2003). Similarly, these technologies
sustain the paradox of universality and specificity discussed in this book, for
events filtered through social media need to be rooted in local circumstances
to gain traction globally (specificity of circumstance tending to increase online
audience engagement). Yet these events simultaneously require such global
engagement in order to be considered newsworthy at the local level; by going
viral, a local situation covered through social media becomes validated as significant to its original public.[2]

The interface of these two tendencies produces what can be termed "representational activism," forms of visually based practices of bearing witness to
human rights violations or struggles, which emphasize the recording, broadcasting via the Internet, and publicizing through social media of material documenting such violations or struggles in the form of still or moving images
(photographs, maps, graphics, illustrations, as well as video footage) that circulate in national and global civil societies. For representational activism, such
material performs two principal functions. First, in a more formalized sense,
it serves as a device of legal prosecution, since it is frequently introduced as
evidence against perpetrators in international courts and tribunals, and thus
officially sanctioned as admissible by such institutions.[3] Second, in an informal manner, this same material can operate as a tool of denunciation in public
spheres, helping to mobilize public opinion against certain situations or in
support of particular demands through concerted human rights campaigns
aimed at moral and political suasion of states, private corporations, and international organizations.[4]

Beyond the realm of human rights *sensu stricto*, the effects of social media
on political activism have generated much academic and popular debate. For
heuristic purposes, we can regroup literature into two salient tendencies that
structure the terms of such debate: techno-idealism and its skeptical counter-
part. Techno-idealists have put forth three sorts of claims. First, they argue that
cyberactivism opens new forms of and avenues for politics, which offer considerable advantages when compared to previous technologies of political
communication. According to them, social media enables self-organization,
the coordination of action or of a concerted campaign among activists and
concerned citizens without the need for large-scale organizational structures
or formal institutional mechanisms. Due to the speed at which information

travels through them, Web 2.0 technologies also permit the rapid mobilization of publics, with almost-instantaneous responses to emerging events or situations, or yet again, quick adaptation to changing circumstances (including a change in tactics). The techno-idealist paradigm asserts that cyberactivism introduces the possibility of more effective, "results-driven" modes of political struggle, for it makes possible targeted campaigns tailored for specific issues and directed toward particular causes, or the targeting of a given actor (a state or corporation) through the visible and vocal expression of public opinion channeled via social media. In addition, the latter are said to offer an unprecedented reach or impact for political activism, since they can be utilized to contact large numbers of followers or viewers, as well as to expand constituencies and audiences receptive to a group's message or general ideology (Rheingold 2002; Shirky 2008).

Second, techno-idealism believes that the spread of social media and of hardware platforms running Web 2.0 technologies could produce a condition of total visibility or absolute exposure, since the ubiquity and portability of recording and broadcasting devices (e.g., mobile phones with cameras and laptop computers) signifies that everyone becomes a potential eyewitness to events or injustices by, for example, uploading a video to YouTube or posting an alert on Facebook or Twitter (Burgess and Green 2009; Gregory 2010). This, in turn, is said to dissuade prospective perpetrators from committing acts of situational or structural violence, as well as to facilitate the collection and circulation of evidence if such acts are committed (and thus assist in the prosecution of perpetrators). Third, techno-idealists assert that the Internet, and social media more particularly, have created a new model of broadcasting that both bypasses conventional communicative intermediaries (principally, the mass media) to directly reach publics and is bottom-up, interactive, and intersubjective in character, thus breaking with older, top-down broadcasting practices based on the passive reception of information by audiences (Jenkins 2006; Kanter and Fine 2010; Pantic 2006; Varnelis 2008).

Although less common in popular and academic discourse, techno-skepticism forms a significant countercurrent that has come to prominence in response to the failures—whether real or perceived—of cyberactivism and social media–driven political campaigns in the last few years (ranging from the misnamed "Twitter Revolution" in Iran to hacker groups such as Anonymous). Essentially, techno-skeptics refute or put into question the assertions of their utopian peers on several grounds, not the least of which is doubting the capacity of web-fueled activism to generate lasting and systemic political transformation at national and global scales. Certain techno-skeptical claims focus on the fact that Web 2.0 activism is strictly suited to low-intensity political engagement, demanding a limited commitment and involvement temporally and ideologically; this so-called digital slacktivism, presumably done in the comfort of one's home or sitting on one's couch, involves gestures such as retweeting a Twitter message, "liking" a Facebook entry, or signing an online petition. Other techno-skeptics have pushed the argument further by maintaining that such forms of political engagement actually detract from more effective and large-scale political struggle or campaigns, which are believed to require mass mobilization in public spaces and high-intensity commitment to a specific cause or injustice (Gladwell 2010; May 2002; Morozov 2009; Morozov 2010).

While both techno-idealism and techno-skepticism put forth compelling ideas, the aim of this chapter is not to take a position on either side of this dispute in order to determine whether to fully embrace or reject Internet- and social media–related human rights activism. This sort of approach, while rhetorically appealing, is at variance with the kind of critical pragmatism being defended here, whereby the effects of such technologically mediated activism are situationally dependent and thus assessed less by uniform pronouncements than by the ways in which actors operating in specific local contexts adapt universal web-based and digital tools for their particular purposes.

Accordingly, this chapter intends to inject a note of ambivalence into the debate by contending that representational activism introduce a series of aporias—that is to say, irresolvable contradictions or insurmountable tensions that are constitutive of this sort of activism itself. Hence, the question becomes not whether aporias can be averted, nor whether Web 1.0 and 2.0 technologies should be employed for contemporary human rights advocacy and struggles— since they already are pervasive—but how to develop practices of representational activism that are fully cognizant of these aporias and attempting to work through them when pursuing human rights causes around the world.

The first part of the chapter proposes a brief overview of some of the dilemmas created by the human rights actors' utilization of visual technologies of representation and communication over the course of the twentieth century, in order to historicize current debates as well as reposition the changing configuration of human rights politics, in the wake of the advent of social media, within a broader, less presentist context. The rest of the chapter is devoted to a consideration of the aporias introduced by new mobile and web-based tools for representational activism, beginning in the second part with an analysis of the tensions introduced when human rights advocacy groups enter into a field of political struggle with powerful governmental and corporate institutions over the representation and diffusion of images, as well as the public degradation of the standing of and trust in digitally based visual material

Fuyuki Kurasawa

as truthful reproduction of reality. In the third part of the chapter, I consider how the growing dependence on new technological platforms is introducing unintended and unforeseen consequences for human rights activists, whether exposing social media users to greater surveillance, compromising victims' well-being, supporting an exhibitionist logic of the spectacle, or contributing to the public invisibility of particular instances of human rights violations. Finally, the fourth part assesses the aporias of analytical and political reductionism that accompany Web 2.0 and mobile technologies, in such a manner that displaces nonrepresentationally oriented modes of politics. All in all, then, the chapter aims to provoke a critical reflection about how such seemingly universal and uniform technologies are transforming human rights politics in order to foster a working through of the constitutive tensions thereby introduced in localized settings.

Historicizing Representational Activism

However tempting it may be to interpret the aporias created by the incorporation of Web 1.0 and 2.0 technologies into human rights politics as unique or unprecedented, we should remember that such aporias have lengthy historical pedigrees. Indeed, the twentieth century was marked by spirited debates about the incredibly rapid and enthusiastic adoption of new means of representation and vehicles of mass communication by human rights groups, whether we think of photography, documentary film, newspaper and magazine advertising, or television; as such, social media are but the latest in a long line of communicative innovations to provoke discussion. This is so because all of these technologies have been characterized by their contested representational nature, which is structured by two ever-present yet opposite tendencies: their being means of reproducing reality with exactitude, in a realist or objectivist understanding of representation; and their being devices of artistic creation whose ties to reality may be jettisoned entirely, in an expressivist or subjectivist understanding of reality.[5] These two tendencies have always existed at the heart of public deliberation about the utilization of means of representation of human rights situations, thus complicating the status of such means as both reliable and effective political tools.

While several instances of this contested character could be given, two of them are particularly interesting for our purposes since they concern localized uses of visual technologies for major human rights causes during the first decades of the twentieth century and are prescient in their anticipation of debates about the representational standing of images in our age. The first noteworthy case is that of the Congo Reform Association (CRA), a group of British- and American-based activists who, between 1904 and 1913, publicly denounced the atrocities committed by the colonial regime of King Leopold II of Belgium in the Congo Free State. The CRA is considered to be the first photographically based international human rights campaign since it relied on the extensive use of photographic evidence to document the abuses against the Congolese people in order to inform Anglo-American publics and mobilize ordinary citizens against King Leopold's rule (Sliwinski 2006). Photographs of maimed Congolese adults and children, whose hands had been cut off by Congo Free State troops, were widely published and reproduced in pamphlets, books such as Mark Twain's satirical *King Leopold's Soliloquy*, and displayed as slides during lantern lectures given by members of the CRA in various cities across the United Kingdom and North America (Twain 1905).

At the same time, the prominence and success of the CRA's actions triggered a visually based countercampaign on the part of King Leopold's regime, which began publishing a series of propagandist periodicals titled "La vérité sur le Congo" ("The Truth about the Congo") in order to discredit the CRA's claims about the Congo Free State by putting into question its photographic material. For instance, a doctored photograph of E. D. Morel, one of the leaders of the CRA, depicted him holding a rifle in a field in the Congo with a dead wild boar a few feet away; the intention was to portray Morel as having deliberately killed the boar, since the Belgian regime claimed that the Congolese subjects captured in the CRA's images had their hands bitten off by wild boars rather than being maimed by colonial soldiers (Grant 2001, 44).

Another significant case for our purposes centered around the Russian famine of 1921–23, which affected between 20 and 25 million people in Southern Russian and Ukraine. In the later months of 1921 and 1922, a controversy erupted in the British public sphere when a conservative and populist newspaper, the *Daily Express*, launched a sustained campaign of criticism of the claims made about the Russian famine by the Save the Children Fund (SCF), one of the major humanitarian and children's rights organizations involved in coming to the aid of the famine's victims. In a set of articles, *Daily Express* journalists raised doubts about the accuracy of reports describing the famine's severity and scale, and thus about the legitimacy of the SCF's appeals for donations by the British public to assist Russians in need.[6] Bolstering the *Daily Express*'s campaign, a January 1922 Pathé Gazette newsreel titled "Charity Begins at Home!" contained footage of well-stocked shop windows and seemingly well-fed Russians, a newsreel that was screened in cinemas prior to feature-length films. In turn, the newspaper used stills from this footage as further evidence that the Russian famine was exaggerated or nonexistent, with

Fuyuki Kurasawa

such stills positioned as ultimate proof of the dubious nature of the emergency.[7] The SCF's response was swift: it commissioned and dispatched a photographer to Russia to shoot footage and take pictures of the famine and its victims— footage that became the documentary film *Famine: The Russian Famine of 1921*, widely screened across Britain and intended to provide a visual record to disprove the *Daily Express*'s claims.[8] This is to say that the debate over the famine's very existence largely was conducted via images in the British public sphere.

Aside from being visually anchored, what matters about the controversies around the Congo Free State and the Russian famine is that they presaged three issues whose relevance persists for representational activism: the contestation of the evidentiary status of images and their standing as objective or accurate reflections of reality; the presence of contradictory or irreconcilable interpretations of such images by various groups and institutions; and the selection or manipulation of visual material to suit the purposes of concerned parties and specific actors.

Despite the presence of such debates throughout the twentieth century, there is no doubt that the first decades of the twenty-first century have produced a reconfiguration of the interface between visuality and the global politics of human rights in at least three notable respects. First, the social ubiquity of Web 1.0 and 2.0 technological platforms in the Euro-American world has spurred human rights–related NGOs and social movements to harness the potential of these platforms in innovative ways to meet organizational or political objectives. Most obvious among these uses is the now virtually obligatory Facebook pages and Twitter feeds supplied by these actors, with the comparative influence of each being gauged by their numbers of online followers; regular communication with and mobilization of constituencies thus becomes much easier and cost-efficient than in the past. Although these pages and feeds facilitate conventional appeals for donations, they also have created opportunities for the emergence of novel fund-raising tools, such as so-called human rights Twestivals through which Twitter users are encouraged to meet up in person for a day in selected cities around the world to raise money for a particular human rights cause (Twestival 2011). Moreover, these same NGOs and social movements regularly post and broadcast online visual evidence of severe human rights violations, often bypassing conventional media by collecting and disseminating such material themselves in the hope of reaching the general public.

For instance, in one of the most highly publicized human rights causes of recent times, Amnesty International published on its website, in August 2007, photographs of military equipment being flown into Darfur by Sudanese government aircraft. These actions directly violated the peace agreements signed at the time and undermined the claims of Omar al-Bashir, the Sudanese president, who had denied such government involvement in assisting the Janjaweed militias' attacks on Darfuri civilians (Amnesty International 2007). Online mapping and geotagging software, such as that offered via Google Earth, have inspired particularly interesting efforts. Staying with the situation in Darfur, the United States Holocaust Memorial Museum's website has created interactive, searchable maps of the region, with clickable locations that expand to reveal recorded testimonials from victims, photographs of destroyed and damaged villages, as well as time-lapsed satellite images tracing the damage done to these villages over time (USHMM 2009).

The second major development of the last decade concerns the trickling downward of visual technologies for the reproduction of reality and their increasing portability, which makes these technologies adaptable to a variety of local settings. Indeed, a dominant trend has been the mass incorporation of photographic and video recording devices in all kinds of consumer and personal electronics products, ranging from cell phones with cameras to laptops with webcams and compact digital video cameras. The multiplication of such recording devices has meant that the practice of collecting evidence of human rights violations or advocating in favor of a human rights cause by members of the general public has been popularized, appearing to many to be a mere extension of the now commonplace habit of visually documenting one's everyday activities. As a direct result of the diffusion and accessibility of these portable cameras, the production of images of human rights issues has become much more decentralized and flexible than in the past; whereas the prohibitive cost, technical complexity, and sheer bulk and weight of earlier cameras limited their flexibility and made them the province of professionals (mainly journalists and filmmakers), ordinary citizens are now regularly employing them for such purposes and adapting their uses to the specificity of local circumstances. Furthermore, there has been a proliferation of websites facilitating the uploading and broadcasting of visual material about human rights, from generalized ones such as YouTube and Vimeo to dedicated or specialized ones such as Demotix (a citizen journalism website that frequently features human rights–related images) and the website of Witness (an NGO advocating the use of video for human rights campaigns).[9]

Similarly, the spread of Internet-enabled mobile communication devices (i.e., cell phones and laptop computers) accessing Web 2.0 services and running certain software has stimulated the invention of new forms of human rights activism on the ground during an event, where victims or eyewitnesses can immediately transmit photographs and live video feeds to audiences and media organizations. Skype, Twitter, Facebook, Flickr, and Ustream are merely

Fuyuki Kurasawa

some of the better known of the constantly changing and proliferating tools utilized for such purposes, often in conjunction with one another; for example, a tweet will contain a link to a live Ustream feed or a series of uploaded photographs on Flickr or Facebook. Accordingly, if it is imprudent to follow the hyperbole of certain breathless Western journalists and analysts who declared that the Iranian protests during the summer of 2009 or the "Arab Spring" of 2011 constituted "Twitter Revolutions"—a technologically determinist argument that perceives Twitter as a causal factor or independent variable—it would be equally problematic to simply dismiss the current role of social media as vital tools to be harnessed by representational activism.

Third, this same representational activism has been transformed by the speed at which visual material about human rights can now circulate and be reproduced, with images instantaneously traveling around the world and being downloadable or viewable by large numbers of people. Apart from dealing with the fact that most geographical borders are rendered irrelevant with regard to the distribution of photographs and video, human rights actors no longer have to contend with time lags in the broadcasting and reception of images to document and strengthen their claims about human rights violations. In fact, audiences are now expecting to be provided with live or recently shot pictures of such violations as credible and "impactful" evidence in order to be prompted or convinced to pay attention and lend their support to certain human rights campaigns.

Together, the new applications of web-based technologies, the popularity and portability of image-producing software and hardware, and the speed of circulation of visual material are transforming the ways in which human rights politics are being performed. At the same time, these three developments introduce a set of aporias for representational activism that have barely begun to be reflection upon.

Entering the Terrain of Representational Politics

The first aporia to be noted here is created by the fact that social movements and NGOs are engaging in Internet-fueled struggles about public awareness of human rights violations on an uneven terrain, occupied by institutions with considerably greater reach and resources (namely, states and private corporations). Accordingly, these same institutions can deploy a variety of communicative and representational tactics that directly counter the campaigns of human rights groups and even aim to discredit such groups.

Among the crudest of these tactics is governmental censorship and monitoring of the Internet—something that is achieved not by avoiding the latest technologies but by exploiting and mining them intensively. Thus, in many parts of the world, states block or filter access to the Internet and cellular phone networks while closely scrutinizing online traffic and social media activity related to human rights causes (e.g., the Chinese government with regard to Tibet, the Iranian government with regard to opposition movements, etc.), thereby severely restricting the range of possibilities for representational activism.[10] Another common strategy consists of states or corporations attempting to control the representation of a situation of mass human rights violations and monopolize its framing, which can go as far as to make alternative interpretations of it virtually impossible. In this vein, governments have sought to restrict journalistic access to certain locations and ban the taking of still or moving images in them (e.g., the requirement that reporters be embedded with units of the U.S. military during the Iraq War, or the absence of visual material from within Guantanamo Bay).[11]

Beyond censorship, the large institutional actors faced by human rights groups can utilize the Internet, and particularly social media, to manipulate visual evidence in new ways. As such, these technologies can be enlisted to produce blatantly false or highly distorted information about a certain event, by helping to circulate doctored images or deliberately misleading interpretations of such images—which can rapidly flood online platforms and become defining representations of this same event. Although communicative and representational tools have always carried the potential to be exploited for such purposes, as the historical cases described earlier make clear, these tendencies are amplified considerably by the decentralized nature of Web 2.0. The erosion of the verifiability of the credibility of sources of information, the proliferation of these sources, and the unclear "traceability" of the point of origination of information all facilitate organized, image-based campaigns of misrepresentation. Once such images become viral by being viewed, reproduced, and sent across the Internet by thousands or millions of users, it becomes difficult to discover who initially created and sent them, and more significantly, to counter whatever framing of a situation they present. Paradoxically, the globalization of these images renders their embeddedness in particular, localized settings more difficult to authenticate.

At the same time, states and private corporations can exploit social media platforms to rapidly respond to evidence presented by eyewitnesses and human rights activists, thereby broadcasting counternarratives that seek to discredit such sources or provide different explanations of images purporting to capture human rights violations. For instance, during the protests that shook Iran in

Fuyuki Kurasawa

the summer of 2009, still and moving images of a young woman shot by the Iranian Basij, Neda Agha-Soltan, "went viral" and became an icon of the so-called Green Movement. In response, the Iranian government—via bloggers as well as Twitter and Facebook users associated with it—used the Internet and mobile phone networks to circulate rumors that she had been killed by protestors or foreign agents working in Tehran.

The uneven terrain of representational politics is also one in which human rights activists are exploiting web-based and mobile platforms that have been rapidly commodified because they are colonized and appropriated by large corporations and entertainment conglomerates. Consequently, even when dispensing with a consideration of the perils of censorship and manipulation, the messages of human rights–based NGOs and social movements, as well as the images that they produce and circulate, can be completely drowned out on the Internet by the "noise" of advertising and "infotainment." One need only compare the number of views for a video of a situation of human rights abuse denounced by a particular organization on YouTube to that of the latest scandal involving a Hollywood or Bollywood star to grasp the problem of saturation and widely asymmetrical impact or clout of what is considered noteworthy on new technological platforms.[12]

Thus, in addition to making human rights actors confront the tactics of powerful institutions, being present in the realm of representational politics introduces an aporia related to the growing public suspicion of visual material in our age. Despite the existence of debates about the authenticity of images throughout the twentieth century, the invention of photography and film were meaningful inventions for activists and advocates because they were publicly perceived in the Euro-American world as unimpeachable sources of objective evidence of human rights violations. In the early decades of the last century, then, these technologies were generally perceived as trustworthy mirrors of reality that by virtue of perfectly reproducing reality were more reliable than words. As captured in the common expression "the camera does not lie," images were understood as artifacts that acted as public arbiters of truth and instruments of validation of the latter (Cosandey 1998, 32). In his satirical *King Leopold's Soliloquy*, Mark Twain could thus have the king himself lament that "[t]he kodak has been a sore calamity to us. The most powerful enemy that has confronted us, indeed. . . . the incorruptible *kodak* . . . The only witness I have encountered in my long experience that I couldn't bribe. . . . Ten thousand pulpits and ten thousand presses are saying the good word for me all the time and placidly and convincingly denying the mutilations. Then that trivial little kodak, that a child can carry in its pocket, gets up, uttering never a word, and knocks them dumb!" (Twain 1905, 39–40).

This faith in the camera's truth-telling qualities has been seriously eroded in the digital age, to the point that a virtual inversion of its previous status has taken place over time: audiences now believe that the camera (or the image) potentially always lies, that is to say that it is an unreliable witness and possible source of distortion or manipulation of reality—as much as it is a means to exactly mirror it. The availability and ease of use of digital editing software and filters for still and moving images (e.g., Photoshop and Final Cut Pro) means that large numbers of computer and mobile phone users have access to and are familiar with the altering of such images, while the practice of modifying them has become commonplace, for instance, through the editing of a video to be uploaded onto YouTube or the touching up of a photograph to be posted on one's Facebook page.

Equally significant is the way in which digital technology enables a decoupling or severing of the relation of correspondence between an image's textual signifiers (the words used to explain the reality being represented) and its visual signifieds (the reality thereby represented), to the extent that a picture of a particular event may be discursively resignified to purportedly represent an utterly different event. Hence, either deliberately (by aiming to deceive audiences through visual hoaxes) or incidentally (by misunderstanding what is being portrayed), captions or didactic text accompanying an image can completely recontextualize it by claiming that it represents something that bears no resemblance to the original situation it captured. Once such a redeployment of meaning is initiated, social media facilitates the viral spread of such false or mistakenly resignified images, which exponentially become further entrenched in online public discourse as more and more persons view, comment, and recirculate them (by reposting them to their Facebook pages, retweeting them, etc.).[13] Another form of decontextualization can occur when NGOs or social movements employ images of a specific human rights incident or campaign as visual signifiers of general human rights causes, since this drive toward representational universality may rupture the link between a picture and its specific points of temporal and spatial reference—thus inadvertently undermining the reliability of visual material as evidentiary indicators of localized events or circumstances.

Cumulatively, these practices are changing audiences' relation to the viewing of visual material of all kinds, including photographs and videos of human rights abuses. Skeptical publics are looking at such material to make sense of it and decipher what it signifies yet also putting into doubt its veracity and accuracy. Consequently, the task for representational activism becomes not merely one of distributing images and exposing the public to them but also to authenticate them as reliable signifiers of a particular event or situation, to

Fuyuki Kurasawa

demonstrate that human rights–oriented social movements and NGOs are authoritative sources of evidentiary information, and to cultivate audiences that can rely on the claims made by these groups.[14]

The Unintended Consequences of New Technologies

Representational activism's reliance on Internet- and mobile-based technologies has created at least four types of unanticipated and inadvertent aporias, which can produce outcomes that fundamentally contradict the political intentions of human rights actors: (1) increased entanglement into mechanisms of surveillance, (2) eroding the standing of victims, (3) advancing the exhibitionist character of the spectacle, and (4) contributing to the public invisibility of certain events. Each of these should be discussed in turn.

Foremost among these unintended consequences are activists and eyewitnesses being ensnared into denser networks of surveillance through the very technologies that they are employing. Amidst the discussions of cyberwarfare and cyberactivism pursued by Internet hackers acting as individuals or loose collectives, what is frequently overlooked is the fact that many of the online mechanisms and strategies initially developed to spy on states or corporations, or to undermine their computer networks, are being redeployed in a manner that turns them against human rights activists on the ground. Their very dependence on universally available social media platforms—which are indispensable for the purposes of organization, mobilization, and information-sharing—is precisely what makes them locally vulnerable. Aside from having their communications monitored, intercepted, or disrupted via viruses or coordinated denial of service attacks, groups and persons involved in human rights struggles become traceable themselves. This is so because their identities and locations can be tracked through a variety of means (the Internet service providers or mobile telephone networks that they use, the IP addresses assigned to their computers, as well as the GPS capabilities of their cellular phones, etc.), which have enabled crackdowns by authoritarian governments on human rights activists and oppositional figures in many countries (Comninos 2011, 9–14).[15]

Another set of unintended consequences to be accentuated by representational activism's utilization of the new information and mobile technologies consists of the possible compromising of victims of human rights abuses, which takes two forms. First, NGOs' and social movements' release and diffusion on the Internet of images exposing such abuses are perceived as hostile acts by the states perpetrating them, often prompting governments to take countermeasures against sociopolitical groups and the media outlets broadcasting the photographs or video footage supplied to them. Chief among these steps is expulsion from or denial of entry into the relevant country, which can worsen the circumstances of victimized populations by reducing the presence of eyewitnesses to observe and document mass human rights violations, limiting media coverage of them, and preventing access to those needing humanitarian assistance.[16]

Second, the circulation and large-scale distribution of pictures of human rights abuses facilitated by the Internet and mobile phone networks introduce numerous ethical questions about the dignity of those portrayed in them. Regardless of the fact that it is sometimes impossible for photographers and filmmakers to obtain the consent of victims captured in their images (notably in cases of mass violence), the public display of such subjects' suffering and its repeated viewing by strangers may be experienced by them as a second form of violation, a revictimization of sorts. The risks of this rise steeply when a localized and circumstantially based image of a victim is transformed into a digital icon of the events in which he or she is involved and thereby is universalized by "going viral," or when such an image is decontextualized in order to be exploited as a generic representation of human rights abuses (for fundraising purposes or public awareness of an NGO or social movement's campaign, most frequently).

The third inadvertent effect of representational activism's dependence on new technologies is associated with the prospect of falling into the trap of the conventional paradigm of visual exposure, according to which the threat of visually documenting and publicly revealing large-scale human rights violations serves to deter potential perpetrators of such violations. For most of the twentieth century, this paradigm focused much civil society activity about human rights around the slogan "The Whole World Is Watching," since bearing witness was believed to apply moral pressure to guard against grave abuses of these rights ("shaming through showing"), or at the very least to supply evidence to prosecute those perpetrating them or take military action against them.

While this remains so in several instances, the ubiquity of Web 1.0 and 2.0 technologies has also precipitated a shift toward a new visual paradigm, which inverts its predecessor's assumptions about deterrence through shaming (Keenan 2004, 445–47). In this new worldview, that of the exhibitionist spectacle, exposure and broadcast of human rights violations on a national or global scale via the Internet and social media platforms as well as traditional media sources are sought after and act as incentives to commit these violations. Indeed, to reformulate the anarchist motto, the camera becomes an instrument

Fuyuki Kurasawa

of propaganda by the visually depicted deed, since the online circulation and viewing of images of large-scale violence becomes a means to advance the perpetrators' objectives: to strike fear in the targeted populations, to incite or recruit followers, to demoralize the enemy, and so on. This is the essential representational tactic that underpinned both Al Qaeda's World Trade Center attacks in New York City and the U.S. military's Shock and Awe campaign in Iraq (Retort 2006), two counterbalancing events intended to be perceived as geopolitical strikes yet just as importantly as spectacles. Hence, the covert nature of human rights abuses has been supplanted, in many instances, by an exhibitionist logic seeking not to hide them but, on the contrary, to amplify their transmission in order to have them acquire online viral status. One could even go so far as to contend that, in certain cases, these abuses would not take place without the presence of cameras and the publicization via social media that such a presence affords.

Fourth, the use and power of social media may well unintentionally marginalize mass human rights violations that do not enter into representational activism's purview. In our age, the aforementioned ubiquity of cameras and their habitual usage in social life sustains an illusion of visual totalization, namely, the belief that all human rights violations can be recorded and broadcast—and thus, that we have reached a technological and sociopolitical moment where nothing escapes the camera's gaze (and, by extension, the public's attention). Furthermore, human rights actors' dependence on the Internet and social media platforms to publicize human rights abuses creates the conditions under which instances of such abuses not featured via these technologies are likely to disappear from public view and thus fail to have a social existence in the Euro-American world.[17]

The public invisibility of certain human rights violations can manifest itself in various ways. A situation can be unrepresented due to the absence of eyewitnesses on the ground, whether survivors, journalists, or human rights activists able to film or photograph, or because of the capacity of perpetrating state institutions to prevent images from being taken or block their broadcast. In addition, an event can remain publicly invisible despite its being captured by cameras, if diffusion of still or moving pictures of it is limited or nonexistent; while footage or photos of this event may well be available, human rights or media organizations may decide not to broadcast them if it is determined to be less significant (because deemed to be of negligible interest to an NGO's constituency or to attract few "eyeballs" to television newscasts or newspaper websites). Yet selectivity equally applies to the reception of a particular case of human rights abuses by Western audiences, which, regardless of the coverage that activists and the media devote to it, may well ignore or remain indifferent to it. Consequently, while images of this case may well be present in public spheres, their circulation and impact on public opinion can remain limited; a story or campaign illustrated with a plethora of pictures can "die" or be buried amid the flood of other items when, failing to capture the attention of viewers and Internet or mobile phone users, it is not sufficiently "crowdsourced" by being retweeted or reposted on Facebook.[18]

A grave human rights violation can also be publicly invisible due to its unrepresentable character, meaning the impossibility or difficulty of visually conveying and thus doing justice—in both the literal and figurative senses of that phrase—to that of which it consists. As such, an image fails to fully reproduce the experiential dimensions of an event, transmitting to Western audiences traces or approximations of the then-and-there of situational violence. Likewise, this same image cannot evoke the situational violence that underpins most human rights abuses by visually symbolizing the global injustices that lie at the root of such abuses; the institutional and structural factors that directly or indirectly cause many violations of socioeconomic and civil-political rights in the world are left outside of the camera's lens. Limit-experiences and their systemic sources are excesses that by virtue of existing beyond the visual frame remain invisible.

The public invisibility that can result from or be worsened by Web 1.0 and 2.0 technologies points to the need for representational activism to tread cautiously when designing its campaigns and struggles around such platforms. Indeed, the fact that a situation of human rights abuses is socially and visually invisible can make both its legal inscription and public recognition as an injustice more difficult. Given the aforementioned evidentiary weight of images, it becomes arduous for activists to constitute an event that is unrepresented or unrepresentable as an object of juridical and political discourse, a crime to be institutionally prosecuted or publicly denounced. Although the absence of photographs or video footage of human rights violations can hamper their entering into the field of legality by being pursued as cases by national and international courts, the lack of social media traction may also stand as an obstacle to their occupying a space in public discourse that can mobilize civil society groups, concerned citizens, and politicians within Euro-American societies.

The Perils of Reductionism

The popularity of Internet and mobile technologies among representational activists engaged in human rights struggles generates another set of aporias, related to what could be termed analytical reductionism. Paraphrasing McLuhan's famous dictum, if the medium is the message (McLuhan 1994), then these technological platforms' privileging of speed and brevity of communication leads, de facto, to a simplification of analysis of human rights situations. In other words, the technical and operational requirements of the platforms partially determine the contents of what is communicated by human rights–based NGOs and social movements, whose emphases become twofold: to provide rapid and frequent textual and visual updates about particular situations to online and mobile followers, and to do so in a manner that is concise (with the 140-character maximum length of non-URL tweets or the limited length of most YouTube videos illustrating this latter point). These are not only objective requirements of the communicative form of social media but are also circumstances prompted by the expectations of audiences habituated to quick, constant, and brief alerts about human rights–related events rather than long-form explanations or descriptions of them.

While such features of digital and mobile communications offer tremendous advantages over their earlier equivalents, they also limit opportunities for detailed analyses of human rights violations, which cannot be fitted into the constraints of the social media genre. Hence, since they involve a multiplicity of causal factors, such complex emergencies and conflicts at the root of most human rights situations today cannot be neatly "summed up" in a tweet or Facebook posting with an image or a short video link.[19] Moreover, detailed studies of the systemic causes of human rights abuses, and particularly debilitating modes of structural violence present in most of the world (gender-based domination, extreme poverty related to the operations of global capitalism, and the like), are not amenable to being translated into Web 2.0-ready formats; thus, representational activism's reliance on these communicative formats may inadvertently skew it away from providing structurally oriented and contextualizing explanations of the abuses against which it is campaigning and the issues that it is promoting.

The tendency toward analytical reductionism encourages human rights actors to engage in simplified explanations, which can render aforementioned complex emergencies into unidimensional moral tales that attribute responsibility according to a binary logic of victim and perpetrator. However, ambiguous situations, where moral and political responsibility cannot be distributed along such a neatly dichotomous structure, are difficult to render through practices of representational activism communicated via Internet and mobile platforms. To take but one instance, in the aftermath of the Rwandan genocide in 1994, several human rights and humanitarian NGOs (along with media organizations) illustrated the refugee crisis spawned by the genocide with images of refugee camps in the border regions of countries adjacent to Rwanda (Zaire, Tanzania, Uganda, etc.). In these images, the refugees were described through accompanying captions or presumed by viewers to be survivors fleeing the genocide and thus symbolically constituted as victims of it. Yet approximately one million Hutus fled Rwanda while Paul Kagame's RPF forces gained ground and eventually took power, joining the large numbers of displaced Tutsis in these border regions. Among these Hutus were many groups of *génocidaires*, who blended into the refugee camps while using them as bases to rearm and launch counterattacks against the RPF. Hence, humanitarian and human rights agencies found themselves in the perverse situation of seeking protection for and lending assistance to some of these *génocidaires* (Terry 2003, 155–215).

Aside from the particularities of this case, what is significant is that representational activism—notably in its mobile- and social media–driven emphases on concision, "directness," and instantaneous impact—has a limited capacity to convey a state of affairs in which the same person or group should be understood simultaneously as victim and perpetrator, in which innocence and guilt are ambiguous and shifting categories that cannot be explained through a picture or a brief message on Twitter or Facebook.

Another form of reductionism that constitutes an aporia for representational activism is found in the political rather than the analytical realm. Here the act of visually bearing witness to and capturing human rights violations overshadows a more expansive form of political struggle seeking to defend and realize human rights around the world. On the one hand, we should question the unbridled and technologically deterministic stance of techno-optimists, who tend to view the new communication platforms as panacea for the challenges of human rights advocacy, by valuing the interactivity intrinsic to social media and hardware portability as generating a new form of politics in and of themselves. On the other hand, we need not agree with the dismissive tone of techno-pessimism, which characterizes Web 2.0 activism as effortless and ineffective "slacktivism" demanding very little political commitment.

Instead, it would be useful to consider the contributions of social media platforms according to a model that differentiates between different modes of political engagement. Accordingly, the comparative advantages of Internet and mobile technologies vis-à-vis other modes of communication (from crowdsourcing to the decentered and rapid circulation of information) favor breadth over depth of engagement, for they are well suited to mobilize large numbers of persons for low-intensity, generalized acts requiring minimal levels of commitment (the signing of online petitions, the sharing of a link or retweeting of a message, etc.). These acts can be effective in shifting public opinion or pressuring official institutions, without necessarily being geared toward converting such actions into higher-intensity, localized ones grounded in greater levels of commitment (the joining of marches, the pursuit of legal action, the volunteering for a cause, etc.).[20]

Given how new technological and communicative platforms are oriented toward and expand the possibilities of representational activism, what risks occurring is an elevation of the latter into an end in itself for human rights politics and, thus, an understanding of it as both a necessary and sufficient mode of political intervention. In this way, human rights NGOs and social movements could be transformed into entities whose primary function becomes that of visually bearing witness to and documenting human rights abuses, thereby transforming them into bystander organizations whose forms of denunciation and intervention in public spheres are limited to photographing and filming human rights violations, distributing images via mobile and web-based tools, and encouraging publics to view these images. Although important as a constituent part of human rights politics, visual witnessing cannot become the raison d'être of such politics, displacing other kinds of political practice and effectively narrowing the field of possibilities for action. Instead, it should be understood as a means, or catalyst, to provoke and inspire other modes of struggle designed to undermine existing structures of inequality and domination undergirding human rights abuses, as well as to create alternative practices and forms of social organization (a new architecture of global governance, workers' self-management, etc.).

Conclusion

In this chapter, I have argued that neither techno-idealism nor techno-skepticism consider the complex range of ways in which emerging web-based and mobile communication platforms are reshaping practices of human rights–related representational activism and the paradoxical ways in which the universal and local co-exist through these platforms. *Pace* these positions' tendency toward technological determinism, I have introduced a stance of critical pragmatism grounded in a principle of the radical indeterminacy of Web 2.0, according to which the latter has no universal technological essence that defines it as intrinsically emancipatory or, conversely, controlling. Rather, the effects of these technologies depend upon how they are applied by human rights actors in a variety of localized, specific circumstances and with regard to different situations, as well as the sorts of publics they reach and the latter's interpretations of and responses to particular discourses and images.

Accordingly, critical pragmatism advocates an ambivalence toward these new technologies, whereby their mass adoption by human rights NGOs and social movements should not occur without working through the aporias explained throughout this chapter.

While such a process of working through cannot transcend these aporias, which are constitutive aspects of representational activists' use of social media, it can assist human rights actors in being reflective about them and thereby aiming to avert their most problematic or troubling outcomes. Although a full discussion of such strategies goes beyond the scope of this chapter, a few ideas can be suggested here. In the first place, to resist the potential for governmental or corporate censorship, or the manipulation of evidence of human rights abuses, civil society actors can support the development of Internet access activism, such as the OpenNet Initiative, which provides software and proxy servers for users facing repressive governments to bypass online filtering and blocking.[21]

Furthermore, human rights groups must be prepared and willing to offer supplementary information and evidentiary material to counter the sophisticated misinformation campaigns launched by state or corporate institutions, as well as to make sure that whatever visual artifacts they produce are verifiable or confirmed by independent sources. And while opposition to the commodification of the Internet is outside the purview of human rights activism, NGOs and social movements can address it by supporting publicly owned or open-source technological platforms, as well as legislation that would treat social media services (such as Facebook and Twitter) as public utilities required to supply services to their users in a manner buffering governmental or corporate pressures. If public suspicion of the evidentiary status of the image in the digital age is inevitable, representational activism can contribute to the cultivation of engaged audiences that are visually literate, which is to say, capable of exercising critical judgment by discerning more reliable sources (such as newspapers of record) from their less trustworthy counterparts (such as partisan blogs) and verifying for themselves, if need be, the authenticity of a photograph or video purporting to capture a particular situation (via websites such as TinEye).[22]

Human rights organizations can also parry some of the unintended consequences of their growing reliance on new technologies, notably by supporting software that protects the identities and locations of eyewitnesses and victims of human rights abuses whose "traceability" has increased by virtue of using social media tools. This can also mean adopting precautionary policies and guidelines, in order to ensure that the public release of visual evidence of human rights violations not worsen the circumstances of victims or inadvertently promote the propagandist aims of perpetrators of such violations. Indeed, under certain circumstances, it may be preferable for human rights advocates to abstain from publishing certain images if the risks are greater than the potential gains from exposure. For its part, the aforementioned aporia of greater public invisibility of certain cases of human rights abuses can be tackled by representational activists drawing particular attention to what remains unrepresented or unrepresentable today, notably forgotten or overlooked events and situations that tend to never "trend" on social media platforms. Specifically, through such platforms, such activists can organize campaigns about neglected cases of human rights violations or symbolically expand the meaning of such violations to include forms of structural violence and systemic socioeconomic factors conventionally understood to be outside of the scope of human rights struggles (such as extreme poverty, gender-based domination, structural adjustment programs, etc.).

Representational activists can parry the reductionist tendencies that their extensive use of social media fosters by acknowledging the limitations of the latter modes of communication, which should be viewed less as substitutes than as complements for platforms that favor long-form explanatory and analytical material, such as documentary films and articles of investigative journalism in newspapers and magazines (whether in hard copy or online). Therefore, instead of diverting much of their communicative resources to Web 2.0 applications, human rights NGOs and social movements can exploit these applications' reach and speed to provide online links to and publicize more elaborate written or narrated pieces about certain human rights situations. When well utilized, such pieces can counter the trends toward analytical simplification and brevity that are core traits of social media—traits that cannot be overcome through the mere circulation of an image or a brief alert about human rights abuses. In other words, analytical reductionism can be tempered by the judicious application of social media and mobile tools, and in such a way that recognizes their flaws in order to encourage publics to seek out communicative media providing more analytical depth, nuance, and complexity than a Facebook post or a tweet.

The temptation to embrace representational activism as an end in itself for human rights politics, and the accompanying visually determinist belief that capturing and broadcasting images is a sufficient mode of sociopolitical practice, can be corrected by putting visuality back in its place. Images, and the Internet and mobile platforms used to produce and diffuse them, are nothing more—and nothing less—than catalysts for informing and mobilizing publics, which can prompt the latter to support and get involved in struggles to realize human rights and global justice. If and when this is understood clearly, human rights advocates will be in a position to maximize the promises of social media without fearing that its technological characteristics are driving the politics that they are intended to serve; at that point, representational activism will have come of age.

Notes

Research and writing of this chapter were made possible by a Standard Research Grant from the Social Sciences and Humanities Research Council of Canada. I would like to thank Michael Christensen, Marcia Oliver, Philip Steiner, and Steve Tasson, all of whom provided skilled research assistance. Gratitude is also due to the audiences to whom different versions of this chapter were presented, at the Mid-Term Conference of the Canadian Law and Society Association (Toronto, February 2010), the Sawyer Seminar on Human Rights at the University of Wisconsin (Madison, October 2010), and the Annual Meetings of the Canadian Sociological Association (Fredericton, May 2011).

1. In this chapter, a deliberate overlap between human rights and humanitarianism is suggested, since most conflict-generated humanitarian emergencies (refugee crises, famines, etc.) have roots in violations of socioeconomic or civil-political rights. Thus, as the Make Poverty History campaign argues, financial aid and humanitarian assistance to poor countries and vulnerable populations is a matter of justice—and thus rights—rather than charity.

2. This is a Web 2.0 version of the "boomerang effect" of transnational activism; see e.g., Keck and Sikkink 1998.

3. For instance, video footage has been used extensively during the International Criminal Tribunal for the Former Yugoslavia, in order to prosecute Slobodan Milosevic and his associates. See Delage 2006, 296–303.

4. In this vein, the most widespread strategy employed by activists is that of "naming and shaming" institutions and persons perpetrating or complicit with large-scale human rights violations.

5. At the origins of cinema, this contestation would take shape in the very different visions of the Lumière brothers and of George Méliès (Morin 1956).

6. The *Daily Express*'s campaign led SCF flag-sellers in London to be threatened with being thrown into the River Thames as well as to protests outside the SCF's headquarters (Mahood and Satzewich 2009). See also the SCF's own narrative of the events: http://www.savethechildren.net/alliance/about_us/index_byyears .html#1920s, accessed December 3, 2010.

7. The lead story on the cover page of the January 5, 1922, issue of the *Daily Express* was thus titled "A Close-Up of the Russian Famine," with the following subtitles: "The Camera Does Not Lie," "No Famine in Moscow and Petrograd,"

and "Enlightening Film." It was accompanied by three photographs: the first of men unloading sacks from a ship (with the caption "Landing English Foodstuffs at a Port"), the second of a shop window filled with goods of all kinds (with the caption "A Well-Filled Shop Window in Moscow"), and a third showing a group of smiling girls (with the caption "Do These Children Look as though They Need British Food?").

8. The SCF extensively publicized the documentary film in its bulletin, the *Record*, in addition to refuting claims that any of the footage was staged (Save the Children Fund 1922, 151). See also Mahood and Satzewich 2009.

9. See, respectively, http://www.demotix.com and http://witness.org, accessed November 27, 2011.

10. For a description of the range of measures taken by the Iranian state in the aftermath of the contested June 2009 presidential election, see Faris and Heacock 2009. More recently, the Electronic Frontier Foundation reports that the Iranian government has increased its efforts to block or filter domestic Internet traffic, notably by preventing access to HTTPS websites such as Twitter, Facebook, and some Google applications. See Galperin 2012.

11. It is in this context that the actions of Wikileaks and Edward Snowden have been perceived as a threat to states, since the former aim to undermine the latter's informational and representational monopolies, as well as to warn ordinary citizens about online government surveillance.

12. A further problem emerges from the commodification of iconic images of human rights abuses as a way to shock public opinion and thus gain publicity. The designer John Galliano used the widely circulated photographs of torture of Iraqis by U.S. military personnel at the Abu Ghraib prison as inspiration for part of his fall 2008 menswear collection. Some of the models were wearing hoods similar to those of the tortured prisoners, with blood-spattered torsos. See http://www.style.com/fashionshows/complete/F2008MEN-JNGALLNO?viewall=true, accessed February 1, 2012.

13. Among the many instances of the spread of false images, one can cite an instance that took place during the writing of this chapter in January 2012, when a photograph claiming to show a large group of Christians burned to death by Sunni Muslims in Nigeria began recirculating on Facebook and various websites: see, for instance, SIOTW 2011. In fact, the image was that of the corpses of Congolese victims of a fuel tanker explosion in July 2010 in the Democratic Republic of Congo; see Manson 2012. I would like to thank Helen Androlia for drawing my attention to this case.

14. This does not mean that human rights actors should encourage publics to blindly trust them, but rather that they encourage practices of critical visuality; see the conclusion to this chapter.

15. Although difficult to confirm with certainty, it appears that several prominent Twitter- and Facebook-based activists operating inside Iran during the

protests in the summer of 2009 were tracked down and arrested by state authorities because their computer and mobile phone usage exposed their whereabouts. Recently, computer users in Syria report that their computers have been infected with spyware; see Brumfield 2012. Furthermore, several Western companies have been providing authoritarian regimes in various parts of the world (and perhaps Western governments as well) with electronic surveillance and spying software; specific client governments include Egypt (under Mubarak), Libya (under Qaddafi), Iran, and Bahrain, among others (Timm 2012a; Timm 2012b).

16. For instance, while not directly cited as a reason by the Sudanese regime, Amnesty International's online publication of photographic evidence of official military assistance to the Janjaweed militias in Darfur in August 2007 may well have contributed to the al-Bashir government's decision to expel several Western humanitarian NGOs from the country in March 2009.

17. Here, *contra* Baudrillard, I am not suggesting that there is no reality outside of its representation (i.e., that an event has no independent *ontological* existence; see Baudrillard 1995). Rather, I am claiming that the *social* existence of this same event—its presence in public spheres—depends upon its visually being represented.

18. The ongoing situation in the Democratic Republic of Congo—which has received virtually no Western media coverage nor any strong public response despite the efforts of several photojournalists and NGOs—is arguably the most egregious instance of public invisibility of mass human rights violations in the last two decades. More than 5.4 million people have died there from conflict-related causes since 1998, making it the worst conflict in the world since the end of World War II; see IRC 2012. On the work of photojournalists to inform and alert Euro-American audiences about the situation in the DRC, see Nachtwey et al. 2006.

19. At best, such a tweet or posting can provide a link to a fuller analysis of a specific event located on a website. This points to several potential problems with this sort of link-heavy usage: social media is converted into a mere promotional tool for more detailed writing or images found outside of its confines; the accumulation of links provided to followers or friends on social media platforms grows exponentially and risks saturating the recipient; and the follow-through of audiences (i.e., the number of recipients who actually click on a link and read or view all the material to which it refers) may well be limited.

20. It should be specified that breadth and depth of political engagement are merely two modes of political engagement, neither one of which is inherently superior nor more effective than the other; the mobilization of large numbers of minimally committed supporters can be just as impactful as that of a small number of highly committed ones, and vice versa. Of course, the most effective forms of political organizing, whether in the field of human rights or any other, combine both breadth and depth.

21. See http://opennet.net, accessed February 8, 2012.

22. See http://www.tineye.com, accessed February 8, 2012.

References

Amnesty International. 2007. "New Photos Expose Sudan Arms Violations." August 24. http://www.amnesty.org/en/news-and-updates/new-photos-expose-sudan-arms-violations-20070824.

Baudrillard, Jean. 1995. *The Gulf War Did Not Take Place*. Bloomington: Indiana University Press.

Brumfield, Ben. 2012. "Computer Spyware is Newest Weapon in Syrian Conflict." *CNN*, February 17. http://www.cnn.com/2012/02/17/tech/web/computer-virus-syria/index.html?hpt=hp_t2.

Burgess, Jean, and Joshua Green. 2009. *YouTube: Online Video and Participatory Culture*. Cambridge: Polity Press.

Comninos, Alex. 2011. "Twitter Revolutions and Cyber Crackdowns: User-Generated Content and Social Networking in the Arab Spring and Beyond." Paper presented at the Association for Progressive Communications, June.

Cosandey, R. 1998. *Eloquence Du Visible: La Famine En Russie 1921–1923, Une Filmographie Documentée. Archives (Institut Jean Vigo)* 75/76.

Delage, Christian. 2006. *La Vérité Par L'image: De Nuremberg Au Procès Milosevic*. Paris: Denoël.

Falk, Richard A. 2000. *Human Rights Horizons: The Pursuit of Justice in a Globalizing World*. New York: Routledge.

Faris, Rob, and Rebekah Heacock. 2009. "Cracking Down on Digital Communication and Political Organizing in Iran." *OpenNet Initiative*, June 15. http://opennet.net/blog/2009/06/cracking-down-digital-communication-and-political-organizing-iran

Galperin, Eva. 2012. "Iran Ratchets Up Its Internet Censorship." *Electronic Frontier Foundation*, February 11. https://www.eff.org/deeplinks/2012/02/iran-ratchets-its-internet-censorship.

Gladwell, Malcolm. 2010. "Small Change: Why the Revolution Will Not Be Tweeted." *New Yorker*, September 28. http://www.newyorker.com/reporting/2010/10/04/101004fa_fact_gladwell?currentPage=all.

Grant, Kevin. 2001. "Christian Critics of Empire: Missionaries, Lantern Lectures, and the Congo Reform Campaign in Britain." *Journal of Imperial and Commonwealth History* 29, no. 2: 27–58.

Gregory, Sam. 2010. "Cameras Everywhere: Ubiquitous Video Documentation of Human Rights, New Forms of Video Advocacy, and Considerations of Safety, Security, Dignity and Consent." *Journal of Human Rights Practice* 2, no. 2: 191–207.

International Rescue Committee (IRC). 2012. "Congo Crisis." http://www.rescue.org/special-reports/congo-forgotten-crisis.

Jenkins, Henry. 2006. *Convergence Culture: Where Old and New Media Collide*. New York: New York University Press.

Kanter, Beth, and Allison H. Fine. 2010. *The Networked Nonprofit: Connecting with Social Media to Drive Change*. New York: Jossey-Bass.

Keck, Margaret E., and Kathryn A. Sikkink. 1998. *Activists Beyond Borders: Advocacy Networks in International Politics*. Ithaca, NY: Cornell University Press.

Keenan, Thomas. 2004. "Mobilizing Shame." *South Atlantic Quarterly* 103, no. 2/3: 435–49.

Kurasawa, Fuyuki. 2007. *The Work of Global Justice: Human Rights as Practices*. Cambridge: Cambridge University Press.

LSE Centre for Civil Society and Centre for the Study of Global Governance. 2001. *Global Civil Society 2001*. Oxford: Oxford University Press.

Mahood, L., and V. Satzewich. 2009. "The Save the Children Fund and the Russian Famine of 1921–23: Claims and Counter-Claims About Feeding 'Bolshevik' Children." *Journal of Historical Sociology* 22, no. 1: 55–83.

Manson, Katrina. 2012. "Fuel Tanker Explosion Kills over 230 in Congo." *Reuters*, July 3. http://www.reuters.com/article/2010/07/03/us-congo-democratic-explosion-idUSTRE6620H220100703.

May, Christopher. 2002. *The Information Society: A Sceptical View*. Cambridge, UK: Polity Press.

McLuhan, Marshall. 1994. *Understanding Media: The Extensions of Man*. MIT Press.

Morin, Edgar. 1956. *Le Cinéma Ou L'homme Imaginaire*. Paris: Minuit.

Morozov, Evgeny. 2009. "Iran: Downside to the 'Twitter Revolution.'" *Dissent* 56, no. 4: 10–14.

———. 2010. "The Myth of the Techno-Utopia." *Wall Street Journal*, February 20. http://online.wsj.com/article/SB100014240527487039830045750739 11 147404540.html.

Nachtwey, James, Gary Knight, Simon Robinson, and Nicolas de Torrente. 2006. *Forgotten War: Democratic Republic of the Congo*. Millbrook, NY: de.MO.

Pantic, Drazen. 2006. "Anybody Can Be TV: How P2P Home Video Will Challenge the Network News." In *Reformatting Politics: Information Technology and Global Civil Society*, edited by Jon Anderson, Jodi Dean, and Geert Lovink, 55–68. New York: Rowman and Littlefield.

Retort. 2006. *Afflicted Powers: Capital and Spectacle in a New Age of War*. London: Verso.

Rheingold, Howard. 2002. *Smart Mobs: The Next Social Revolution*. Cambridge, MA: Perseus.

Save the Children Fund. 1922. *Record* 2, no. 10. February. Reprinted in *Western Aid and the Global Economy, Archives of Major Aid Agencies, Series One: The Save the Children Fund Archive, London*, edited by Hugo Slim and Patricia Sellick. Woodbridge, CT: Primary Source Microfilm/Thomson Gale. 2002. Reel 1.

Shirky, Clay. 2008. *Here Comes Everybody: The Power of Organizing Without Organization*. New York: Penguin.

Sliwinski, S. 2006. "The Childhood of Human Rights: The Kodak on the Congo." *Journal of Visual Culture* 5, no. 3: 333–63.

Stop Islamization of the World (SIOTW). 2011. "Christians Burnt Alive by Sunni Muslims in Nigeria." October 15. http://www.siotw.org/modules/news _english/item.php?itemid=498.

Surman, M., and K. Reilly. 2003. *Appropriating the Internet for Social Change: Towards the Strategic Use of Networked Technologies by Transnational Civil Society Organizations.* New York: Social Science Research Council.

Terry, Fiona. 2003. *Condemned to Repeat? The Paradox of Humanitarian Action.* Ithaca, NY: Cornell University Press.

Timm, Trevor. 2012a. "Spy Tech Companies & Their Authoritarian Customers, Part 1: FinFisher and Amesys." *Electronic Frontier Foundation.* https://www .eff.org/deeplinks/2012/02/spy-tech-companies-their-authoritarian-customers -part-i-finfisher-and-amesys.

————. 2012b. "Spy Tech Companies & Their Authoritarian Customers, Part 2: Trovicor and Area SpA." *Electronic Frontier Foundation.* https://www.eff.org/ deeplinks/2012/02/spy-tech-companies-their-authoritarian-customers-part -ii-trovicor-and-area-spa.

Twain, M. 1905. *King Leopold's Soliloquy: A Defence of His Congo Rule.* Vol. 2. Boston: P. R. Warren.

Twestival. 2011. http://www.twestival.com/info.html.

United States Holocaust Memorial Museum (USHMM). 2009. "Crisis in Darfur Update." http://www.ushmm.org/maps/projects/darfur.

Varnelis, Kazys, ed. 2008. *Networked Publics.* Cambridge, MA: MIT Press.

8

The Human Right to Water in Rural India

Promises and Challenges

PHILIPPE CULLET

Introduction

India has made tremendous progress over the past few decades with regard to drinking-water supply in rural areas. Thus, while coverage in rural areas was estimated at 18 percent in 1974 (Black and Talbot 2005, 5), it has increased to at least 72 percent (Planning Commission 2012, 35). This first basic measure of access to water indicates that there has been tremendous improvement in the realization of the human right to water in rural areas of India. At the same time, full realization is yet to be achieved.

Turning to the legal framework, the human right to water is well established in India, having been recognized by the Supreme Court of India for a number of years (Supreme Court of India 1991). Yet there is little substance to the right beyond its formal recognition (Muralidhar 2006, 65). The case law is not particularly detailed with regard to the content of the right, and the Parliament of India has never adopted framework legislation that would provide specificity to this right.

In strict legal terms, India has thus little beyond the formal recognition of the right to water. Yet this does not reflect its importance in practice. Indeed, the crucial role of drinking water for survival has led the government of India and state governments to introduce a number of initiatives over the past several decades, which amount at least in part to attempts to foster the realization of the right.[1]

One of the hallmarks of the framework for drinking water supply in recent years is that it has been shaped mostly through administrative directions of the executive. The absence of a legislative framework giving content to the right to water raises questions concerning the content of the right in the context of ongoing neoliberal reforms. On the one hand, the dichotomy between positive and negative duties that was a hallmark of the categorization of rights during the Cold War has been largely sidelined in favor of a broader understanding of human rights, which encompasses economic and social rights. On the other hand, while courts have clearly indicated that the human right to water includes various positive duties of the state, policy reforms over the past fifteen years have specifically sought to take the state away from "providing" toward only "facilitating."

The shift in the state's own understanding of its human rights–related duties has important consequences for the majority of rights holders. Indeed, for the overwhelming majority of the rural population, the involvement of the state over the past few decades has impacted very positively on the realization of the right to water. This has happened either by ensuring that water is available at a lesser distance from the home or by insuring increased overall availability. This positive contribution does not mean that there were no shortcomings. One of the elements that has been particularly lacking and that affects the long-term realization of the right is the lack of attention given to operation and maintenance of existing infrastructure.

The progressive withdrawal of the state from direct provision hurts first of all the most vulnerable members of society. This should not come as a complete surprise since some of the reforms are specifically premised on users getting the supply they are ready to pay for. Unfortunately this results in making the poor bear the burden of adjustment of ongoing reforms by linking the realization of the human right to willingness to pay (Cullet 2009a, 157). In other words, ongoing reforms, which are premised at a macro level on the need to realize the human right to all, end up in many cases disadvantaging the poor, who suffer in the long term from a reduced level of realization of the right while being further impoverished because they have had to reallocate additional resources toward access to water. This is a priority that will nearly always trump everything else, in particular health expenditure, which is one of the key areas likely to suffer in a country like India, where the overwhelming majority of health costs are borne by individuals.[2]

The story of the human right to water in rural India is an excellent illustration of the need to make sure that human rights be conceived not only as abstract constitutional or international law claims but also in the form of very specific and local measures that actually make the right experienced by people on a daily basis a reality. There is no opposition between the two but rather an intrinsic relationship that make them inseparable. The fact that human rights cannot be looked at only from a relatively general level of abstraction also means that their realization cannot be seen separately from the more specific context within which it happens. Political, policy, or historical factors thus play an immense role in the way in which the right is realized in a specific locality. This explains, for instance, why the human right to water that has been recognized consistently for the past twenty-odd years in India is today implemented on the ground in a completely different way, if not sometimes opposed to what was being done up to the end of the twentieth century.

This chapter starts by identifying the broad content of the human right to water in India and the law and policy framework that informs drinking-water supply in rural areas. It then looks at the changing policy framework that has been in continuous evolution since the late 1990s. This is used as a basis for identifying some impacts of ongoing reforms on the right to water in theory and practice, and to proffer some suggestions on the future path that needs to be taken to guarantee universal implementation of the right.

From a Judicially Recognized Human Right to the Framework for Its Implementation

The recognition of the human right to water in India is well grounded. The real issues that arise concern the translation of this broad entitlement into laws and concrete measures, which make the right a daily reality for every person in the country. This section highlights the broad contours of the judicially recognized right to water and introduces what is in effect a skeletal legal framework for drinking-water supply.

The Human Right to Water

The Constitution of India does not specifically include a human right to water. Yet a number of judicial pronouncements have made it clear that the right indeed exists in India. The Supreme Court has repeatedly derived a right to water from the right to life (Supreme Court 1991). Courts have also derived the right to water from article 47 of the constitution. In the Hamid Khan case, the complaint focused on the health consequences of the supply of water with excessive fluoride content. The High Court found that under article 47 the state has a duty "towards every citizen of India to provide pure drinking water" (Madhya Pradesh High Court 1996, para. 6).

Further, courts have found on repeated occasions that the right to water includes a duty on the part of the state to provide water. Thus, in *Vishala Kochi Kudivella Samarkshana Samithi v. State of Kerala*, the High Court found that

> [w]e have no hesitation to hold that failure of the State to provide safe drinking water to the citizens in adequate quantities would amount to a violation of the fundamental right to life enshrined in article 21 of the Constitution of India and would be a violation of human rights. There-fore, every Government, which has its priorities right, should give fore-most importance to providing safe drinking water even at the cost of other development programmes. Nothing shall stand in its way whether it is lack of funds or other infrastructure. Ways and means have to be found out at all costs with utmost expediency instead of restricting action in that regard to mere lip service. (High Court of Kerala 2006, para. 3)

The cases mentioned above confirm that the right is well established. Yet the actual content of the right has not been elaborated upon in detail in judicial decisions. Further context is thus to be found in legislation and subsidiary legal instruments.

Laws Regulating Rural Drinking Water Supply

Drinking water is acknowledged as the primary concern in the water sector.[3] Yet recognition in legal terms is largely limited to the recognition of the human right to water. Indeed, there is no framework drinking-water law to complement the recognition of the right to water, and as a result there is neither any general set of principles that apply to drinking water sup-ply throughout the country nor specific rules giving content to the human right to water.[4]

The absence of broad drinking-water legislation notwithstanding, a num-ber of more specific initiatives have been taken over time. Thus, following the adoption of the seventy-third constitutional amendment various states have either confirmed or adopted legislative provisions giving *panchayats* (village councils) control over water supply at the local level. Different formulations are used, and various acts give a diverse set of competences to panchayats. There is nevertheless broad agreement among panchayat acts in giving control to these councils over drinking-water supply at the local level (Himachal Pradesh Panchayati Raj Act 1994). Some acts are more detailed than others. Some spec-ify the kind of activities that panchayats can engage in, such as constructing, repairing, and maintaining tanks or wells, streams, and watercourses, and specify their powers, such as the capacity to contract someone for water supply (Karnataka Panchayat Raj Act 1993). While panchayat acts are not detailed with regard to water-supply rights and obligations of the panchayats, they provide a general binding framework within which all water supply at the local level must be organized.

Some states have also adopted sectoral legislation that addresses drinking water from the perspective of the regulation of one specific body of water. This is, for instance, the case of Karnataka, Madhya Pradesh, and Maharashtra whose groundwater legislation focuses specifically on drinking water (Karnataka Ground Water 1999; Madhya Pradesh peya jal parirakshan adhiniyam 1986; Maharashtra Ground Water Regulation 1993). These acts focus on water conservation and availability. They thus neither include any list of principles governing drinking-water supply in general nor specifically regulate water supply in detail.

In addition, the Union has introduced various quality standards for drinking-water supply. These include the 1991 Bureau of Indian Standards Water Quality Standards (BIS Specification 1991), and the Manual on Water Supply and Treatment issued by the Central Public Health and Environmental Engineering Organization (CPHEEO Manual 1999). While these are in principle applicable countrywide, the absence of any legislation directly referring to these standards means that to date their legal status is partly inchoate. They are applicable but not legally binding on water service providers.

Filling the Regulatory Gaps: Government-Led Initiatives

The limited framework existing to give shape to the human right to water implies that there are significant gaps in the regulatory framework. This has been filled at different levels and in different ways over time. At the most general level, a number of states have adopted state water policies. These documents make general reference to drinking water and all give it the highest priority in terms of intersectoral allocation of water (Kerala State Water Policy 2008).

At the Union level, the government of India felt increasingly compelled to involve itself in rural drinking-water supply. Since this supply falls in principle under the competence of states, the Union decided to use a mix of administrative directions and financial incentives to make its mark at the local level. Over time, while states have retained the overall mandate over rural drinking-water supply, the influence of the Union framework has been increasingly visible throughout the country.

From a legal point of view, the key dimension of the different instruments adopted by the government over time is that they create no rights and obligations. These should thus be considered as subsidiary instruments. Yet, in practice, the frameworks of the government have had a disproportionate influence. This can be explained in part by the financial incentives offered by the Union and in part because the framework proposed by the Union is similar to what international development agencies propose and implement through the projects they finance in individual states.

ARWSP and Early Reforms

The first key framework put out by the Union to foster better drinking-water supply in rural areas was the Accelerated Rural Water Supply Programme (ARWSP). The ARWSP guidelines first introduced in 1972 provided, for a number of years, the core framework used by the Rajiv Gandhi National Drinking Water Mission in guaranteeing the provision of drinking water to all habitations in the country (ARWSP Guidelines 1999–2000). Some of the salient points of the guidelines included:

- Defining different levels of coverage in terms of quantity. Noncovered habitations were defined as having access to less than ten liters per capita per day (lpcd). Partially covered habitations were those having access to 10 to 40 lpcd. Covered habitations were defined as having access to 40 lpcd.
- Specifying that the source of water had to be within 1.6 kilometer or 100-meter elevation in mountain areas. The water was not to be affected by quality problems even though no specific standards for determining quality were included. Another criterion was that a given public source of water, such as a hand pump, was not to be used to serve more than 250 people.
- Acknowledging the direct link between drinking water for human beings and water for cattle. Consequently, in a certain number of states especially affected by drought, the guidelines mandated that an additional 30 lpcd should be provided for cattle.
- Acknowledging the minimum level of 40 lpcd as a minimum level of coverage, which should be increased over time.

The progressive implementation of the ARWSP was carried out until the mid-1990s. Since then, a string of reform efforts eventually led to abandoning the ARWSP altogether in 2009. The first harbinger of the reforms was a pilot project sponsored by the World Bank whose principles were adopted in the Swajaldhara Guidelines in 2002. The latter were used as a template for reforms, which eventually led to a complete rethinking of the existing policy framework and the adoption of an entirely new set of guidelines known as the National Rural Drinking Water Programme (NRDWP).

Kicking off the Reforms: The Swajal Project and the Swajaldhara Guidelines

The Uttar Pradesh Rural Water Supply and Environmental Sanitation Project (Swajal project), a World Bank–funded project started in 1996, was one of the important drivers of change in the rural drinking-water sector. The Swajal project introduced a number of important policy propositions that have become the norm for rural drinking-water supply. It advocated in particular the shift from a supply-driven to a demand-driven approach, and the introduction of cost recovery of capital costs and operation and maintenance.

The Swajal project and related initiatives taken in the late 1990s, such as the Sector Reform Project, were generally assessed positively by policy makers. This led to the formulation of the Swajaldhara Guidelines, which extended during the Tenth Five-Year Plan the key principles of the Swajal project to the whole country (Ministry of Rural Development 2002). The Swajaldhara Guidelines were premised on the fact that the understanding of water as a social right was misplaced and that it should be seen instead as a socioeconomic good (ibid., sec. s1[1]). Further, the guidelines were based on an understanding that the delivery of the social right by the government did not sufficiently take into account the preferences of users and was ineffective in ensuring the carrying out of operation and maintenance activities. This then called for a demand-led approach. The link between the demand-led approach and the new conception of water as an economic good was succinctly brought together in that the guidelines argued that the idea of demand-driven system needed to take into account the preferences of users "where users get the service they want and are willing to pay for" (ibid., sec. s1[2]). The imposition of full cost-recovery of operations and maintenance, in addition to the replacement costs on the communities, was expected to generate a sense of ownership and insure the financial viability of the plans.[5]

Consolidating the Reforms: The NRDWP

The experience gathered during the Tenth Five-Year Plan led the government to suggest an entirely new framework for rural drinking-water supply. In a bid to demarcate the new policy principles from earlier reforms, it has been given a new name and is now known as the National Rural Drinking Water Programme. The NRDWP brings a number of key changes to the policy framework for drinking-water supply in rural areas (NRDWP 2010).

Philippe Cullet

First, the NRDWP sees water as a "basic need" (ibid., sec. 2). In a general sense the fulfillment of basic water needs contributes to the realization of the human right to water—or at least its core content. Yet from a legal perspective, the notion of basic needs is different from that of a human right. In other words, legal instruments that choose to speak the language of basic needs do not speak the language of human rights.

Second, the NRDWP goes farther than simply abandoning the language of human rights. In fact, it operates a U-turn on the policy followed since the 1970s by suggesting that measuring access to water in terms of a quantity of water per capita per day is inappropriate.[6] The NRDPW suggests moving from a fixed minimum to the concept of drinking-water security.

Drinking-water security is not given a specific definition, but it is opposed to the per capita norm followed earlier. Indeed, the NRDWP specifically states it is necessary to "move *ahead* from the conventional norms of liters per capita per day (lpcd) norms to ensure drinking water security for all in the community" (ibid., sec. 4). The basic unit now considered is the household. The NRDWP bases the shift from the individual to the household on the fact that "[a]verage per capita availability may not necessarily mean assured access to potable drinking water to all sections of the population in the habitation" (ibid., sec. 7). It does not, however, explain how the shift guarantees better coverage in a given habitation.

The new framework is startling from the perspective of the right to water. The key concern is that the focus on the individual makes way for a focus on the household. In addition, the foreword to the guidelines specifically indicates that "norms and guidelines need to be flexible" and further states that flexibility is preferable to the "adoption of universal norms and standards" (ibid., iv). This makes sense in terms of giving panchayats the opportunity to manage drinking water in the way most suited to local conditions. However, in terms of broad regulation, this does not fit within the framework of the right to water that is essentially based on guaranteeing the exact same realization of the right (at least its "core" content) to everyone.

Third, the NRDWP emphasizes the need for infrastructure that provides water from outside a given village through a grid fed by pipelines or other means of connecting major water sources (ibid., sec. 6). Alongside the focus on conjunctive use of surface and groundwater, and reliance on multiple sources of water, a grid can make an important contribution to the provision of water. It could also lead to more equity among regions since everyone could, in principle, be provided the same amount of clean water regardless of their geographical location. This would constitute a major step forward in making sure that the right to water is realized in the same way for everyone. At the same time, this is a momentous change from reliance on local sources of water and should be integrated in a much broader policy discussion. From the point of view of the principles and concepts being proposed, there is a tension, or maybe even an opposition, between the move to foster decentralization and participation, and the move toward having a grid covering all villages. The latter will imply a new level of centralization, which has in fact never been present in rural drinking-water supply until now. This may be a positive factor to the extent that the whole new framework is conceived with appropriate safeguards and accountability. It cannot, however, be introduced under the guise of participation and decentralization, and the two streams thus need to be clearly distinguished.

Toward Further Reforms: The Strategic Plan to 2022

The NRDWP is still relatively new. Yet the Ministry of Drinking Water and Sanitation has already moved toward adopting even more sweeping reforms. This comes in the form of a strategic plan for the period leading up to 2022 (Strategic Plan 2011–22).

This strategic plan does not imply rescinding the NRDWP but can be seen as an additional framework guiding the entire sector for the next decade. The overall conceptual framework of the strategic plan is highlighted in a section titled "aspirations," which calls for all rural households to have access to piped water supply in adequate quantity with a metered tap connection providing safe drinking water. The implication of this aspiration is a complete redrawing of the physical map of water supply throughout the country. As indicated in the plan, what is envisaged is a large-scale abandonment of hand pumps whose contribution to water supply is predicted to decline from 70 percent to 10 percent while the contribution of community standposts is meant to decrease from 30 percent to 10 percent (ibid., 4).

Interestingly, the strategic plan seems to reverse in part the NRDWP decision to abandon a per capita measurement of water supply by suggesting that the goal by 2022 should be that every person should have access to 70 lpcd within 50 meters (164 ft.) from his household. This is, however, not conceived as a universal norm. Indeed, the plan goes on to identify three different levels of service: the first one includes basic piped water supply with a mix of household connections, public taps, and hand pumps and is designed for 55 lpcd. The second one comprises piped water supply with all metered, household connections and is designed for 70 lpcd or more. The third option—to be adopted "in extreme cases"—includes hand pumps, protected open wells, protected ponds supplemented by other local sources, and is designed for 40 lpcd (ibid., 3).

Philippe Cullet

The plan does not indicate how these choices will be made. It specifies, however, that the first two options are based on at least partial cost recovery, leaving each state to decide on the basis of "affordability and social equity" the cost ceiling (ibid.). The third "extreme case" option is the one where water is still provided free of cost. This seems to imply that the level of service provided will depend on the ability of water users to pay for it, as was the case for more than a decade with the Swajal project and Swajaldhara guidelines.

The plan is clearer than the NRDWP by specifically recommending what it calls "outsourcing." The participation of the private sector is thus openly called for in rural water supply for the first time. This will likely usher a revolution in the way the rural water supply sector functions.

In fact, the plan is directly linked to another scheme, the Provision of Urban Amenities in Rural Areas Scheme (PURA 2011). This scheme proceeds from an idea first debated in 2003. As the name implies, it seeks to ensure that rural areas get some of the basic amenities enjoyed in urban areas. It is specifically premised on delivering these amenities through public private partnerships.

PURA is conceived not only as a way to bring in private sector finance to rural areas but also as a way to rethink the disbursement of existing public sector funding, and in particular to guarantee convergence of different schemes such as the NRDWP and the Nirmal Bharat Abhiyan. PURA is particularly significant in the context of this chapter because the first amenity covered is drinking water and sewerage (ibid., 7).

One of the striking features of PURA is that it includes different categories of amenities. In the first category are amenities falling under the purview of the Ministry of Rural Development. This includes, besides water and sewerage, construction and maintenance of village streets, drainage, and solid waste management. This is supplemented by "add-on projects," which include village-related tourism or integrated rural business centers. PURA calls for at least one add-on activity to be included in every project. The mixing of social service delivery by the private sector with purely commercial activities is a novelty for the rural water supply sector. In principle, the two need not conflict, but in practice the likelihood that private sector actors may focus on the commercially viable sectors to the detriment of basic needs provision cannot be excluded.

The possibility of schemes going awry confirms the need for a regulatory framework that provides general guidance for activities and projects contributing to the realization of the right to water. Ongoing proposals may generally point toward ways to fulfill the right. Yet the crux of the matter lies in the finer details. Thus, as witnessed in earlier efforts at turning rural drinking water into an economic good under the Swajal project and the Swajaldhara Guidelines, it is not enough to simply rely on community involvement to ensure equitable results. The results of pilot projects showed that the poor were largely excluded from improved water-supply infrastructure because they could not pay the capital cost contribution demanded, leading to an increase in inequality in access to water along socioeconomic lines rather than to the provision of amenities to people most in need (Sampat 2007).

Implications of Ongoing Policy Reforms for the Realization of the Right to Water

Ongoing policy reforms for rural water supply have the potential to contribute to the realization of the right to water. This could probably be said of any policy framework concerning drinking water in any country since the stated aim is unlikely to ever deny water to anyone. In this context, what matters is the underlying framework that animates the reforms and the stated or unstated policy aims pursued besides or beyond the human right to water rhetoric.

In the context of the ongoing policy reforms, reforms are not based specifically on the idea of a human right to water. Further, in the case of the NRDWP, a specific exclusion of the mention of the human right to water was introduced between the first and second version of the policy framework. There are thus several areas of concern with regard to the realization of the right to water, in particular for the most vulnerable and socioeconomically disadvantaged individuals.

Threat to the Universal Entitlement

In the conception of fundamental rights adopted by the Indian Constitution, the right to life and, by extension, the right to water are rights that every individual possesses. There is in theory no doubt that entitlements contained in fundamental rights are held to the same extent by every individual, as confirmed by the equality and nondiscrimination clauses (Constitution of India 1949, art. 14 and 15).

This is crucial in a context where secondary legal instruments increasingly talk of a "need" rather than a "right" when referring to water (NRDWP 2010). In legal terms there is an important difference between a need and a right. While a right is universal, a need may be "targeted." Millennium Development Goals (MDGs) illustrate this well (UNGA Res. 2000). The MDGs are not informed by a universal perspective in the sense that they target only half of the people whose basic water needs were not met in 2000. This will correspond to a basic level of realization of the right to water for these people. Yet the MDGs exclude half of those whose right to water is not realized from their purview. This lack of a universal perspective distinguishes MDGs from human rights.[7]

Ongoing water-supply policies seem to operate in the same conceptual framework of targeted benefits rather than universal entitlements. This is, for instance, seen in limited exemptions for the poor, such as in the case of lifeline tariffs (Asian Development Bank 2001, para. 46). Here, they single out the poorest and most marginalized, which is unwarranted in a situation where a vast majority of the population is poor. What should be done instead is to have a universal entitlement to the provision of the basic content of the right, supplemented with exceptions whereby the rich may be excluded from certain benefits (Drèze and Khera 2010). If this is the case, the exclusion should be focused on that quarter of the population earning more than twenty rupees (Rs) a day (NCEUS 2007).

The universality of the entitlement is also threatened by the division of the population into rural and urban residents. While this is not particularly problematic in view of the many different issues that arise in urban and rural areas, it cannot be an excuse for an understanding of the right as having a different content for these two different sets of people. This is regrettably what happens when the government generally suggests that the basic level of the realization of the right to water is equivalent to a minimum of 40 lpcd in rural areas (70 lpcd in the future) and different quantities in urban areas ranging from 70 lpcd to 150 lpcd according to the size of the city (ARWSP Guidelines 1999; CPHEEO Manual 1999, 11). While the Strategic Plan (2011–22) seems to bring the basic supply level in rural and urban areas to a similar minimum level, this is deceptive since the 70 lpcd for rural areas will not apply to everyone.

Threat to the Recognized Duty to Provide

The right to water, which has been repeatedly recognized by the courts, has been shaped around the state's duty to provide to its citizens. This is not particularly unexpected since it is generally recognized that the state has a duty to guarantee the realization of human rights, given that it alone commands the necessary economic and institutional resources necessary to ensure those rights and because the state is generally responsible for safeguarding constitutional rights (Drèze 2004).

While article 47 of the constitution does not specifically mention water, there has never been any doubt that the state has a major role to play in the realization of the human right to water, as confirmed by the case law analyzed earlier. Until the past decade, there had in fact been little discussion around this because the government made water supply one of its key duties. This led successive governments to at least attempt to provide the infrastructure in rural areas, such as hand pumps, that gave in the overwhelming majority of cases free access to water.

Policy reforms that seek to turn the state into a facilitator rather than a provider do not necessarily mean that the state is abdicating its responsibility to ensure the realization of human rights. However, in a context where these changes are happening nearly entirely through administrative directions of the government, they require close scrutiny.

First, the current discourse around socioeconomic rights has progressed, at least in theory, toward a strengthening of the duties of the state. This is, for instance, the case where the right to education legislation has confirmed the obligations of the state with regard to the provision of free and compulsory education (RTE 2009). In the case of the right to food, the public-interest litigation that has been going on for a decade has already led to a series of orders that have imposed on the state additional obligations to provide, such as in the case of midday meals in schools (Supreme Court of India 2001). This has been written into the National Food Security Act, 2013 (National Food Security Act 2013).

Second, in the context of water the government has put in significant effort and resources over several decades that contributed to the realization of the right to water (ARWSP 1999); this was done in a context where there was little if any talk of a right to water. Yet the actions of the government were motivated by an understanding that providing water to everyone was one of its primary obligations (Rajasthan Municipalities Act 1959, sec. 98). With all its faults and shortcomings, in a span of a few decades, the ARWSP assured that rural areas made tremendous progress toward the realization of the basic content of the right.[8] From this perspective, a withdrawal of the state from such provision needs to be justified by more than cost reasons.

Controversies over whether the realization of the right to water implies a duty for the state to "provide" rather than simply facilitate "access" is partly linked to the fact that policy and international legal instruments have tended to suggest that there is only a right to access water (ECOSOC 2002, para. 12.c.ii). Yet in reality there is little to debate. First of all, courts have clearly established the duty of the state to provide basic water. Second, in practice there is no alternative to provision by the state since imposing full cost recovery

Philippe Cullet

of capital costs on users would end up automatically denying the fulfillment of the right to the majority of the population.

The duty of the state to provide does not imply that it is the only actor involved and responsible. Indeed, the fact that state has a primary responsibility to ensure that sufficient safe water is provided does not mean that everyone else is absolved of any obligation. Thus, despite the state's duty to provide, everyone is obliged to make sure that no one is severely affected by lack of water, implying that there is not only a duty to share equitably common sources of water but also those individual sources (Drèze 2004, 1726).

Looking Ahead: Ensuring the Realization of the Right to Water in the Context of Policy Reforms

The past two decades have been momentous in terms of the evolution of the law and policy framework concerning drinking water. The existence of the human right to water in India has been confirmed on various occasions and in different contexts by the courts. While courts have not developed the content of the right in detail, there is no doubt that the right is part of everyone's human rights in India. Beyond this in-principle recognition there is very little legislation that confirms and expands the right. Yet the government of India took a number of policy measures over the years that constituted steps toward its realization. In particular, the ARWSP established a framework for providing water in rural areas, which was both bold and significant. The 1970 decision to put the minimum quantity of water constituting the lowest threshold at 40 lpcd reflected a good understanding of the challenges involved. As a result of these different law and policy measures, significant steps had been taken toward the realization of the core content of the human right to water for a great number of people by the end of the twentieth century. These steps, however, were far from adequate: millions of people still did not have access to sufficient water, but it was headed in the appropriate direction. In this sense, there was progress toward the progressive realization of the right.

The reforms undertaken over the past decade can be analyzed from different angles. First, administrative directions of the government have failed to engage specifically with the right to water. That the 2009 version of the NRDWP mentioned the human right to water reflects the fact that court strictures have at least been considered by the government, if not formally integrated into its administrative directions.[9] Second, policy reforms have in principle not affected the basic content of the human right to water defined by courts because they come down in the form of administrative directions that do not create legally binding rights and obligations. At the same time, there has been a major shift in the policy framework concerning drinking-water supply in rural areas that is not without impacts on the realization of the right to water. The paradigm shift that has been implemented progressively over the past decade has led, for instance, to a focus on demand-led rather than supply-led schemes, and an emphasis on efficiency rather than equality. The focus has also been on redefining water as a socioeconomic good rather than a social right. The latest changes in the policy framework have further sought to move away from conceiving water provision as an individual entitlement, one that could be measured in terms of certain benchmarks such as a minimum quantity per person per day in favor of the vaguer concept of drinking water security that only considers entities from the household level upwards.

These changes may not necessarily be problematic from a human rights perspective. Indeed, different policy perspectives can support the realization of the right to water. At the same time, there is a limit to the flexibility that governments have in this regard. The following two points illustrate this.

First it is now widely acknowledged that any measures to foster the realization of a human right must primarily focus on the situation of the poorest, thereby contributing to the overall realization of the right, but starting from the people who are most disadvantaged in this regard.[10] In this context, the experience with reforms over the past decade does not indicate that the policy framework is either geared toward a focus on the most disadvantaged or able to preferentially foster the realization of the right for the most marginalized (Cullet 2009b). This is related to the emphasis on the need for individuals to pay the costs of running the infrastructure providing access to water or/and to pay part of the costs of any new infrastructure. The implementation of ongoing reforms seems to have the effect of bypassing the poorest because of the emphasis on financial investment as the primary driver of better access. In effect, it is first of all the richer members of any given community who get additional water supply because they can afford it. In the case of piped supply, where community taps are part of the planning, they tend to be closed off early by the locals running the program, usually because of nonpayment of related charges (ibid., 50). This is problematic because even if the poor do not suffer from the new measures put in any place, they do not benefit from them. Additionally, in the long term the poor will be affected when the maintenance of their existing sources of water supply is sidelined in favor of maintenance of the newer infrastructure created under ongoing reforms.

Philippe Cullet

Second, whereas the government has the choice of the policy measures it wants to implement in order to foster the realization of human rights, it must be undertaken within the existing rights framework. At present, that framework happens to focus mostly on individual entitlements. In this context, the move away from an individual entitlement measured in terms of a minimum quantity of water in favor of a nonquantified standard applying to no smaller a unit than the household is a step away from the existing human rights framework. Leaving aside the possibility to have a collective right to water, something that no country seems to have yet considered, the move away from an individual entitlement in favor of a collective notion has already been seen to lead to inappropriate results in South Africa in the context of the free water policy (South Africa 2001, sec. 3). In this case, it is the poorer households that suffer because they are often the largest, in part because more people cohabit a smaller space than wealthier households. As a result, the poorer households lose out in any household-based measure, which goes against the idea of preferentially alleviating the situation of the least well off first (Smith 2006).

The overall outcome of the reforms is to foster better water supply to parts of rural communities. The focus of the reforms on availability of money as the yardstick that drives better access ends up making the new policies an instrument favoring the wealthier members of a given community over the poorer ones. This is problematic in the context of the realization of human rights and the focus on poverty eradication where the situation of the poorest is the most important issue to address. In addition, the move away from an individual entitlement tends to dilute the content of the right without helping the poorest households.

The more general problem that emerges is that the policy framework for reforms effectively only pays lip service to human rights. The constructive interpretation suggested earlier that sees reforms as proposing a different way to realize the human right to water goes farther than what the reforms themselves seek to do. Indeed, the move away from a social right toward the concept of water as an economic good is a direct reflection of the Dublin Statement (Dublin Statement on Water and Sustainable Development 1992). At the national level, there is no doubt that human rights are not subordinated to anything else. The Dublin Statement, which is not even a piece of soft law endorsed by the UN, has no bearing on what states must do at the national level. The only thing that matters in this context is respect for the constitutional framework, which happens to mandate that human rights prevail over other rights. There is thus a need to reconceive ongoing reforms so that they fit within the human right to water framework rather than the other way around.

Conclusion

The human right to water is everybody's concern. This is reflected in the increasing emphasis given to the supply of drinking water by the government. This is particularly true with regard to water supply in rural areas where the Department of Drinking Water and Sanitation, which was formerly within the Ministry of Rural Development, was set up as a separate Ministry of Drinking Water and Sanitation in 2011. There is further confirmation of the increasing importance given to rural drinking-water supply with a significant increased allocation in the 2012–13 budget.[11] The reason for this increased importance of rural drinking-water supply is not necessarily linked to the human right to water. Yet it reflects at least the recognition of the importance of the challenges that the country faces.

This chapter has considered the right to water mostly from the point of view from the contributions of the judiciary, legislative, and executive branches to the human right to water. This does not imply that they evolve in a vacuum. In fact, civil society has been very visible in the water sector for several decades in different forms. The bulk of water sector civil society organizations are implementing NGOs who do not concern themselves directly with influencing policy developments. There is nevertheless a smaller but very important set of groups that work on various issues related to drinking water or the right to water. These include groups for whom the right to water is the overarching concern within the context of more specific struggles, such as campaigns against big dams. These groups also include those that focus specifically on drinking water and have mounted various campaigns against privatization of water services in urban areas. Many of these groups have been very influential, but there have been few groups among them focusing specifically on rural areas.

The relatively low profile given to rural drinking-water policy by civil society groups is partly due to the multiplicity of situations arising in different areas of the country and even of a given state. This does not mean that the formalization of the right to water and the various policy initiatives of the government have not been noted by civil society. In fact, there have already been several attempts at mounting a national campaign on the right to water. The various attempts have not yet coalesced into something as strong and visible as the right to food campaign. Nonetheless, the past few years have seen an increasing interest among groups around the country for issues related to the right to water. The desire to engage with such issues is an extremely positive sign, one that will hopefully lead to civil society being able to better influence future law and policy developments concerning the human right to water in rural areas. This may take some time to become effective, but the urgency

Philippe Cullet

of the challenges posed by drinking water supply will ensure that civil society will be increasingly present and visible on this front.

Notes

1. For instance, the Accelerated Rural Water Supply Programme (ARWSP), created for rural areas, is described in more detail later in the chapter.

2. A recent estimate is that private expenditure accounted for 67 percent of the total expenditure on health in 2009; see High Level Expert Group Report 2011, 97.

3. One of the formal signs of this is the first priority given to drinking water in all the existing state and national water policies.

4. The only proposal for drinking water focused legislation at the Union level is limited to certain issues linked to water quality and would not constitute a comprehensive drinking-water legislation if it is adopted (Department of Drinking Water Supply 2007).

5. For more details on the Swajaldhara Guidelines, see Cullet 2009b.

6. Note that the guidelines indicate that the overall goal is to "provide every rural person with adequate safe water for drinking, cooking and other domestic basic needs." See NRDWP 2010, sec. 1.

7. On the links between MDGs and human rights, see Alston 2005.

8. See Black 2005, which estimates that coverage in rural areas increased from 18 percent in 1974 to 94 percent in 2004.

9. The two mentions are found at sections 2 and 12(1) of NRDWP 2009 and are no longer found in NRDWP 2010.

10. This is in fact what the World Commission on Environment and Development called for in its definition of sustainability. See Report of the World Commission on Environment and Development 1987.

11. There was a 27 percent increase in allocation for rural drinking water and sanitation in the union budget of 2012–13 (from $2.03 billion to $2.59 billion).

References

Accelerated Rural Water Supply Programme Guidelines (ARWSP Guidelines). 1999–2000. Government of India. http://www.ielrc.org/content/e9914.pdf.

Alston, Philip. 2005. "Ships Passing in the Night: The Current State of the Human Rights and Development Debate Seen Through the Lens of the Millennium Development Goals." *Human Rights Quarterly* 27, no. 3: 755–829.

Asian Development Bank. 2001. *Water for All: The Water Policy of the Asian Development Bank.*

Black, Maggie, and Rupert Talbot. 2005. *Water: A Matter of Life and Health.* New Delhi: Oxford University Press.

Bureau Indian Standards Specifications for Drinking Water (BIS Specification 10500: 1991). 1991. Bureau Indian Standards, New Dehli.

Central Public Health and Environmental Engineering Organisation (CPHEEO Manual). 1999. *Manual on Water Supply and Treatment*. 3rd ed. New Delhi: Ministry of Urban Development.

Committee on Economic, Social, and Cultural Rights, General Comment (ECOSOC). 2002. *The Right to Water: International Covenant on Economic, Social and Cultural Rights*. UN Doc. E/C.12/2002/11.

Constitution of India. 1949.

Cullet, Philippe. 2009a. *Water Law, Poverty and Development: Water Law Reforms in India*. Oxford: Oxford University Press.

———. 2009b. "New Policy Framework for Rural Drinking Water Supply: The Swajaldhara Guidelines." *Economic and Policy Weekly* 44, no. 50: 47–54.

Dublin Statement on Water and Sustainable Development. 1992. International Conference on Water and the Environment, Dublin.

Drèze, Jean. 2004. "Democracy and Right to Food." *Economic and Political Weekly* 39, no. 17: 1723–31.

Drèze, Jean, and Reetika Khera. 2010. "The BPL Census and a Possible Alternative." *Economic and Political Weekly* 45, no. 9: 54–63.

High Court of Kerala. 2006. *Vishala Kochi Kudivella Samarkshana Samithi v. State of Kerala*. 2006 (1) KLT 919.

High Level Expert Group Report. 2011. Universal Health Coverage for India. Planning Commission of India.

Himachal Pradesh Panchayati Raj Act. 1994. http://www.ielrc.org/content/e9410.pdf.

Karnataka Ground Water Regulation for Protection of Sources of Drinking Water Act. 1999. http://www.ielrc.org/content/e9905.pdf.

Karnataka Panchayat Raj Act. 1993. http://www.ielrc.org/content/e9312.pdf.

Kerala State Water Policy. 2008. http://www.ielrc.org/content/e0804.pdf.

Madhya Pradesh High Court. 1996. *Hamid Khan v. State of Madhya Pradesh*. AIR 1997 MP 191.

Madhya Pradesh peya jal parirakshan adhiniyam. 1986. http://www.ielrc.org/content/e8603.pdf.

Maharashtra Ground Water Regulation Drinking Water Purposes Act. 1993. http://www.ielrc.org/content/e9301.pdf.

Ministry of Rural Development. 2002. Guidelines on Swajaldhara. http://www.ielrc.org/content/e0212.pdf.

Muralidhar, S. 2006. "The Right to Water: An Overview of the Indian Legal Regime." In *The Human Right to Water*, edited by Eibe Riedel and Peter Rothen, 65–81. Berlin: Berliner Wissenschafts-Verlag.

National Commission for Enterprises in the Unorganised Sector (NCEUS). 2007. *Report on Conditions of Work and Promotion of Livelihoods in the Unorganised Sector*. New Delhi: Ministry of Small Scale Industries, Government of India.

National Rural Drinking Water Programme (NRDWP). 2009. *Movement Towards Ensuring People's Drinking Water Security in Rural India. Framework for Implementation 2009–2012.* http://www.ielrc.org/content/e0901.pdf.

———. 2010. *Movement Towards Ensuring People's Drinking Water Security in Rural India. Framework for Implementation.* http://www.ielrc.org/content/e1002.pdf.

National Food Security Act. 2013. *Gazette of India*, Extraordinary, Part II, Section 1, September 10.

Planning Commission. 2012. *Report of the Steering Committee on Water Resources and Sanitation for Twelfth Five Year Plan 2012–2017.* Government of India.

Provision of Urban Amenities in Rural Areas (PURA). 2011. A Public Private Partnership (PPP) Scheme Guidelines.

Rajasthan Municipalities Act. 1959. *Rajasthan Gazette*, Part IV-A, Extraordinary, September 14.

Report of the World Commission on Environment and Development. 1987. *Our Common Future.* UN Doc. A/42/427.

Right of Children to Free and Compulsory Education Act (RTE). 2009. *Gazette of India*, Extraordinary, Part II, Section 1, August 27.

Sampat, Preeti. 2007. "'Swa'-jal-dhara or 'Pay'-jal-dhara—Sector Reform and the Right to Drinking Water in Rajasthan and Maharashtra." *Law Environment and Development Journal* 3, no. 2: 103–25. http://www.lead-journal.org/content/07101.pdf.

Smith, Laila. 2006. "Neither Public nor Private—Unpacking the Johannesburg Water Corporatization Model." Social Policy and Development Programme Paper, no. 27. UN Research Institute for Social Development.

South Africa. 2001. *Regulations Relating to Compulsory National Standards and Measures to Conserve Water.* http://www.capetown.gov.za/en/Environmental ResourceManagement/publications/Documents/Regulations-for-National -Water-Conservation_2001.pdf

Strategic Plan. 2011–22. *Ensuring Drinking Water Security in Rural India.* Ministry of Rural Development, Department of Drinking Water and Sanitation: Rural Drinking Water.

Supreme Court of India. 1991. *Subhash Kumar v. State of Bihar.* AIR 1991 SC 420. http://www.ielrc.org/content/e9108.pdf.

Supreme Court of India. 2001. *People's Union for Civil Liberties v. Union of India.* Writ Petition (Civil) No. 196. Supreme Court Order. November 28.

United Nations General Assembly Resolution (UNGA). 2000. 55/2. United Nations Millennium Declaration, UN Doc. A/RES/55/2.

9

A Very Promising Species

From Hobbes to the Human Right to Water

RICHARD P. HISKES

Since Kant the foundation of human rights has been grounded on certain features of individuals, which are construed as conferring human dignity, the protection of which is the main justification for and purpose of human rights. Most often those features are subsumed under the general heading of rationality, and, according to Kant, the possession of which renders humans uniquely capable of moral autonomy and therefore worthy of dignity. This construal of human rights, among other things, severely limits the number of rights according to several commentators such as Hart, Cranston, Feinberg, and others, sometimes to only a handful, or in Hart's case, to a single human right to liberty.

In this chapter I argue that a second, competing foundation for rights is also anticipated within liberalism by Thomas Hobbes and elaborated upon by several twentieth-century schools of political thought, including feminism, postmodernism, and liberal communitarianism. These three appear to be rather strange bedfellows (not to mention as Hobbesian inheritors), but what they share provides a different basis for human rights. It is a foundation laid in two different features of human experience: the capacity of human beings to enter relationships based upon shared promises; and second, the existential condition of vulnerability that results from this capacity. For Hobbes it is these two aspects of human personality in the state of nature that provide the logic of natural rights at the same time as they make life there "nasty, brutish and short," rendering necessary the social contract.

Though not unrelated to the capacity to reason, the ability to have relationships that cause vulnerability, in response to which persons need and therefore deserve rights, opens the door both to new and new types of human rights. It is my argument that if the capacity for relationships that delivers rights uniquely to human beings is a dynamic feature of human personality and itself capable of evolution and growth, it is logical to assume that the kinds of relationships for which humans are capable can also grow. Thus, as human relationships evolve, both in terms of interactions with each other and with, perhaps, their environment, it is entirely possible that new rights will emerge, for instance environmental human rights, and that some rights might even be the property of whole groups rather than only of individuals. I specifically explore the emergence and meaning of the human right to water as a uniquely "relational" right anticipated by Hobbes's account of the logical foundation of rights. Therefore, an appreciation of this new foundation for human rights allows the domain of human rights to be a vital and dynamic one that anticipates change and growth even in the number of rights that are legitimately conceived as core human rights.

Hobbes and the Relational Logic of Human Rights

The relational underpinnings of human rights begins with Hobbes, and not only because, as Alan Gewirth (1996, 106) notes, all modern rights doctrines begin there. It is a commonplace to recognize the seeds of liberalism—and therefore of modern rights theory—in *Leviathan*, since as the first state of nature/social contract theorist, Hobbes initiates the idea that even outside of society individuals have rights. But most discussions of Hobbes's approach to rights (e.g., Gauthier 1969, Gewirth 1996, Hobbes 1651, or Tuck 1979) focus almost exclusively on either Hobbes's defense of the right to life or to property. It is certainly true that Hobbes spends much of his time on these, at least implicitly, but I contend that a more fundamental right in Hobbes's system is logically implied by the capacities of human beings: the right to cooperate, or more specifically for Hobbes, the right to contract with each other by exercising the uniquely human capacity to make promises. It is because the exercise of this right is singularly—and tragically—lacking in the state of nature that it is necessary for humans to sign the social contract and depart into society, one characterized by the artifact of the modern state.

The right to contract and its absence in the state of nature has been remarked upon by some Hobbes scholars (Gauthier, Barry), but it is perhaps not readily apparent why this is the most basic right in Hobbes's view. Most scholars follow Gewirth (1996) in quoting Hobbes's famous statement concerning life in the state of nature as being "poor, solitary, nasty, brutish and short," as his declaration that the denial of the most fundamental right—the right to life—is what makes rational individuals complete the contract establishing the state. But it is the paragraph of the Leviathan that precedes that closing sentiment that makes clear Hobbes's general point that the state of nature denies not so much human *life* as human *capacities*, and it is those capacities that make a human life uniquely deserving of rights.

In this passage Hobbes is bemoaning the enormous wastefulness of life in the state of nature. In their necessary obsession with private security, individuals there realize that whatever non-security-related individual talents they have are worthless since they do not have the time or the resources to pursue them. Collectively, the various areas of potential human excellence remain unfulfilled, and human life as a result is not significantly different than that of animals.

> In such condition, there is no place for Industry; because the fruit thereof is uncertain; and consequently no Culture of the Earth; no Navigation, nor use of the commodities that may be imported by Sea; no commodious Building; no Instruments of moving, and removing such things as require much force; no Knowledge of the face of the Earth; no account of Time; no Arts; no Letters; no Society; and which is worst of all, continuall feare, and danger of violent death; And the life of man, solitary, poore, nasty, brutish, and short. (Hobbbes 1651, 186)

The abilities to achieve these things are all uniquely and singularly human; in the state of nature they are unused.

The reasons for this lack of exercise of human abilities in the state of nature are, of course, much commented upon by Hobbes scholars. Essentially, however, they boil down to two: first, the inability to establish relationships of trust that would make collective cooperation possible to achieve all these distinctively human ends; and second, a shared vulnerability bred again from lack of trust and the inability to read others' minds, where human plans and motivations are easily hidden from the understanding of would-be contractual partners.

Richard P. Hiskes

Hobbes makes it clear that what is necessary to make human life livable and productive is a force powerful enough to make individuals behave civilly. But he frames the need for force in a particular way, as Brian Barry (1968) makes clear. For Hobbes, the problem of order and human development is essentially found in the inability of people in the state of nature to enter into cooperative relationships—specifically promissory contracts—which would make collective action possible. Without an external authority powerful enough to enforce contracts, human reason dictates that contractual cooperation is irrational, since all contracts are by their very nature unequal and therefore unacceptable in a place where everyone considers oneself equal to everyone else. Contractual inequality reveals itself in the fact that for every contract one party must act first, at which point she is at a disadvantage (i.e., unequal) having already completed her part of the arrangement and now vulnerable to the subsequent action (or inaction) of her contracting party. Hobbes relates the dilemma of the natural state:

> For he that performeth first, has no assurance the other will performe after; because the bonds of words are too weak to bridle mens ambitions, avarice, anger, and other Passions; which in the condition of mere Nature, where all men are equall, and judges of the justness of their own fears cannot possibly be supposed. (Hobbes 1651, 186)

Without someone to force the *other* party to honor the obligations of the contract to keep his or her promise—no rational person would enter a contract. As cooperation languishes, the human achievements of collective life that wait upon such relations are never realized.

Barry construes Hobbes's argument in the context of what is necessary for the concept of obligation to become real in the state of nature, and he broadens Hobbes's claim not only to contracts but to *all* promises and therefore to justice and morality as a whole—what Hobbes calls "the qualities that relate to men in society" (Hobbes 1651, 188). But whether the key is obligation or simply cooperation, it is clear that what the sovereign brings is the opportunity for human beings to realize their fundamental nature as beings capable of forming equal relationships with each other that are productive of all that is uniquely human. It is that aspect of right's nature that establishes both the basic right of all to protect their lives and the subsequent rights of society.

For Hobbes, then, human rights are grounded in two things: first, the human capacity to make promises for the purpose of entering into rational agreements for collective action in the future; and second, the fact of our vulnerability in doing so without a common arbiter to guarantee that the obligations proceeding from those agreements will be fulfilled. Reason plays its role here certainly, but it is not the logical basis for rights themselves. Reason provides the understanding of what is lacking in the natural state—and the vision of what might be possible once it is left behind. But that level of understanding and capacity for reimagining how one might live—both the products of reason—do not grant rights on which to build human relations. If they did, leaving the state of nature would not be necessary, and life there would not be as miserable as it is. Rather, rights emerge *from* relationships and more fundamentally from the ability—and necessity—to engage in them for the human experience even to occur. Without both the rights and the relationships, we remain in the subhuman, "brutish" presocial state. Rights are the logical consequence—and requirement—of our relational nature.

Notice here that Hobbes is crediting the collective—or emergent—phenomenon of relationship itself at least as much as the individual capacity to enter them, with the production of rights. Here is where his focus on contract is most emphatic and telling. All contracts involve the creation—and exchange—of private rights and duties, but the *capacity* to contract—to enter into a promissory relationship with mutual rights and duties—is what sets humans apart from animals and is what logically implies that there be must be some rights accorded to them even before the production of social order and the myriad contracts that ensue. Society guarantees many more rights both by securing contracts and fulfilling the right to peace, but it must be created itself by (social) contract—a uniquely human event. Only humans possess the "natural" right to create the social contract and the obligations that ensue, because, again, only humans have the capacity to enter such relationships based on promise.

In basing rights on the capacity to promise and enter relations that produce, among other things, collective goods, Hobbes is also anticipating how the idea of rights will alter the modern notion of human identity. As other liberal thinkers (and eventually the authors of the Universal Declaration of Human Rights (UDHR 1948) will ground the notion of human dignity on the idea of individual rights, the unique human ability to make public promises (i.e., contract) and enter relationships thereby will become essential to many rights arguments today as an exercise that manifests and protects human dignity and identity. The best current example is the demand for gay marriage rights. If making significant public promises is so essential a part of human identity as Hobbes claims, then denying the opportunity to those who make such meaningful public professions constitutes an egregious assault on their dignity as human beings. Indeed, for Hobbes it would be a denial of their identity as humans. No wonder then that gay marriage is such a fervently sought right—it is the manifestation of the very thing that Hobbes claims is the basis of all rights: the capacity to promise.

Hobbes's understanding of rights provides a foundation for liberal society in the sense that it (or rather the sovereign) guarantees the sanctity of individual liberty to contract with others. Of course, Hobbes's view also establishes an authoritarian government, necessary in his opinion so that there be only one enforcer of rights. Locke would carry the right to private liberty into the public realm as well, by giving citizens the liberty to choose and also withdraw support for their governors. But Locke's understanding of rights differs from Hobbes's in that Lockean rights are held privately by individuals as part of themselves whether or not they are in relationships with others. The best example here is Locke's foundation of the right to property within the actual body and labor of each individual. What grants ownership is the "mixing" of one's labor—one's *self*—with the thing to become property. For Hobbes, property is the result of the *relationship* of exchange, produced by contracts enforced by the sovereign—there is no property (and no right to property) without relations.

Unlike Locke and, later, Kant, Hobbes establishes the existence of rights as the logical consequence of the human capacity for relationships. That capacity produces a few rights itself, mostly the right to liberty to protect oneself in the state of nature. But the capacity to enter relationships portends many more rights to come, both in the event of the social contract and all the subsequent relationships possible in the society it creates. From a standpoint within the Hobbesian state of nature, most human rights have yet to emerge.

Hobbes, of course, complicates matters considerably by arguing that the emergence of new rights under the sovereign matters only to the sovereign because in the society of the Leviathan only the sovereign can be said actually to possess rights. The social contract in Hobbes's formulation transfers all natural rights from citizens to sovereign in exchange for the return to citizens of a now protected and enforced right to contract (and, following Barry, to enter into other promissory relations as well). Locke will provide a different relationship between liberal citizens, their rights, and the government, but Hobbes's relational foundation of rights in the state of nature still pertains in Hobbesian society since the right to contract is, as MacPherson (Hobbes 1651) argues, the supreme liberal right.

It might be objected that I am overstating the relational nature of rights in Hobbes because in his view only the right to contract is truly an emergent, relational right, and that is the only right that citizens retain in society. In some sense this is a fair objection in light of Locke's later expansion of the number of innately held rights. But I think a better understanding of this paradox relies on the language of contemporary human rights. What is missing in Hobbes's treatment of rights is the conceptualization of the state as itself the "addressee" of individual rights. Human rights today are addressed (in documents like the UDHR) specifically to governments as the protectors of those rights, and, often, their violators as well.

Today the human rights regime charges every state with protecting the human rights that its citizens possess, usually by restricting or directing the state's own behavior. Clearly Hobbes does not view the sovereign as the addressee of citizens' rights *except* the right to contract. This limits the number of what Hobbes sees as the rights of citizens since the sovereign is above any such charge that might come from being the addressee of rights. Nevertheless, the foundation of all rights in the state of nature remains relational. In society the relation that dominates is that between the sovereign and citizens, thereby limiting the number—but not the nature—of those rights.

It is the "emergent" character of Hobbesian human rights that fully sets them apart from the more reductionist Lockean and Kantian view. Most rights for Hobbes, except the liberty to protect one's life and to make promises, we are not born with; they are yet to come from the exercise of our ability to enter relationships with others. But they are also emergent in Hobbes's view in that unlike Locke and Kant they do not come from inside individuals (or from what God or nature has imbued there) but from *between* them—from their interactions. This is a somewhat uniquely collectivist foundation for individual rights, which meets the contemporary social science definition of emergent phenomena—things that appear only in the context of groups or group behavior, groups being understood minimally as simply individuals-in-relations.

It is this doubly "emergent" nature of rights, as "new" and as oddly collectivist—irreducible to individuals in isolation—that Hobbes offers to human rights theorists today. In doing so, Hobbes perhaps inadvertently lays the groundwork for a dynamic conception of rights, which can embrace the possibility of new relationships between people and even with nature itself that are productive of newly emergent, "environmental" human rights. In the process, Hobbes opens the door through which diverse approaches to human identity and politics can meet and join in a shared understanding of human rights and possibilities. It is to the latter Hobbesian product that we turn first.

Emergent Identity and Emergent Rights

Except for Hobbes, state of nature theory in general, and especially as expounded by Locke and Tom Paine, specifically denies the possibility of emergent rights since part of the theory is that no new rights are gained in society. For both Locke and Paine this is a crucial step in the justification of revolution, since government is denied any role significant enough to deliver such important goods as rights. This is one reason both Locke and Paine rely on the language of "natural" rights, to make it clear that what rights there are emanate directly from human nature and therefore pertain before social or political relations exist.

Hobbes is notably silent on this issue, and the use of the modifier "natural" except when preceding "law" is mostly absent from *Leviathan* as well.[1] But it is obvious that Hobbes certainly understands that only in civil society can anyone possess "contractual" rights: it is their absence that leads man to opt out of the state of nature. Furthermore, if life in the state of nature is subhuman due to their absence, and only becomes human through their enforcement by the sovereign, it is difficult not to conclude that the right to contract is perhaps a "natural" right but one that only emerges in society.

At a minimum we should conclude that Hobbes's view of rights is more expressly political than that of Locke, Paine, and perhaps even Kant, and is therefore more in line with our current understanding of "human" rights. Compared to the Enlightenment view of natural rights, human rights today are unquestionably political in definition, since, as Carl Wellman (1995) argues, they presume the existence of governments and exist primarily to stipulate what the relations between governments and individuals should be. The difference between natural and human rights can be overstated, but, as Jeremy Waldron (1987) points out, use of the modifier "human" makes it clear that the justification for rights no longer lay in alleged features of human nature. In fact, for Waldron, using the term "human" rights "leaves open the question of justification, or worse still, takes the mere existence of a broad consensus on these matters to be a sufficient reason for avoiding the task of justification altogether" (163).

Certainly the Universal Declaration of Human Rights (UDHR 1948) is a political document, and many of the rights listed there appear nowhere in early liberal lists of "natural" rights. But that does not go very far in establishing how it has become acceptable to speak of the "new" rights emerging from documents like the UDHR when the classical doctrines invoked in its preamble would not countenance such an emergence. The concept of human rights in view in the UDHR shares with natural rights theories a belief that rights are grounded in the capacity (and need) of human beings for dignity. The UDHR links dignity with two other features of human identity—our endowment of reason and moral conscience. It states that "All human beings are born free and equal in dignity and rights. They are endowed with reason and conscience and should act towards one another in a spirit of brotherhood" (UDHR, art. 1).

So far this is not much different from Locke and Kant's grounding of nat-ural rights in the special identity of human beings. But what is different is the understanding of the *sources* of human identity that underlies the UDHR is in direct opposition to state of nature theory. The UDHR presumes societies and governments as the starting point of all rights, not the state of nature; therefore it invokes the nature of the *relations* between people that guarantee rights—equality and a spirit of brotherhood. These relations are productive of human rights because they produce the identity of rational and moral per-sons. Unlike Locke and Kant but echoing Hobbes, the UDHR assumes these aspects of human identity appear only in society, not in some primordial pre-existing state. In short, if the idea of human rights does not rely on the state of nature for its notion of identity, it is logical to assume that the identity of individual persons that qualifies them for human rights is constructed through the relations within which the lessons of conscience and dignity are learned. In other words, it is through the relations that individuals participate in that their identities are created, that is, they emerge. As emergent identities, indi-viduals are then worthy of human rights. Human rights are emergent because the human identity that logically entails them (as in Hobbes) is itself an emer-gent product of human relationships.

In a sense then, all human rights except (as in Hobbes) the rights to life are emergent rights, since they rely on human relationships and the identities created thereby. But I argue in the next section that environmental human rights in general, and the human right to water in particular, are emergent rights for other reasons as well, having to do with the harms to which they respond and the interconnections between persons and nature that they pre-sume. But these two rights also share—or best exemplify—the patrimony of Hobbes that virtually all contemporary human rights manifest. Therefore in an ironic way they bring us back to nature for the realization of some of our most important rights. I also explore further the emergent nature of human rights and how it is embraced or implied in several contemporary political the-ories. Nature guarantees that as human relationships change and evolve, the rights to which humans are entitled will evolve with them.[2]

A recent impetus for changing our understanding of the foundations of human rights comes from Richard Rorty's (1993) well-known critique of human rights foundationalism in general. For Rorty, the view of human rights as grounded in specific human attributes such as reason effectively excludes from human rights consideration other cultures, which do not share the West-ern attitude that rationality is the defining mark of our species. Emphasizing human rights in moral arguments about human dignity and desert for Rorty means that in practice human nature is defined as manifested in "people like

Richard P. Hiskes

us." Consequently it is easy to deny rights to people significantly different than "us" on the grounds that they are not really human. Rorty's example of the dehumanization of Croats by the Serbs is simply one instance of a sad contemporary litany of crimes against humanity—crimes Rorty concludes will never be prevented by human rights arguments or practices.

Rorty's argument is provocative, but its power as a critique of human rights dissipates if the foundation of human rights lies not in human rationality (or other individualistic attributes) but in the universal ability of humans regardless of cultural context to enter moral relationships with other persons. Those relations, as commented on by a variety of different scholars representing very different schools of political thought, are characterized specifically by the "sentiment" and sympathy that Rorty prefers to human rights as a basis for morality. If this is true, then it is not the idea of human rights that gets in the way of morality, as Rorty would have us believe. Rather, the problematic issue is human rights' reliance upon an outdated and solipsistic understanding of human nature or identity that promotes human rights as based upon the private characteristics of individuals construed as abstract rights holders rather than as individuals in relations with others.

As one of the first human rights theorists to reject the Kantian basis of human rights, Jack Donnelly (1989, 18) insists that "human nature is a social project as much as it is a given." Furthermore, Donnelly claims that human rights belong to persons because of social practices aimed at preserving dignity. Dignity is itself a product of social conventions that sustain a view of human nature seen as emerging "out of a wide range of given possibilities through the interaction of natural endowment, individual action, and social institutions" (ibid.). The range of possible relationships from which rights emerge for Donnelly means that although different cultures in their varied social practices may disagree on which relationships give rise to rights, there can still be consensus globally on the possibility and reality of at least some rights. Furthermore, the production of rights by such interactions means that human rights can be as dynamic as human nature itself, evolving and multiplying in response to "changing ideas of human dignity, the rise of new political forces, technological changes, new techniques of repression, and even past human rights successes" (ibid., 26).

In his reconceptualization of human identity to fit the emergent and dynamic nature of rights, Donnelly is joined by an eclectic group of theorists from several philosophical camps, including neo-pragmatism, communitarianism, and especially twentieth-century feminism. Pragmatists like Rorty argue that human rights need a less abstract foundation to account for the diversity of human experience across time and cultures, and especially to encompass nonrationalistic elements of behavior like sentimentality. Donnelly's foundation for human rights opens up the concept of human identity to variation depending on social context, therefore grounding the concept in a way that fits well with the pragmatist demand for a less abstract view of human nature.

In the late 1970s communitarians like Michael Sandel and Charles Taylor launched their own critiques of the liberal understanding of the abstract individual as rights bearer. Sandel (1982) argued that liberalism's attachment to social contract theorizing ignored the obvious fact that real community is "constitutive" of individual identity—not the other (Kantian) way around, and that community is more a realm of shared meaning than mere self-interest. Similarly, Taylor (1989) insisted that individual identity is inexplicable without reference to communities of discourse that are, in his titular concept, "sources of the self." Communities incorporate interactions productive of "webs of interlocution" without which human subjectivity itself is incoherent as a concept. "I am a self only in relation to certain interlocutors: in one way in relation to those conversation partners who were essential to my achieving self-definition; in another in relation to those who are not crucial to my continuing grasp of languages of self-understanding—and, of course, these classes may overlap. A self exists only within what I call 'webs of interlocution'" (ibid., 36).

For communitarians, only such "situated" selves could be said to have rights, since only such persons could be said to have "personhood" in the first place. It is in the web of interaction that defines one's communal situation where rights are produced.

Though opposed ideologically and philosophically to the conservative communitarianism of Sandel and Taylor, contemporary feminism shares with it—and with pragmatism as well—an insistence on the relational, emergent nature of individual human identity. In recent work both Seyla Benhabib (2002) and Carol C. Gould (1998, 2004) trace the emerging feminist view of the "intersubjective constitution of the self" (Benhabib 2002, 51) or of "embodied politics" (Gould 2004, ch. 3) to the critique of rationalist individual identity advanced by both communitarian and feminist theorists.

Broadly speaking, feminism's argument for an emergent, relational approach to identity differs from the postmodern and communitarian arguments in terms of how it locates the source of its model of identity. Gender difference is the starting point of course, as both Gould and Benhabib begin with the living experiences of women—their roles as caregivers, nurturers, and close providers for completely dependent infants—to generalize a different picture of human identity. Such a starting point is fundamentally at odds with liberal and other characterizations of individuals as intrinsically autonomous beings.

Richard P. Hiskes

Gould's concept of the self as "individual-in-relations" borrows much from Iris Young's (2002) insistence that identity is a product of relations with others. As Young insists, an individual sense of self is derived from recognition by others within a web of relations that both enable and restrain all participants, granting rights to all at the same time that everyone's alleged autonomy is restricted. Thus, the whole idea "that a person's autonomy exists independent of others and from which they are excluded except through mutual agreements is a dangerous fiction" (ibid., 33). For Gould this means that true individuality is always that of the "individual-in-relations," where individual uniqueness derives from every person's unique set of relationships with others. Individual persons remain "ontologically primary" according to Gould, because each person chooses her own relations, "but the relations among them are also essential aspects of their being [that] do not exist independently or apart from the individuals who are related. Rather, they are relational properties of these individuals" (Gould 2004, 120). Rights too then also become "relational properties" of persons, both intrinsic to each person as a self-in-relations, and also produced ontologically and universally by the very capacity for and practice of interrelationship.

This convergence of three such widely divergent approaches to politics represents a shared departure from the traditional understanding of the foundation of rights. As social phenomena, human rights are produced by the situationally defined identities of their holders. Rather than rendering human rights completely relative to (different) cultures, however, this relational understanding of rights makes clear that rights are *universally* the products of human relationships of which only—and all—humans are capable. But those relations are themselves defined differently both across cultures and across time. For Donnelly (2007), this constitutes the "relative universality" of human rights: they are the relative (contextually produced) manifestations of a universal human capacity to enter a variety of different relations.

The debate that Donnelly's recent work has produced is too much focused on *space*, however—how different cultures around the globe produce different rights via different relations.[3] At least as interesting is how rights have changed across *time*, as the recognition of new relationships have raised prospects of new rights yet to emerge. I have argued elsewhere (Hiskes 2005, 2009) that the science of ecology postulates both a general relationship with our environment and a connectedness with all other living humans and with future generations as well, which also produce new rights, specifically environmental rights including the human right to water. Within that argument lies the extension of Hobbes's original insight that the capacity to relationally define new rights within society is limited only by the extent of human knowledge.

As knowledge grows, so will our awareness of the relationships that encumber us—and grant us rights.

The Emergence of Environmental Human Rights and the Right to Water

We can conclude that following Hobbes and the twentieth-century schools of thought that endorse his initial insight, human rights are emergent initially because the unique human identity to which they attach is itself an emergent feature of each rights holder, produced by the sum of his or her relations. In this section we explore two additional emergent features of contemporary rights. First, the science of ecology teaches that the interactions of people today with their natural environment are similar to the complex interconnections that make up Taylor's "webs of interlocution." Though this has probably always been true, it is modern science's recognition of this relation that gives rise to environmental rights. Second, since all rights, as Harmon (1980) points out, are in response to real or potential harms, the structure of environmental harms as themselves distinctly emergent means that the rights that are meant to protect people against them are emergent as well.

By its very nature the environment calls attention to the interconnectedness of all human life and the impacts it has as a whole on natural systems. Ecology teaches this lesson of interconnectivity more than any other; one of its corollaries is that impacts on the environment such as pollution are ontologically emergent. That means that for practical purposes it is unproductive to try to separate out each individual contribution to the phenomenon of, for instance, water pollution. In other words, pollution is an emergent phenomenon, a product of our collective life and a harm for which we are essentially all to blame as contributors.

As a response to environmental harms, environmental rights are emergent in three ways. First, as discussed earlier, all rights to some extent are emergent products of human relationships. Second, environmental rights are "new" rights, the product of new knowledge including the science of ecology. The recognition of environmental rights derived from ecology does not necessarily mean that humans never had such rights before, but that the awareness of all rights waits upon the development of knowledge in at least two areas, scientific and moral.

Environmental rights can emerge as rights only when knowledge of the social impacts of human life upon the environment is attained. When energy sources are recognizably threatened with depletion, when degradation of the air, water, and soil becomes impossible to ignore, when, in short, human knowledge about how life impacts the environment and vice versa becomes widespread, the awareness of the necessity of environmental human rights grows. It is, in short, the understanding of environmental harms caused by humans that gives rise to environmental rights. Environmental rights also wait upon what Edith Brown Weiss (1989) names a moral knowledge that supplements our scientific, ecological awareness of environmental interconnections and how we are entwined with them. She identifies the "evolution of public conscience" to a point where awareness of the harmful environmental effects of human behavior becomes widespread and results in moral outrage. "When this evolution has achieved a certain maturity" sufficient to undergird a public demand for action, then "legal obligations and rights are formulated" (103).

Not only knowledge about them but the actual environmental harms both to us and to nature are themselves emergent as collective effects. The depredations visited upon the natural world are the products of collective behavior of individuals *in relations.* This is the third way in which environmental rights are emergent rights. They are the products of the relations between individuals—both locally and globally—that have impacts on the natural world. These relations can be legal, contractual ones as in corporations in a free enterprise system, the very ones Hobbes envisioned in society and lacking in the state of nature. But families also have collective environmental impacts, as do social groups under a variety of definitions. The point here is that as a species our impacts on the environment emerge from behavior patterns generated by the relationships by which we act jointly in ways that affect the world around us. Societal norms and patterns of consumption, corporate decisions about resource usage or production, and family decisions about property use or purchase all carry effects for the surrounding environment.

Elsewhere (Hiskes 2005, 2009) I have explored environmental rights specifically referring to the rights to clean air, water, and soil. As emergent phenomena environmental rights also invoke an intrinsically group focus, both because the harms to which they respond are collectively produced and because they include future persons as well. Perhaps more than any other right, environmental rights specifically concern the rights of future generations, who can only logically be construed abstractly as a group. Culturally as well we tend to think of the future in terms of future persons to whom we are related either by family or as future members of our community, thereby dissipating the abstractness of future generations by making them part of "us." Politically this recognition of the rights of future persons needs to be embodied in constitutions that guarantee rights to all citizens now and in the future. In making such claims, politics manifests the "social contract" of which early liberals first spoke, invoking a group identity (a society "in relations") that persists across time and extends into the future.

It is somewhat ironic given the international, border-transgressing nature of environmental harms like air and water pollution to argue for the inclusion of environmental rights within national constitutions. But constitutions are where citizens and nations proclaim their beliefs and values, which endure across generations. Constitutional rights in an important sense are promises to future citizens, guarantees (with judicial clout) that certain bedrock values will continue to define national identity long after the founders are gone. In a modern politics where shortsightedness and transitory political gain tends to rule behavior, the long-term demands of environmental harms and their concomitant rights require the transgenerational promise of constitutionalism.

The irony of constitutional protection for environmental rights mirrors the general "human rights paradox" that frames the approach to human rights taken in this book and named in its title. Environmental rights are uniquely global—universal in more than the traditional human rights sense because their scope is global: the natural environment is not segregated according to national or political borders. This is especially true for the right to water, whose "flow" interconnects all holders of this right in the same way that all earth's water sources are interconnected. But of course, human rights protection is the business of national governments as the addressees of human rights, so it is natural that we look to constitutions to provide our "local" protection. And to complete the picture of what in the introduction to this book is referred to as the "mélange of the global and the local," environmental human rights embrace in their global reach even future generations.

Environmental rights are especially future-oriented compared to all other rights, since most environmental harms lie in the future, and future persons are uniquely vulnerable to the environmental assaults launched by the living. But more than this, the environmental rights of the living are contingent upon the existence of the same rights in the future. In other words, it is by protecting the environmental rights of future generations that the same rights even exist today. This is a uniquely reciprocal relationship posited by the whole idea of environmental rights. Other rights, such as the right to free speech, do not manifest this level of interconnectivity between present and future persons. My right to speak freely does not depend in any real sense on whether after I am dead the right persists or is rescinded for the rest of social history. But given the unique relationship to time encapsulated within the idea of environmental rights my current rights to clean air, water, or soil intrinsically depend on protecting the same rights for future generations.

Richard P. Hiskes

A moment's reflection will elucidate the special, inextricable relationship that environmental rights presume across generations. Given the extended length of time that both environmental harms and ameliorations require to deliver their effect, any policies aimed at preserving the environment must seriously take into account the interests of citizens living several generations in the future. In the case of radioactive waste pollution, the relevant time span is hundreds, even thousands, of years, but even more prosaic forms of environmental damage and cleanup pose decades of effort.

Nevertheless it is undeniable that environmental protection or sustainability policies are rarely predicated on the foundation of rights. Even when they are, the rights under consideration are almost always those of present generations, since rights of nonexistent persons have no legal standing. But given the relational character of all human rights, and the particularly pervasive interconnectedness of environmental harms across generations, it is increasingly clear that the interests of future generations in present environmental impacts ought to be elevated to the level of rights. Since the purpose of rights is to protect people from harms to which they are vulnerable, who is more vulnerable than the group of future persons responsible for cleaning up the environmental messes we leave behind? If we the living have environmental rights to protect us from those same harms that persist into the future, why do future generations not have the same rights?

If the response is that future people *will* possess environmental rights when they are in fact living in the world, consider what an inadequate response that is in terms both of protecting the rights of the living and of the future. Unless harms to the environment that we create today are ameliorated within the current generations' lifetime, all future persons will enter the world with their environmental rights already under assault. Too bad for them perhaps, but the living also jeopardize their own environmental rights by not recognizing that environmental harms deny the rights of the future. Our environmental safety and security depends specifically on honoring the future's rights, since policies initiated to honor our rights will of necessity need to be extended far into the future. If the argument for doing so is based on environmental rights, it will logically include recognition of the rights of future generations as well as living citizens. In Hobbesian terms, environmental rights are the promises the living make to future generations within their reciprocal relationship of environmental protection.

More than logic recommends this recognition of the environmental rights of future generations, however. It is in our self-interest both individually and collectively to invest future persons with the power of rights with which they as a group can restrain our environmental choices today. Their vulnerability imparts a moral obligation on us but, more than this, it is the level of our environmental interconnectedness with future persons that ought to raise our obligation to the level of a claim of rights, not mere altruism. We have a relationship with the future defined by the interconnectedness of nature itself. This means that our relationship with the future in preserving environmental goods is a reciprocal one—serving the future's interests by protecting its environmental rights reflexively serves our interests and honors our rights as well.

Nowhere is the relational interconnectivity across generations that gives rise to rights more clear than in the recent arguments surrounding the promulgation of an international human right to water. As one aspect of environmental rights, the right to water requires that we be concerned not only with our own needs but with those of others, including of future persons. Water literally floods the spaces between all people in their communities, nations, and continents; it also flows through time. The water we consume today reappears tomorrow in either potable or polluted form through the workings of a global ecosystem. Water connects us spatially across the globe and through time, since all of us, whether we live in the desert or amid the Great Lakes, are part of the same water supply that persists into the future. If a human right to water exists, it must be because of these intimate relations between all people that nature's interconnectivity bequeaths. By the same token, then, the holders of such a right must simultaneously be both the living and the not yet born.

Currently there is much discussion and a growing consensus concerning the reality of a human right to water.[4] In 2003 the UN Committee on Economic, Social, and Cultural Rights (UN CESCR) officially adopted General Comment 15, which declared that "the human right to water is indispensible for leading a life in human dignity [and] entitles everyone to sufficient, safe, acceptable, physically accessible and affordable water for personal and domestic uses" (UN CESCR 2003, 1–2). Such declarations do not carry the force of law, of course, and some detractors of the proposed right to water echo Maurice Cranston's famous (1967) admonition that most human rights fall into a "supposed" category rather than a real one. One such critic is Stephen Tully, who argues (2005) that article 11 of the 1966 International Covenant on Economic, Social, and Cultural Rights specifically denies an interpretation that would support the adoption of new rights not named in the Covenant. One can almost hear the echoes of Jeremy Bentham's nineteenth-century ridicule of any imprescriptible moral rights as elevated nonsense ("nonsense upon stilts") that ignores essential facts about the human condition, which cannot be altered by the proclamations of new rights: "wanting is not the same as having; hunger is not bread" (Bentham 1987).

Richard P. Hiskes

Nevertheless, arguments for a human right to water are beginning to cascade within human rights scholarship and law. Malcolm Langford (2006) identifies an imminent "world water crisis," which many ecologists and policy makers, including the authors of General Comment 15 (UN CESCR 2003), agree will lead by the year 2025 to 1.8 billion of the world's population living with severe water deprivation. Langford acknowledges that the argument for a human right to water can be construed several ways: as part of a general environmental human right, as a specific right regarding access, or as a claim against government privatization of water delivery. Before General Comment 15, arguments varied but generally drew from a broad reading of article 25 of the UDHR that delineates a human right "to a standard of living adequate for the health and well-being of himself and his family, including food, clothing, housing and medical care and necessary social services" (UDHR 1948). The right to water is not singly specified by this reading, but as Peter Gleick (1999) observes, the list should not be taken as exhaustive of the component elements of an adequate standard of living" (88).

The human right to water is explicitly named in two prominent and widely ratified human rights documents, the Convention on the Elimination of All Forms of Discrimination Against Women (CEDAW 1979), where it is incorporated into a general right of development, and the Convention on the Rights of the Child (CRC 1989), as part of the right to health. Both types of arguments have been pursued by human rights scholars (see Filmer-Wilson 2005; Shue [1980] 1996), but one additional argument presented by the legal team of Scanlon, Cassar, and Nemes (2004) extends the argument for the right to water to future generations as well. They argue that the right to water embraces not only the consumption "rights of people but also the needs of the [larger] environment with regard to river basins, lakes, aquifers, oceans and ecosystems surrounded watercourses. Realistically, a right to water cannot be secured without this broader respect" (27).

Scanlon et al. are not offering here a deep ecology defense of the rights of inanimate objects. Rather, they are calling attention to the inescapably borderless nature of water systems that brings all people across the globe and across time into relationship with each other and with nature in their shared need of its bounty. Therefore, ensuring the right to water "for present and future generations requires that a long-term view be taken. A greater integration of environmental principles . . . and human rights principles will be required" (ibid., 27).

As stated before, these environmental human rights such as the right to water need to be included in national constitutions, both because of the nature of constitutions as embodying trans-generational values and concerns, and because constitutional rights have teeth when it comes to enforcement (Hayward 2005). An enforceable, constitutionally protected right to water offers opportunities to make decisions that will encourage conservation in all aspects of citizens' lives together. One example includes golf course siting and management. If future citizens have a constitutionally rights-based claim on the water we waste today, expending anywhere from 500,000 to 1,000,000 gallons a day on average to keep the greens lush and the fairways glowing becomes a practice actionable in court (Hiskes 2010).

As a fundamental human need, the case for water as a most *basic* right in Shue's ([1980] 1996) sense of the word incorporates a realization that such rights are never held in isolation. Just as all of humanity is connected by its reliance on one global water system, the rights that emerge both regarding water and all other natural resources are products of their capacity to enter cooperative relations with each other, and with those yet to come.

Conclusion: The Emerging Social Contract of Human Rights

The human right to water is not yet fully established either in international or constitutional law nor in public consciousness, although consideration of it is undeniably on the rise. Partly this is due to the growing realization that the effects of water scarcity and deprivation are already upon us and visibly so, not only in the third world but also, for example, in the Western United States. Still, such recognition sounds more like hunger than bread in Bentham's rendering—clearly many need the right to water; does "wanting" make it so?

The answer, obviously, is no. Emergent human rights as a concept do not imply that for every new desire a corresponding human right will emerge to slake it. As Bentham and, later, John Stuart Mill recognized, such a system of social entitlement would put individual liberty at ever increasing risk. Since the human right to liberty is something all liberals, utilitarian or deontological, agree upon, any new human right that severely jeopardized it would bring its validity into question.

As Hobbes first understood, it is not desire or need that verifies the rights that do legitimately exist. What rights humans possess is determined by what logic requires them to have in order to realize their identity as beings superior in important ways to animals. That realization produces all those uniquely human excellences absent in the natural state (in Hobbes's iteration, industry, culture, navigation, architecture, transportation, knowledge, art, etc.) but

Richard P. Hiskes

possible in society once the opportunities for collective action, cooperation, trust—for human relations based on shared promises—are secured. These capabilities are what define human identity but can only be achieved by humans in relations with each other. Whatever realization of those capabilities requires then—whatever those relationships require—is protected by right. For Hobbes, there is nothing natural to man about the solitary state of nature; unlike for Locke and other social contract theorists, we are only fully human in society when fully interconnected within a web of relationships that define both ourselves and our rights.

No single right manifests that same level of deep interconnection and relationship than does the human right to water. Similarly, no genre of rights insists more upon the fundamental relatedness of all humans with each other and with nature than does the group of environmental rights. Therefore, environmental rights including the right to water are the most basic of all human rights, but not because as isolated individuals we need what they protect in order to survive. They are the most basic of rights because they protect the relationships that *produce* us as human beings. They are what our relational nature logically requires as necessary prerequisites of every human capability, abilities refined not in isolation, not singly, but within communities endowed with the protections that rights provide. Environmental rights are the most emergent of human rights and therefore the most essential for the protection of us all, in both our individual and collective identities as the most emergent of species.

Notes

1. Hobbes's concept of natural law is itself a huge topic to explore. However, two features of Hobbes's understanding of natural law are worth commenting on since they have distinct relevance for my argument. First, Hobbes states that in its entirety natural law constitutes simply a "tendency toward peace." Second, natural law is to be distinguished specifically from natural right, almost as opposites; they differ, he says (1651, 189) as much as obligation and liberty. Thus natural law by itself does not produce rights, except perhaps—and minimally, the right to liberty: the "Right of Nature . . . the Liberty each man hath, to use his own power, as he will himselfe, for the preservation of his own Nature; that is to say, of his own Life" (ibid.).

2. For a fuller discussion of these issues, see Hiskes 2009.

3. See for instance Michael Goodhart's (2007) response to Donnelly's argument. For a full treatment of different cultural representations of contemporary human rights see Gould 2004 and Brysk 2002.

4. What follows in brief here is elaborated upon in Hiskes 2010.

References

Barry, Brian. 1968. "Warrender and His Critics." *Philosophy* 43:117–37.

Benhabib, Seyla. 2002. *The Claims of Culture*. Princeton, NJ: Princeton University Press.

Bentham, Jeremy. 1987. "Anarchical Fallacies." In *"Nonsense Upon Stilts": Bentham, Burke, and Marx on the Rights of Man*, edited by Jeremy Waldron, 46–69. London: Methuen.

Brysk, Alison, ed. 2002. *Globalization and Human Rights*. Berkeley: University of California Press.

Convention on the Elimination of Discrimination Against Women (CEDAW). Adopted December 18, 1979, G.A. Res. 34/180, U.N. GAOR 34th sess., art. 14, UN Doc. A/34/46 (1980), 1249 UNTS 13.

Convention on the Rights of the Child (CRC). Adopted November 20, 1989, G.A. Res. 44/25, UN GAOR, 44th sess., art. 24, UN Doc A/44/49 (1989), 1577 UNTS 3.

Cranston, Maurice. 1967. "Human Rights, Real and Supposed." In *Political Theory and the Rights of Man*, edited by D. D. Raphael, 43–53. New York: Blackboard.

Donnelly, Jack. 1989. *Universal Human Rights in Theory and Practice*. Ithaca, NY: Cornell University Press.

———. 2007. "The Relative Universality of Human Rights." *Human Rights Quarterly* 29:281–306.

Filmer-Wilson, Emilie. 2005. "The Human Rights-Based Approach to Development: The Right to Water." *Netherlands Quarterly of Human Rights* 23:213–41.

Gauthier, David P. 1969. *The Logic of Leviathan*. Oxford: Clarendon Press.

Gewirth, Alan. 1996. *The Community of Rights*. Chicago: University of Chicago Press.

Gleick, Peter H. 1999. "The Human Right to Water." *Water Policy* 1:487–503.

Goodhart, Michael. 2007. "Neither Relative Nor Universal: A Response to Donnelly." *Human Rights Quarterly* 30:183–93.

Gould, Carol C. 1998. *Rethinking Democracy*. New York: Cambridge University Press.

———. 2004. *Globalizing Democracy and Human Rights*. New York: Cambridge University Press.

Harmon, Gilbert. 1980. "Moral Relativism as a Foundation for Natural Rights." *Journal of Libertarian Studies* 4:367–71.

Hayward, Tim. 2005. *Constitutional Environmental Rights*. Oxford: Oxford University Press.

Hiskes, Richard P. 2005. "The Right to a Green Future: Human Rights, Environmentalism, and Intergenerational Justice." *Human Rights Quarterly* 27:346–67.

———. 2009. *The Human Right to a Green Future: Environmental Rights and Intergenerational Justice.* New York: Cambridge University Press.

———. 2010. "Missing the Green: Golf Course Ecology, Environmental Justice, and Local 'Fulfillment' of the Human Right to Water." *Human Rights Quarterly* 32:326–41.

Hobbes, Thomas. 1651. *Leviathan.* Edited by C. B. MacPherson. New York: Penguin Classics, 1982.

Langford, Malcolm. 2006. "Tragedy or Triumph of the Commons? Human Rights and the World Water Crisis." http://www.law.monash.edu.au/castan centre/Events/2006/ conf-06-langford-paper.html.

Rorty, Richard. 1993. "Human Rights, Rationality, and Sentimentality." In *On Human Rights: Oxford Amnesty Lectures,* edited by Stephen Shute and Susan Hurley, 111–34. New York: Basic Books.

Sandel, Michael J. 1982. *Liberalism and the Limits of Justice.* Cambridge: Cambridge University Press.

Scanlon, John, Angela Cassar, and Noémi Nemes. 2004. "Water as a Human Right?" IUCN Environmental Policy and Law Paper 51.

Shue, Henry. (1980) 1996. *Basic Rights.* Princeton, NJ: Princeton University Press.

Taylor, Charles. 1989. *Sources of the Self.* Cambridge, MA: Harvard University Press.

Tuck, Richard. 1979. *Natural Rights Theories: Their Origin and Development.* Cambridge: Cambridge University Press.

Tully, Stephen. 2005. "A Human Right to Access Water? A Critique of General Comment 15." *Netherlands Quarterly of Human Rights* 23:35–63.

United Nations Committee on Economic, Social, and Cultural Rights (UN CESCR). 2003. *General Comment No. 15,* Committee on Economic, Social and Cultural Rights, 29th sess., 1, UN Doc. E/C.12/2002/11.

Universal Declaration of Human Rights (UDHR). 1948. Adopted December 10, 1948. G. A. Res. 217A(III). UN GAOR, 3rd. Sess., art. 3. UN Doc. A/RES/3/217A.

Waldron, Jeremy. 1987. *"Nonsense Upon Stilts": Bentham, Burke, and Marx on the Rights of Man.* London: Methuen.

Weiss, Edith Brown. 1989. *In Fairness to Future Generations: International Law, Common Patrimony, and Intergenerational Equity.* Dobbs Ferry, NY: Transnational.

Wellman, Carl. 1995. *Real Rights.* New York: Oxford University Press.

Young, Iris. 2002. "Two Concepts of Self-Determination." In *Human Rights: Concepts, Contests, Contingencies,* edited by Austin Sarat and Thomas R. Kearns, 25–44. Ann Arbor: University of Michigan Press.

Acknowledgments

This book has been many years in the making, and we have many to thank. The first to acknowledge are the ten extraordinary scholars who contributed chapters to the book. Every edited volume depends on the quality, flexibility, and promptness of its contributors. Our collaborating authors shone in all three dimensions. We cannot thank them enough for their intellectual engagement with the book, their scholarship, and their responsiveness. Even more than that, the book is what it is because of them.

The Mellon Foundation deserves special thanks as well. The book stems from an eighteen-month-long John E. Sawyer Seminar called "Vulnerability and Resilience: Rethinking Human Rights for the 21st Century," which the Mellon Foundation funded. While the themes of *The Human Rights Paradox* are not the same as those conceptualized at the start of the seminar, the ideas unearthed during the seminar are what gave rise to the book. The seminar was the inspiration and discovery path for the book, and without the Mellon's generous support neither the seminar nor the book would have happened.

As part of the seminar, more than three dozen scholars visited Madison. Their sustained engagement, passionate debate, and scholarship allowed us to explore new grounds in the human rights field. In addition to the volume's contributors, the following scholars and practitioners made the seminar rich: Anne Aghion, Jay Aronson, Brett Logan Carter, Michael Carter, Sheena Chestnut, Harri Englund, Michel Feher, Michael Goodhart, Paul Gready, Andrew Lakoff, Bronwyn Leebaw, Andrew Linke, Dyan Mazurana, Sally Merry, Sam Moyn, David Petrasek, Hari Osofsky, Kaushik Sunder Rajan, Alexandra Scacco, Adam Sitze, Joseph Slaughter, Charis Thompson, Molly Todd, Lars Waldorf, Eric Weitz, and Ann Marie Wilson. In addition, we are grateful to the scholars, particularly José Zalaquett, who could not come to Madison for the Mellon Sawyer Seminar but who sent in thoughtful memos that advanced our thinking.

In addition to the external presenters, the seminar benefited from scholars drawn from the University of Wisconsin–Madison campus. Their excellent comments helped to craft an intellectual community around human rights for the seminar, the book, and beyond. They include Sumudu Atapattu, Lori DiPrete Brown, Jo Ellen Fair, Fran Hirsch, Linda Hogle, Alexandra Huneeus, Sharon Hutchinson, Rick Keller, Nancy Kendall, Helen Kinsella, Heinz Klug, and Miriam Thangaraj.

Throughout the Sawyer Seminar and the book-writing process, we depended greatly on the assistance of three dedicated and intellectually stimulating graduate students, each of whom has a very promising academic career around human rights. They are Tamara Feinstein, Brett Kyle, and Debbie Sharnak. As intellectual colleagues, their contributions and ideas were invaluable to the seminar; as organizers, they were also gracious hosts to visitors and participants.

Gwen Walker at the University of Wisconsin Press has been a guiding light for the book series in which this volume is a part. She came to many of the Sawyer seminars, and she has been a highly valued intellectual colleague throughout. She provided helpful feedback as the volume developed as well as a trenchant reading of an earlier draft of our introduction, all of which greatly improved the book. We are also deeply grateful to the two anonymous readers, whose reports were detailed, thorough, and enormously helpful.

At the University of Wisconsin–Madison, the Department of Political Science and in particular Debbie Bakke made the logistics of the Sawyer Seminar and later the book possible. The Division of International Studies also jump-started the Human Rights Initiative, which was instrumental in spawning the Sawyer Seminar.

Contributors

Jo-Marie Burt is an associate professor of political science at George Mason University, as well as director of Latin American Studies and co-director of the Center for Global Studies. As a Senior Fellow at the Washington Office on Latin America (WOLA), she works on transitional justice issues and has organized and participated in international observation missions to the trial of former Peruvian president Alberto Fujimori and the genocide trial of former de facto president General Efrain Ríos Montt in Guatemala. She has published widely in academic and journalistic venues on political violence, transitional justice, and state-society relations in Latin America, and is coeditor of *Politics in the Andes: Identity, Conflict, Reform* (2004) and author of *Political Violence and the Authoritarian State in Peru: Silencing Civil Society* (2007). She is currently directing a research project on human rights prosecutions in Peru and is completing a manuscript on the Fujimori trial.

Bridget Conley-Zilkic is the research director for the World Peace Foundation and lead researcher on the How Mass Atrocities End project. She previously worked as research director for the U.S. Holocaust Memorial Museum's Committee on Conscience. She led the museum's research and projects on contemporary threats of genocide, including curating the interactive installation *From Memory to Action: Meeting the Challenge of Genocide Today*. She received a PhD in Comparative Literature from Binghamton University in 2001.

Philippe Cullet is a professor of international and environmental law at SOAS, University of London, the Convenor of the International Environmental Law Research Centre (IELRC), and a Senior Visiting Fellow at the Centre for Policy Research (CPR), New Delhi. He has published widely in environmental law, natural resources law, water law and policy, human rights, and the socioeconomic aspects of intellectual property. His monographs include *Water Law, Poverty and Development—Water Law Reforms in India* (2009), *Intellectual Property and Sustainable Development* (2005), and *Differential Treatment in International Environmental Law* (2003).

Richard P. Hiskes is a professor of political science and honors professor at Grand Valley State University. He is the author of many books and articles on political theory and particularly human rights theory. His 2009 book, *The Human Right to a Green Future: Environmental Rights and Intergenerational Justice*, was named the Best Book in Human Rights Scholarship from the American Political Science Association. He is the former editor and now associate editor of the *Journal of Human Rights*. His forthcoming book (2014) is titled *Human Dignity and the Promise of Human Rights*.

Fuyuki Kurasawa is an associate professor of sociology at York University in Toronto, and Faculty Fellow of the Center for Cultural Sociology at Yale University. He is the author of *The Ethnological Imagination: A Cross-Cultural Critique of Modernity* (2004) and *The Work of Global Justice: Human Rights as Practices* (2007), and currently is researching the history of the visual representation of humanitarian crises as well as the use of social media by human rights campaigns.

Meghan Foster Lynch is an assistant professor in the Department of Political Science at Temple University. In addition to human rights, her research interests include civil war and genocide, political psychology, and research methodology.

Phuong N. Pham is a research scientist at the Harvard School of Public Health and associate faculty and director of Evaluation and Implementation Science at the Harvard Humanitarian Initiative. Dr. Pham is a pioneer in utilizing epidemiologic methods, statistics, and innovative technologies to address emerging complex international issues at the intersection of public health, complex emergencies, human rights, transitional justice, and peace building. She cofounded KoBoToolbox and Peacebuildingdata.org.

Geoffrey Robinson is a professor of history at UCLA, where he teaches and writes about political violence, popular resistance, and human rights, primarily in Southeast Asia. His major works include: *The Dark Side of Paradise: Political Violence in Bali* (1995); *East Timor 1999: Crimes against Humanity* (2006); and *"If You Leave Us Here, We Will Die": How Genocide Was Stopped in*

East Timor (2010). Before going to UCLA, he worked for six years at Amnesty International's Research Department in London. He is currently writing a book about the mass killing and incarceration of up to one million people following a 1965 military coup in Indonesia.

Steve J. Stern is Alberto Flores Galindo and Hilldale Professor of History at the University of Wisconsin–Madison. He researches and teaches Latin American history, and has published numerous books and articles. Among recent awards, he received the Bolton-Johnson Prize from the Conference in Latin American History in 2007 for *Battling for Hearts and Minds: Memory Struggles in Pinochet's Chile, 1973–1988* and was elected to the American Academy of Arts and Sciences in 2012.

Scott Straus is a professor of political science and international studies at the University of Wisconsin–Madison. His most recent book is *Remaking Rwanda: State Building and Human Rights after Mass Violence*, which he co-edited with Lars Waldorf. Straus's research focuses on the dynamics and determinants of large-scale violence against civilians, in particular genocide.

Noa Vaisman is an International Junior Research Fellow and a Marie Curie Fellow at Durham University. She conducted ethnographic fieldwork in Buenos Aires, Argentina, and has written on such topics as human rights, new technologies and the body, sociality, and temporality. She is currently working on a book about the generation of the children of the disappeared in Argentina.

Patrick Vinck is a research scientist at the Harvard School of Public Health and associate faculty with the Harvard Humanitarian Initiative. At Harvard, Vinck leads the Program for Vulnerable Populations, where he focuses on managing and implementing empirical studies and evaluations on the prevalence of trauma and exposure to violence in conflict-affected societies, and the association with peace, justice, and reconstruction. He also conducts research on vulnerability analysis, food security, and displacement. Vinck also co-founded KoBoToolbox (www.kobotoolbox.org), a digital data collection project to advance social research.

Index

DRC. *See* Democratic Republic of the Congo
Dublin Statement, 219
Due Obedience Law (Argentina, 1987), 129, 132, 133, 134
Dyer, Samuel, 156, 157

East Timor, 14–15, 31–57; Amnesty International's role in, 37, 39–41, 43, 45; anticolonial movement in, 32; and asylum seekers' action, 45; Catholic Church in, 38, 41, 43, 46, 52, 56n7; CAVR in, 50–51, 57n22; diplomacy and human rights in, 39–42; genocide/humanitarian crisis in (1975–81), 33–34, 35–39, 52, 56nn4–5; human rights history/turning points in, 33–35, 37–39, 46, 48, 52–54; international human rights community's role in, 43–46, 48, 53, 54–55; intervention in/independence for, 32, 46–52, 53; John Paul II's visit to, 42; judicial process in, 49–50; justice for Indonesian officials in, 48–51, 57n17, 57n21; research on, 55–56n1; revolutionary ideals in, 38–39, 41; Santa Cruz massacre (1991), 42–43, 55, 56n11; Serious Crimes Unit (SCU) in, 50, 57n19, 57n21; UN's role in, 44–45, 46–48, 49, 51, 53–54, 56n14; and Western embrace of human rights, 42
East Timorese Church, 38, 56n7
ECCC (Extraordinary Chambers in the Courts of Cambodia), 108–9, 118, 149
Enlightenment, 32, 231
escrache, 130–31, 132–37, 141, 143nn12–13, 144n18, 145n27
ESMA (Navy Mechanics School; Argentina), 132, 139–40, 145nn27–28

ethnic cleansing, 61
evolution of public conscience, 237
exhibitionary complex, 65
Extraordinary Chambers in the Courts of Cambodia. *See* ECCC

Facebook, 177, 178, 180, 183, 184–85, 192–93
Familiares de Desaparecidos y Detenidos por Razones Políticas (Argentina), 138
Famine: The Russian Famine of 1921, 183
Fattah, Ezzat A., 113
Federación Ecuménica para la Paz (FEDEPAZ; Peru), 171n12
feminism, 224, 233–34
FIDH (International Federation of Human Rights), 155
Final Stop Law (Argentina, 1986), 129, 132, 133, 134
Flickr, 184–85
Ford, Gerald, 36
Foreign Assistance Act (United States, 1961), 56n3
Foucault, Michel, 67
free speech, 238
Fretilin (Revolutionary Front for an Independent East Timor), 35, 38, 40, 41
Friedman, Thomas, 4
"From Madness to Hope: The 12-Year War in El Salvador," 170n4
From Memory to Action: Meeting the Challenge of Genocide Today (USHMM), 75–76
Fronton prison uprising (Peru, 1986), 163–64
Front pour la Démocratie au Burundi (FRODEBU), 85
Fujimori, Alberto, 5–6, 22, 148–58; background of, 150–55; coup by, 150, 152; in exile, 155; extradition

to Peru, 17–18, 155–58, 168, 170n8; overview of, 148–50; precedent set by, 157–58, 168; repression/human rights abuses under, 150, 152 (*see also* Colina Group); sentencing of, 148, 157, 170–71n11; trial/conviction of, 148–49, 154, 156–58, 162, 170n11, 171n15

Fundamental Rights Agency of the European Union (FRA 2011), 73–74

future generations' rights, 237–40, 241

Galliano, John, 199n12
Gama, Paulino, 44
gang members' violent intentions, 98
Garcia, Alan, 160, 163, 164–66, 169
gay marriage rights, 228
General Comment 15 (UN CESCR), 240, 241
genocidas (genocide perpetrators), 144n20
Gewirth, Alan, 225, 226
Giampetri, Luis, 163–65
Gleick, Peter, 241
globalization, 4–5, 22
Goldston, Jim, 149
González, Olga M., 7, 23n2
Goodale, Marc, 12
Google Earth, 184
Gorriti, Gustavo, 156, 157
Gould, Carol C., 234–35
Green Movement, 186–87
Griffiths, Jose-Marie, 77n5
Guatemala, 169
"Guatemala: Memory of Silence," 170n4
Gulu (Uganda), 23
Gusmão, Xanana, 39–40, 42, 45, 48–49, 51, 55, 56n10, 57n17

Habibie, B. J., 47
Hamid Khan case (India), 206–7
Harmon, Gilbert, 236
Helsinki Watch. *See* Human Rights Watch
Hermoza Ríos, Nicolás, 154, 160–61
H.I.J.O.S. (Sons and Daughters for Identity and Justice against Oblivion and Silence; Argentina), 17, 130–41; demonstrations by, 130–31, 132–34; *escrache* by, 132–35, 143nn12–13, 144nn15–16, 144n18; goals of, 130, 131, 140, 141–42; hair-cutting event by, 137–39; importance of, 126; on impunity, 136; interpretation of "truth" by, 131, 135–36; on repression, 136–37; rift within, 137, 143n9; trials/punishment demanded by, 137–39, 141–42, 145n26; on youth, 136
Hobbes, Thomas: on dignity/identity, 228; *Leviathan*, 225, 226, 229, 231, 243n1; liberalism of, 224, 225; on natural law, 243n1; on promises/contracts, 20, 225–26, 227–29, 231, 237; on property, 225, 229; on relational rights, 225, 227–30, 243; on the social contract, 225–26, 228; on the state and rights, 20; on the state of nature, 225–27, 230–31, 242–43
Hoffmann, Stefan-Ludwig, 32, 35
Holocaust, 64, 68–69, 71, 77n8
Holocaust education, 73–74
Holocaust museums, 78n11. *See also* U.S. Holocaust Memorial Museum
HRE (human rights education), 73–74
HROs (human rights organizations): in Argentina, 128–29, 131–32, 137, 142nn4–5, 143n9, 143n11, 145n28; international, 43; in Peru, 150. *See also* human rights

curatorial decisions about displays in, 63; genocide exhibits at, 75–76; human rights activism sparked by, 62–63; human rights discourse, role in, 63, 67, 70–72, 74–75; and human rights on the political landscape, 67–71; memorialization/interruption by, 71–76, 77–78nn10–11; national, 65–66, 77n4; overview of, 61–63; politics of, 63–67, 77n4, 77n7; social trust in, 65, 77n5; South African, 77n7; state and power relations, role in, 63; U.S. Holocaust Memorial Museum, 15, 22, 61–66, 68, 75–76, 76n1, 77n9, 184; visitor engagement at, 15, 63, 65, 66, 77n6. *See also specific museums*

naming and shaming, 69–70, 198n4
National Council of the Maubere Resistance (CNRM; East Timor), 40
National Criminal Court (SPN; Peru), 153–54, 160, 161–63, 171nn17–18
National Food Security Act (India, 2013), 216
National Intelligence Service (Peru), 156
National Museum of African American History and Culture, 66
National Museum of American History, 66
National Museum of the American Indian, 66
natural law, 243n1
natural rights, 225, 231–32
Navy Mechanics School. *See* ESMA
Nazis, 64
Ndadaye, Melchior, 15, 81–82, 84, 85–91, 94–95, 98
Neier, Aryeh, 121–22n1
Nemes, Noémi, 241

NGOs (nongovernmental organizations), 142n2, 177, 183. *See also* HROs; human rights
Nirmal Bharat Abhiyan (India), 213
Nobel Prize, 45–46, 57n15
Northern Uganda. *See* Uganda
NRDWP (National Rural Drinking Water Programme; India), 210–14, 217, 221n6, 221n9
Nunca Más, 128–29
Nuremberg trials, 115

Office of the Director of Information Control (Office of Military Government for Germany; U.S.), 115
Olazabal, Cristina, 166
OpenNet Initiative, 196
Open Society Foundation, 171n12
Ortiz Perea, Luis Enrique, 170n9. *See also* La Cantuta case
"Otros Saberes" Initiative (Latin American Studies Association), 171n12
OV-10 Broncos (aircraft), 35, 36–37

pacification. *See* peace, maintenance of
Paine, Thomas, 230–31
panchayats (village councils; India), 207–8, 211
Paniagua, Valentín, 150–51, 152, 155, 156
Pathé Gazette, 182
peace, maintenance of: via coercion, 88, 92–93, 98; via collaboration, 88, 94–96, 98; via obedience to local leaders, 88–90, 98; via persuasion, 88, 91–92, 98; via prejudice reduction, 88, 93–94, 98
peace, survivors on, 117–18
Pérez, María Hilda, 140
Peru, transitional justice process in: Accomarca case, 160, 166; accountability agenda, 153, 155, 157, 158,

postmodern arguments for, 224, 234; relational logic of human rights, 225–30; relative universality of, 235; social contract, 225–26, 228, 234, 237–38, 242–43; state as addressee of rights, 229–30; Universal Declaration of Human Rights on, 20; to water, 20, 232, 236–37, 238, 240–43. *See also* Hobbes, Thomas

Report of the President's Commission on the Holocaust, 68, 76n1

Rettig Commission (Chile), 151

revolutionary movements, 38–39, 56n8

Rey Rey, Rafael, 164, 165

Rieff, David, 62

Ríos Montt, Efraín, 169

Rivera, Carlos, 164

Roht-Arriaza, Naomi, 127

Rome Statute (1998), 108–9. *See also* ICC

Rorty, Richard, 232–33

Roth, Ken, 69–70

Rumonge. *See under* Burundi

Russian famine (1921–23), 182–83, 198–99nn7–8

Rwanda, genocide in (1994), 24n4, 109, 193–94

Sala Penal Nacional (Special Criminal Court; Peru), 148, 153

Salazar Monroe, Julio, 154, 160

Sandel, Michael, 234

Santa Cruz massacre (East Timor, 1991), 42–43, 55, 56n11

Sarhuinos (Andes), 5–8, 13

Save the Children Fund (SCF), 182–83, 198–99nn6–8

Scanlon, John, 241

Scilingo, Adolfo, 129–30

Sector Reform Project (India), 210

self, conceptions of, 234–35

sentimentality, 233–34

September 11 attacks (2001), 48, 54, 191

Serious Crimes Unit (SCU; East Timor), 50, 57n19, 57n21

Sharpeville massacre (South Africa, 1960), 56n11

Shaw, Rosalind, 12

Shining Path (Peru), 5, 7, 150, 153, 164, 167, 169n2, 170n5, 171n17

Shock and Awe campaign, 191

Shue, Henry, 242

Sikkink, Kathryn, 25n8, 53, 70, 131

situational rights. *See* relational and situational rights

Skype, 184–85

Snowden, Edward, 199n11

social contract, 225–26, 228, 234, 237–38, 242–43

socialism, 33

social media technology, 177–200, 198n5; Amnesty International's use of, 183–84, 199n16; aporias introduced by, 180–81, 185–87, 189–92, 194; authenticity of images, 187–89, 196; boomerang effect, 198n2; broadcasting via, 179, 185; Congo Reform Association (CRA), photographic evidence used by, 181–82; critical pragmatism about, 195–96; and critical visuality, 196, 199n14; crowdsourcing, 19, 192; *Daily Express* criticism of Save the Children Fund (SCF), 182–83, 198–99nn6–8; decontextualization of images, 188, 199n13; Demotix, 184; dialogical character of, 177–78; evidentiary status of images, 183, 188–89, 192, 196; exhibitionism by perpetrators via, 190–91, 196–97; eyewitness evidence discredited via, 186–87; Facebook, 177, 178, 180, 183, 184–85, 192–93; Flickr, 184–85; fund-raising via,

social media technology (*continued*)
183; Google Earth, 184; and governmental censorship/monitoring of the Internet, 185–87, 199n10; human rights and humanitarianism, 198n1; idealists vs. skeptics about, 19, 178–80, 195; image-based misrepresentation, 186; Internet-enabled mobile communication devices, 184; Internet's consolidation, 177; invisibility of some human rights violations, 191–92, 197, 200nn17–18; irreconcilable interpretations of images, 183; for legal prosecution, 178, 198n3; mapping and geotagging software, 184; mass human rights violations, controlling representations of, 186; naming and shaming via, 198n4; OpenNet Initiative, 196; optimism vs. pessimism about, 194; overview of, 177–81; as paradoxically universal and local, 178; portable recording devices, 184, 185;reductionism of, 192–95, 197, 200n19; representational activism via, 178, 180–85; representational politics of, 185–89, 197–98, 199nn11–13, 199–200n15; selection/manipulation of visual material, 183, 191–92; Skype, 184–85; surveillance and tracking of activists, 189, 199–200n15; Twitter, 19, 177, 178, 179–80, 183, 184–85, 192–93; unintended consequences of, 189–92, 199–200nn15–17; Ustream, 184–85; victims of human rights abuses exposed via, 189–90, 196–97, 200n16; Vimeo, 184; Web 1.0 and 2.0 activism, 177–80, 183, 184–85, 194, 198n2; Wikileaks, 199n11; Witness, 184; YouTube, 177, 178, 184

Sons and Daughters for Identity and Justice against Oblivion and Silence. *See* H.I.J.O.S.
South African free water policy, 219
Special Court for Sierra Leone, 149
state of nature, 225–27, 230–31, 242–43
Strategic Plan (India, 2011–22), 212–13, 215
Suharto, President, 36, 40, 42, 46–47
Supreme Court (India), 206
Supreme Military Council (Argentina), 128
survivors, 16–17, 107–22; on amnesty, 117; best practices regarding, 118–21; classification of, 112–13; depression and PTSD among, 112, 117; engaging with, 110–15; expectations/desires of, 109–10, 119; on international justice and reconstruction, 115–18; justice/accountability mechanisms, role in, 107–11 (*see also* ICC); on peace, 117–18; perpetrator-victims, 113, 116; refugees, 112; reparations for, 120; role in policy making, 107–8; surveys of, 113–20; in Uganda, 110–11, 115–16; victims' variety of experiences, 109, 116; as witnesses of violence, 116
sustainability, 221n10
Swajaldhara Guidelines (India, 2002), 209–10, 213–14
Swajal project (India), 210, 213–14
Sword, Kirsty, 45
Syrian spyware, 199–200n15
Sznaider, Natan, 68, 77n8

Tarrow, Sidney, 12
Tate, Winifred, 18
Taylor, Charles, 234, 236

violence: interrupting violent intentions, 98; obedience to orders to commit, 98–99; promoted by local leaders, 101n33; self-preservation vs. ethical norms as deterrent to, 82, 87, 99. *See also* peace, maintenance of

Vishala Kochi Kudivella Samarkshana Samithi v. State of Kerala, 207

Waldorf, Lars, 12
Waldron, Jeremy, 231
water, right to. *See* India, water access in; relational and situational rights
water crisis, 241
Weiss, Edith Brown, 237
Weitz, Eric, 32

Wellman, Carl, 231
Wiesel, Elie, 62–63, 64, 68–69, 71
Wikileaks, 199n11
Williams, Paul, 72–73
Wiranto, General, 50
Witness, 184
Women's Rights Defense Group (DEMUS; Peru), 171n12
World Bank, 209–10
World Commission on Environment and Development, 221n10
world culture/politics, 4–5
World Trade Center attacks (2011), 191

YouTube, 177, 178, 184

Critical Human Rights